Echoes of
KANSAS
BASKETBALL
The Greatest Stories Ever Told

Edited by Matt Fulks

TRIUMPH
B O O K S

Library of Congress Cataloging-in-Publication Data

Echoes of Kansas basketball : the greatest stories ever told / edited by Matt Fulks.
   p. cm.
   Includes bibliographical references.
   ISBN-13: 978-1-57243-868-2 (hard cover)
   ISBN-10: 1-57243-868-1 (hard cover)
   1. University of Kansas—Basketball—History. I. Fulks, Matt.

GV885.43.U52E35 2006
796.323'630978165—dc22

2006011364

This book is available in quantity at special discounts for your group or organization. For further information, contact:

Triumph Books
542 South Dearborn Street
Suite 750
Chicago, Illinois 60605
(312) 939-3330
Fax (312) 663-3557

Printed in U.S.A.
ISBN-13: 978-1-57243-868-2
ISBN-10: 1-57243-868-1
Design by Patricia Frey
Jersey photo courtesy of Peter Kuehl.

CONTENTS

FOREWORD

When I hear the words *Kansas basketball,* I think of the tradition and the history more than anything else. I think of the inventor of the game, Dr. James Naismith, being the first coach here. I think about Dr. "Phog" Allen, who's known as the "father of basketball coaching." I think of the great players—from Clyde Lovellette and Wilt Chamberlain to Jo Jo White to Danny Manning to so many guys through the 1990s. When I think of Kansas basketball, I think of being part of something much bigger than any one person.

It can be a struggle to get new players to understand that. We do our best to educate them about it. We show them old films and stories or quotes from different people. Truth be told, though, the history and tradition make this a tougher place to play than one would think. If a guy grows up outside the Midwest, he doesn't truly understand the passion and mystique until he gets here as a student. Then it takes a new player a while to appreciate that every day that he doesn't give it his best, he's letting down many ghosts that reside in Allen Fieldhouse, along with every student that's ever attended this university, every person who's ever given money to this school, and even the people who have no ties to the school except as fans.

By the time Kansas basketball players are sophomores and juniors, they see the history and mystique in a totally different way. I would bet that you could talk to any past or older current player and they'd say that was the case when they first stepped foot on this campus as a freshman.

As a player or as a coach, you can't escape the history and tradition of Kansas basketball. You can't avoid it; you're a part of it.

Some guys relish that pressure; others don't. One of our freshmen came up to me early in the 2004–05 season and said, "Coach, I can't get away. I can't go to the movies, I can't go anywhere around town. I just want to be able to go hide every now and then."

"You know something," I told him. "Welcome to Kansas. We told you this would happen when we recruited you."

Everyone says that he wants that pressure and notoriety, but there's a lot of responsibility in accepting it, grasping it, and turning it to your benefit.

Recruits aren't overwhelmed by the great players who played here in the 1950s, '60s, and '70s. But, because of those great players and teams, recruits see the passion that exists in the fans. It's a passion that continues to build. When recruits come on campus, they feel that. Today, that passion is off the charts. It gives us a great home-court advantage.

My first baptism into the tradition of the Kansas program came as a player at Oklahoma State during the early 1980s. I loved coming to Allen Fieldhouse more than anywhere else. It wasn't because of the visual of the arena, at least it wasn't back then; but there's something about being on that court that gives players an extra bounce, a special energy. We couldn't wait to get out there for our first practice at Allen Fieldhouse each time we came to Lawrence.

Teams have good home records because they have good players, not because of the building. In my opinion, there are four or five places in America that I've been to that stand out as tough places to play because of the building itself—not just because they have good players. This is one of those places where the building means a lot. It's tough to play here because of the atmosphere and the fans. Then once you throw the great Jayhawks players in the mix we have a tremendous advantage.

Because people equate Kansas basketball with excellence, playing against Kansas in Lawrence is always one of the biggest games on a team's schedule. That's how I felt as a player. That's why we stress to our players that they are always going to get the other team's best shot at KU.

Even though I loved it as an opponent, I didn't truly experience the mystique of KU until 1985–86, the season I was an assistant on Larry Brown's staff. The biggest impression about that season for me was the passion for the program everywhere—on campus, around Lawrence, everywhere.

For me, working with Larry Brown at Kansas, no less, was almost an out-of-body experience. To have a chance to work with that staff, when I was basically the same age as the players, was too good to be true. Think about those coaches—not only Larry, but also R. C. Buford, Ed Manning, Alvin Gentry, Mark Freidinger, and Tommy Butler. That was an incredible staff. Then, to be around those great players, being close to them and seeing things through their eyes, and yet being involved with all of the coaches' activities...I had a pretty good situation.

In fact, I learned more from Coach Brown in that one season than I've learned, probably, from everyone else before and since. First off, he's a great coach. So, when you don't know much, as I didn't, and you're around somebody great, you're going to pick up a lot of things. Larry has an incredible knack for managing people. Besides his staff and players, he knows exactly how to work the officials and work a crowd. Those stories are legendary.

I've borrowed ideas from other coaches who have influenced me, such as Leonard Hamilton and Eddie Sutton, but during that one year with Larry, I learned a ton about building a philosophy, motivating players, and how the game was meant to be played. He's an all-timer in all of those things.

There was one practice when we had been out there for 45 minutes, and the guys were busting their rumps. Coach Brown was riding them hard, and he wouldn't get off them. He was always tough on them, but he was unmerciful this particular day. The players were trying so hard. Finally, Coach threw them out of practice, and then he stormed off. We were in the coaches' locker room and I asked him if he was all right. He said nonchalantly but hurriedly, "Yeah, I'm fine, but I've got to be in Kansas City in 30 minutes, so I have to get out of here." He was not going to waste a chance to get a point across to the players that he expected things to be done a certain way. Throwing them out of practice added the perfect exclamation point.

Another time, the guys weren't helping each other defensively. They weren't talking to each other and working as a team. Coach Brown said, "Okay, let's do this your way. We're going to scrimmage for 40 minutes. Any time that anybody does anything to help a teammate, we're going to stop the clock and it goes back to 40. So I want everybody to be totally selfish and play on your own." Just to help prove his point, the clock would get down to 5, and he'd spot something and push it back to 40. It'd get down to 13, and then he'd put it back up to 40. Down to 20, and then back up to 40. *Five hours later*, he finally called it off. Again, he was proving the point that things were going to be done his way. He was the master at doing things like that.

In the end, his way obviously paid off, as KU won the national title in 1988. Even during the 1985–86 season, though, we had a great run during the NCAA Tournament as a number one seed. Of course, that run took us through Kansas City for the Midwest Regional, where the team had that incredible overtime win over Michigan State in the regional semifinals, where we had been practically dead. Then we beat North Carolina State for a chance to play Duke in the Final Four in Dallas.

Duke had beaten us already that season, in December at the Preseason NIT Tournament, but we felt we could beat them in Dallas. A couple of our guys didn't have their typically good game that day, but it was closely played. The knockout punch hit us late in the game when Archie Marshall went down with a knee injury. Archie was the best player in that game at the time, so I think that was a big blow. Plus it was so deflating because everybody loved Arch and wanted to see him do well. We left the floor that day feeling that we were the best team. To add to the hollow feeling that we had in our hearts, the team that went on to win the national championship, Louisville, was a team that we had beaten twice that year.

Even though I left Kansas after that season and joined Leonard Hamilton's staff at Oklahoma State, I was ecstatic to see Larry and the Jayhawks win the title two years later, beating rival Kansas State, Duke, and then another rival, Oklahoma. It's that pride that you can't escape when you're a part of Kansas basketball. It can be seen everywhere from summer basketball camps, when former players come back, to something as big as a national championship.

Once you're a part of this experience, you're a permanent part of the tradition and history. You're in the same record books as Wilt Chamberlain, who stands out to me more than anyone else at Kansas. Stop and think about how he scored 52 points and had 31 rebounds against Northwestern as a sophomore in his first varsity game. That's unbelievable. Shoot, look at what he did in his first collegiate game, when the freshman team played the KU varsity. Wilt scored 42 points and grabbed 29 rebounds, leading the freshmen to an improbable win. Then, even though he wasn't a track star, Wilt won the then–Big 7 high jump championship. He just ran up to the bar and jumped over it. He also did pretty well in the shot put and triple jump, and he could run the 100-yard dash in less than 11 seconds. He was one of the greatest athletes ever.

Wilt's a permanent part of KU's tradition and history, just like Dr. Naismith and Dr. Allen. I visit with a lot of Phog Allen's former players often, and they all talk about "Doc" in such a reverent way. I could listen to Doc Allen stories all day—and there are a lot of them.

Then there was all of the remarkable success of my predecessor, Roy Williams, who had so many great players. The only thing his teams didn't do, obviously, was win the whole championship, because they definitely accomplished everything else the right way over time.

There's much more than that to Kansas basketball, but those are some of the things that make this place special, that give it its incredible history. Game night helps, but it's all the things that build up to game night and the pride that exists within it. All of it exudes class over the course of time.

In this book, *Echoes of Kansas Basketball*, Matt Fulks has gathered the best collection of printed articles and columns out there, from both local and national sources, to take you on a journey through the program's history. You're going to read about Wilt and Dr. Naismith and Doc Allen, as well as some of the other players, coaches, and moments that make the University of Kansas such a unique place.

As a coach, I sit back all the time and think about the history and tradition of Kansas basketball. I'm very fortunate to be a part of this. Being the coach at Kansas is one of the best jobs in America. The expectations are high, but you should deliver at Kansas. You should put a good product on the floor that has done it the right way—with integrity, within the rules, and with teaching and enforcing the right things on and off the court.

In fact, 100 years from now, when another author compiling the greatest stories about Kansas basketball researches my time as a coach, I want him or her to read about how we did things the right way. That's my top priority. Second, as the head coach, I want him or her to read about how we developed young men to be as good as they could be as student-athletes and for the rest of their lives. If we're able to do those two things, then third, I want him or her to read about how we were able to cut down the nets in April.

It's unbelievable for me to think that I am just the eighth coach in this program's 100-plus-year history. Of course, that's a little skewed because Dr. Allen coached here for so long. But the coaches who have been here have all been successful on the national level. It's an honor to sit in this chair. I wake up every morning, not taking the responsibility and expectations lightly. The University of Kansas is a wonderful place with an incredibly rich basketball tradition. I'm really proud to be here.

—Bill Self

PREFACE

At the outset, the concept for this book seemed simple enough: an anthology of the best and most intriguing writings throughout the history of KU basketball. Hmmm. For a college basketball junkie who grew up in the Kansas City area, the idea was a no-brainer. Indeed, it seemed easy.

Boy, was I wrong. I've never been so wrong. Well, except for the time in 1997 when I thought painting my toenails blue in honor of Scot Pollard would be a cool good-luck charm. (Try explaining that one when you're wearing sandals in a Georgia convenience store.) Although the Jayhawks lost to Arizona that year in the NCAA Tournament, I escaped the convenience store unscathed.

Turns out, sorting through more than 100 seasons of Kansas basketball was frustratingly exhilarating. Frustrating in that there have been so many outstanding players, thrilling games, and championship seasons that picking the perfect ones proved to be tricky at times. Exhilarating in that I found long-lost stories and colorful personalities that I never knew.

The winning tradition at Kansas has led some of the nation's best writers—among them Jimmy Breslin, Frank Deford, and David Halberstam—to author articles about the Jayhawks. At the same time, however, being based in a small town in the northeastern part of Kansas meant that the Jayhawks didn't garner a lot of national press coverage on a regular basis until the 1980s. A couple of the articles from the 1980s and '90s that you'll read in this book actually mention that fact.

There are great players and moments that you won't find here. But *Echoes of Kansas Basketball* isn't meant to be a complete history of the program. There are already so many great historical books on the Jayhawks, such as Blair Kerkhoff's *Phog Allen: The Father of Basketball Coaching*, Mark Stallard's *Tales from the Jayhawks' Hardwood*, and, of course, Max Falkenstien's *Max and the Jayhawks*, that you could fill a field house with them.

This book, however, is a snapshot of KU's basketball history through the words of great journalists, including Bob Broeg, John Feinstein,

Jackie MacMullan, and Joe Posnanski. There are even stories from a couple of Jayhawks legends: Dr. James Naismith and Dr. "Phog" Allen.

My hope is that you'll enjoy reading about and reliving some of the Jayhawks' biggest basketball moments through the feature articles about many of the program's great players, the unique coaches, and the "phog" that surrounds being a Jayhawk. *Echoes of Kansas Basketball* offers a new look at one of the most successful traditions in college basketball history.

—Matt Fulks

ACKNOWLEDGMENTS

Even though a book such as this requires seemingly endless research and reading fuzzy microfilm instead of relying on interviews, a lot of people made *Echoes of Kansas Basketball* possible.

Thanks to Mike Emmerich, Tom Bast, and the rest of the team at Triumph Books for your patience, guidance, and desire to make this book the best book possible.

To *The Kansas City Star*'s Blair Kerkhoff, a former KU beat writer, who offered great words of encouragement during the project. To each of the writers who covered Kansas basketball through the years, either for newspapers, magazines, or book projects. Without your work there would be no *Echoes of Kansas Basketball*.

To Mark Stallard and Ken Samelson, each of whom are compiling books in this Echoes series, for your camaraderie and suggestions as we tackled these projects at the same time. Mark, thanks also for hooking me up with Mike. Thanks to Keith Zimmerman for pointing me in the right direction a couple of times.

To Dave Kelly at the Library of Congress, plus Barry Bunch and Becky Schulte at the University of Kansas Archives. Other librarians and research assistants were invaluable, also, particularly several at the main branch of the Kansas City Public Library and the various branches of the Johnson County Library.

To Chris Theisen, KU's assistant athletics director for media relations, and Mason Logan, an associate media relations director, for helping to put me in touch with Bill Self and for offering advice on locating additional stories.

To Bill Self and Max Falkenstien for your willingness to be involved in this project. The University of Kansas is lucky to have each of you. Max, you are a wonderful part of KU's history. The broadcasts just won't be the same without you.

To my mentor and great friend Tom Lawrence, who was a perfect research assistant and chauffeur in D.C. To Steve Beaumont, Tim and Amy Brown, and Chris Hartwick, who offered either advice on stories or stress relief as I approached deadline. Your support and friendship are appreciated more than you know.

Finally, I would like to thank my parents, Fred and Sharon, along with my wife, Libby, and our three children—Helen, Charlie, and Aaron—for your love and unending support. Thank you, all.

INTRODUCTION

It's been an honor to be associated with the great history and tradition at the University of Kansas for more than 60 years. People say I'm part of that history. I've been around for a lot of it, but I don't know that I'm a part of it. Regardless, it was a wonderful experience for 60 years.

My introduction to sports at KU, though, goes back to when I was a kid, and my dad was KU's business manager of athletics. He directed the ticket sales and handled the money for the players and coaches. He did alone what takes about 30 people today, although it's a bigger operation than it was then. Remarkably, he knew where everybody's seat was in the football stadium and in Hoch Auditorium. There were no computers back then, obviously, so he had all of that memorized.

My love of sports likely began around that time. Being around the KU basketball program for that long has given me a chance to see first-hand the great teams and players, the history and tradition, that make Kansas a unique place.

Of course, there were so many great moments during my time with the Jayhawks. Being able to broadcast the national championship from Seattle to Kansas in the pretelevision days of 1952 was a huge thrill. It was special to see that team win with Clyde Lovellette and all of the great players who surrounded him. Most of the players on that team were from small towns around Kansas, which made it unique. Then, being a part of the 1988 championship with "Danny and the Miracles" was a huge thrill.

Unfortunately, sometimes you remember the downers as well as the uppers. In 1997, Kansas had arguably the best team in the country, with four starters—Raef LaFrentz, Paul Pierce, Scot Pollard, and Jacque Vaughn—who are currently in the NBA, plus Jerod Haase, who was a great player in his own right. But they lost to Arizona in the Southeast Regional in Birmingham. The Wildcats beat three number one seeds on the way to the national championship. That regional championship game sticks out as an unforgettable night.

For me, though, Kansas basketball is not about the tradition and the history as much as it's about all of the great people who I've known and the wonderful friendships I've built over these many years. For instance, one player with whom I have remained close friends for more than 50 years is Al Correll, who was our first black captain in the early 1960s. Al, who's a gifted public speaker, did the broadcasts with me for a few years after he graduated from KU. Then, after living in Topeka and Des Moines, he eventually moved to Tacoma, Washington, where he was the city's director of human relations. We still talk two or three times a month and have retained a very close friendship.

I also have several good friends right here in Lawrence and Topeka who are Olympic champions. Charlie Hoag, who was a two-sport athlete, was a member of the 1952 Kansas national championship team and the gold medal–winning U.S. Olympic team that year. Also, Bill Lienhard, who was on the '52 team, and Bill Hougland, who has Olympic medals from the 1952 and '56 Games, live here in Lawrence. Al Kelley, who was on the 1960 Olympic team, also lives here. It's been a treat for me to get to know these men and so many others, and to still consider them friends today.

I've enjoyed getting to know all of the coaches with their great characteristics. Dr. "Phog" Allen was the athletics director and basketball coach when Dad worked for the university, and he was the basketball coach for nearly a decade after I started broadcasting. Coaches Dick Harp and Ted Owens were good friends of mine. Then there was Larry Brown, who was something unique and won a national championship before Roy Williams and his 15 great years. Now there's Bill Self, who's a good coach and a great recruiter. Besides getting to know these men through radio, we did weekly television shows and played golf together. We went through some great times together, as well as some that weren't so good. As they used to say on ABC's *Wide World of Sports*, we experienced "the thrill of victory and the agony of defeat" together.

It's impossible for me to pick a favorite out of that group, but as everyone knows, Doc Allen was special. More than anything else, Doc was a great motivator. He could put the fire in his guys' bellies and make them want to go out there and win for "dear old KU." I don't know that he was the world's greatest Xs and Os coach, even though he's credited with being the "father of basketball coaching," but he was great at dealing with the kids and inspiring them to reach their maximum potential. That was his greatest asset. Plus, he was one of the best storytellers, which helped him communicate with nearly anyone with whom he came in contact.

Doc's greatest rival school was Missouri. He wanted to beat the Tigers every time out. One year, though, he gained tremendous respect for them, or at least for their coach. During the Big 7 Christmas Tournament in Kansas City in 1951, Win Wilfong, who was a great player at Missouri, fell and was lying on the court. Clyde Lovellette was walking along after the play and came to Wilfong. Instead of jumping over him or walking around him, Clyde stepped on Wilfong's stomach, and kept walking. The crowd at Municipal Auditorium erupted. I just knew we were going to have a riot. Sparky Stalcup, the Missouri coach, came over and grabbed the public address microphone and told everyone to cool it.

"These are good young men and tempers may have got a little short, but this is a fine ballgame and we don't want anything to ruin it," Stalcup said. (Although I don't think Clyde was mad or trying to start a fight. He was just walking and kept on walking. To this day, Clyde's probably the only one who knows whether it was intentional.)

After that game, which KU won 75–65, Sparky and Doc became very close friends. In fact, on more than one occasion, Doc invited Sparky to come and speak at the KU basketball banquet, which Sparky did.

Throughout this book, you're going to read a couple of stories about the rivalry between Kansas and Missouri, which is heated but not always ugly. Remember when Norm Stewart retired from Missouri and he received the rocking chair from KU during the game at Allen Fieldhouse? I also learned firsthand that Missouri fans aren't all bad. At halftime of the game during our trip to Columbia in January 2006—my final trip there as a broadcaster—they introduced me over the public address system and said that it was my swan-song year. I thought for sure the fans would boo the heck out of me. Instead, I got a standing ovation. I didn't hear any boos at all. It was a very nice thing for them to do.

You also will read stories about many of the great players who have come through the university, including Wilt Chamberlain, who was one of the hardest to get to know. I think Wilt put a shield around himself beginning in his youth because of his size and the fact that he was black during a socially tough time in America. He just really was a private person. Plus, there was so much pressure on him when he came to Kansas. I think that pressure culminated when the Jayhawks lost that triple-overtime thriller to North Carolina in the 1957 national championship game. Wilt played one more year at KU and then went on to a wonderful pro career. He didn't return to Lawrence for 39 years.

In January 1998, Wilt made the trip back to Kansas to have his jersey officially retired. By then, he was a different person; he was easy-going and reflective. I'll never forget seeing him wear his KU letter jacket that day. For many guys, the moths would've eaten away at the jacket, but somehow Wilt had kept his all those years and brought it back that afternoon.

To present Wilt to a worldwide audience on CBS that afternoon at halftime was easily one of the highlights of my career. The big guy was so touched and moved by the ceremonies that tears were running down his cheeks. He ended his remarks with "Rock chalk, Jayhawk," which moved that sellout crowd. Less than two years later, Wilt died of a heart attack at his home in California.

The relationships I've developed over the years obviously included members of the media. For *Echoes of Kansas Basketball,* Matt Fulks has gathered a great compilation of stories written by some wonderful sportswriters, many of whom I've considered close friends. There used to be a close-knit group of men who covered the games. We had a great fraternity with men such as *Topeka Capitol-Journal* writers Dick Snider, Bob Hurt, and Bob Hentzen, with whom we took many trips. Joe McGuff, who passed away in February 2006, was a great writer with *The Kansas City Star.* In those days we traveled a lot with the writers, so all of us developed bonds through dinners together, playing cards, and just being around each other.

It was thrilling to be associated with the University of Kansas as a broadcaster for so many years. This is a terrific school with a deep passion for its basketball teams. For me, though, it's been wonderful developing relationships with the people who have made Kansas basketball what it is today.

—Max Falkenstien

The underdog Jayhawks controlled the tempo against heavily favored Oklahoma to claim the 1988 national title in Kansas City. Photo courtesy of Time & Life Pictures/Getty Images.

Section I
THE GAMES

The University Daily Kansan

HOW BASKET BALL CAME TO BE BORN

There doesn't seem to be any other way to lead off a book about the history of Kansas basketball than with an article featuring the school's first coach, who also happened to be the inventor of the game of basketball. Incidentally, this short article was written just 21 years after Dr. James Naismith came up with the idea for the new sport.

"The game of basketball originated partly by the endeavor to create a form of athletic exercise along the line of football and partly by accident," said Dr. Naismith at the gymnasium today.

"It was while I was at the Springfield Training School in Massachusetts in 1891," he continued, "that we discovered that the men who had played on the football team were not taking any interest in gymnasium exercise after the season had closed. They had been used to quick action and pitting their wits against their opponents, and the routine work with the dumbbells and Indian clubs was exceedingly irksome to them. The man who was the leader of the class became discouraged and gave it up, and I was invited to take his place.

"I realized that the men wanted some sort of a game that would be not only beneficial but also interesting. In other words, the men wanted something they could have some fun in. The only thing that I did was to try to find something of that sort."

Tried Dehorned Football

"At first we tried a form of 'dehorned' football, but that was too rough. Next followed soccer and then lacrosse, but none met the requirements of our small gymnasium. One day the question happened to strike me: what makes football rough? and the answer came—the tackling. What makes the tackling? [It's] the only way of stopping the man running with the ball. Why not eliminate the running and that would eliminate the tackling? But you can't play a game and stand still all the while. Then I conceived the idea of letting all the men run except the man with the ball—he would have to pass it before he could run.

"That point settled and experimented with and found satisfactory, the next that came up was the question of goals. An ordinary football goal would be too easy to make; a goal such as used in lacrosse or soccer would likely be easily torn down by sending the ball into it with great force. I thought of the plan of turning the goal up horizontally so that the ball instead of being thrown in forcibly would have to describe an arc before it entered. I thought at first of placing it about two feet off the floor, and then I realized that all a goalkeeper would have to do was to sit on it and it would be impossible for the opponents to score. I then thought of placing it up above the players' heads."

Peach Baskets, Ergo Basket Ball

"I went to the janitor and asked for some sort of a box. It just happened that he procured a couple of baskets (such as peaches are shipped in) about 18 inches across at the top and tapering down toward the bottom. We nailed these up on the gallery, which happened to be just 10 feet high. The name 'basket ball' has clung to the game ever since, and the official height of the goals has remained just 10 feet.

"The game was very successful in giving the men indoor exercise and training, and when vacation came in the summer the men went to their various homes all over the United States and carried the game with them."

F. C. "Phog" Allen, *Better Basketball*

THREE OBSTACLES AGAINST ONE HOPE

Phog Allen disliked Missouri, and he never tried to pretend otherwise. Heck, he despised the Tigers. In fact, legend has it that during the 1920s, Allen told close friends that he would stop coaching if the Jayhawks didn't beat the Tigers in the season finale. Obviously, Kansas won. The following story about the 1922 Helms championship season and how the Tigers played into it came from one of Allen's books, Better Basketball, *which was published in 1937.*

A defeat early in the 1922 season, at the hands of our traditional basketball enemy, Missouri, by a 35–25 score on our home floor; a lost scorebook; and an outstanding star declared ineligible at the 11th hour were three incidents that might have contributed to a definite lowering of morale for the University of Kansas team, now entering Tigertown for its second encounter of the season with Missouri, had we not been able to do something about it. We were hoping and planning for breaks which might turn our misfortunes into a startling victorious upset.

The Missourians had not lost a game, and this, their 16th, was the final game for them. Kansas was not conceded a chance by well-informed dopesters.

To some of the team's more superstitious members, a lost or forgotten scorebook was indeed a very bad omen, and almost as great a calamity as is the southern Negro plantation worker's loss of his prized rabbit's foot.

Arriving at the Missouri Rothwell Gymnasium at noon, we asked Director of Athletics Clevenger if we might borrow or buy a scorebook in which to keep our game record. Clevenger gave us a recently contrived scorebook, distributed at that time by a nationally known sporting-goods company.

In this new book, the substitutes' names followed the names of the regular players. The early-day scorebooks had single spaces only for

4

the five regular players' names to appear in position order, and the substitutes were listed at the bottom of the page. The scorebook plan of today is identical to that of the scorebook given us that night. Then, it was a new idea.

Upon this unfortunate incident of forgetting our scorebook was to hinge one of the turning points of the game, although we did not realize it at that time.

However, hand in hand with our calamities came other factors to strengthen our will to win. It is ever thus, if we will have it so. En route, in a little provincial Missouri town, while our boys were enjoying their toast and a light evening repast at a chocolate table, a partisan Missourian who could not forgo the opportunity shouted to us, "Look out, you, when you go to Columbia tomorrow."

In a few minutes, the waiter brought us a note, saying, "Here is a note from a friend." Upon opening it, we read this cryptic greeting: "To hell with Kansas!"

If we had been laboring under any delusions to the contrary, we were assured now that we were in enemy country. The fellows kept the note to frame as a souvenir, and also wished to frame the fellow who had sent it. However, he had disappeared.

Ordinarily, such unpleasant experiences as these do not tend to build fighting morale among superstitious athletes, unless some plan is devised to counteract them immediately. However, the morale of these Kansas players was, as yet, intact and growing, but there were still other rivers to cross.

That afternoon about 5:00, I received a telephone call from our university stating that our star forward, [Armin] Woestemeyer, had just been declared ineligible for further athletic competition by the eligibility committee.

Woestemeyer, a law student, had failed to register for a possible half hour of credit granted to students who attended moot court, on schedule, in the College of Law. Woestemeyer had attended the court, but had failed to register for credit, and was thus found a half hour short of eligibility for this and future games.

A tough break for us was this, with our regular forward ineligible. Woestemeyer was in my hotel room when the call came. Suddenly remembering the borrowed scorebook with its new plan for writing in the substitutions, I broke the sad news to him but countered with this thought: "Woeste, I am going to use you to win this game. You follow orders and we'll win, even though you are ineligible. At the start of the game, you will be the scorekeeper."

The rules at that time did not require that the lineup be given to the scorekeeper a certain number of minutes in advance of the game. Immediately, we decided not to inform anyone of Woestemeyer's ineligibility. Certainly, as a permissible point of strategy, we would try to keep this misfortune from Missouri until the last.

Our real problem, and greater than this strategic coup, was to keep the morale of our team at the highest pitch. I was planning to use Woestemeyer as scorekeeper, thereby forcing Craig Ruby, Missouri's coach, to keep one of his Tiger aces on the bench to offset the contemplated entry of Woestemeyer into the game.

My next problem was to contact the starting men, privately, one by one, and to impress upon them strongly my contemplated strategy and thus, with their cooperation, to pledge them their chance for success.

The Missouri Tigers were big and powerful. The Kansas Jayhawkers were shorter and lighter. Woestemeyer's loss, with his heft and speed, was a blow to Kansas. To choose between [Byron] Frederick, tall, eccentric, and inconsistent as a player, and [Waldo] Bowman, firebrand but a featherweight, was my problem. We controlled the tip-off, but Missouri's powerful guards would smother [George] Rody and Bowman, two midgets, if we used Bowman at the start.

Just prior to game time, Coach Ruby again asked for my lineup. Of course, I countered with indecision. As I walked among my players who were warming up, I carried my scorebook along with the pages open. Anyone, especially Coach Ruby, could easily read the lineup, if and when he came close enough to read over my shoulder.

The Kansas regular starting lineup, the same as in other games, was written in the book, but Woestemeyer's name appeared immediately under Rody's name and in Rody's substitute position. I was hoping that Coach Ruby would think the error a case of pregame nervousness or unfamiliarity with the new scorebook, rather than a definitely planned bit of strategy to throw him off guard. Evidently, this is exactly what happened.

In order to dispel any idea of a changed Kansas lineup, Woestemeyer, although ineligible, was kept warming up with the other Kansas regulars. Woestemeyer had been the regular starter in all previous games.

Coach Ruby, apparently satisfied that he had obtained the correct starting Kansas lineup, walked over to convey its personnel to his huddled Tigers, who were ready to play. Thereafter, each Tiger pointed out his own Jayhawker, including Woestemeyer, with the following remarks: "I'll take this man," "You take that man," "Let's get 'em!"

Referee Ernie Quigley snappily thrust himself on the court and, with the blast of his whistle, shouted, "Play ball!"

Just at this moment, I hastily penned Frederick's name in the other starting forward's position in the scorebook and tossed the book on the scorers' table. Coach Ruby, hastening to the table, took one nervous look at the lineup, then madly dashed out to his surprised players to inform them of the coup d'état.

Now, instead of the calm, eager, and confident Tigers, the surprise element was manifest. Missouri's defensive and offensive [needed to] be hastily shifted, and there was precious little time to do it.

Border warfare of Civil War days between Kansas and Missouri had deeply seared the free-soil and the slave-state citizens' burning prejudices against each other, and tonight, against this emotional background, this age-old animosity flamed anew.

The game was a sellout. The gymnasium was packed. Missouri versus Kansas! Another scrap! Howling, wild-eyed Missouri rooters, eager for the kill, were there in their deliriums of joy. Of course, they were unaware of the academic fatality that had befallen Kansas in the loss of one of her aces. But, for them, it was enough just to be there for the joust. The Missourians had been waiting a long time for this moment, and apparently it had arrived. They had a great outfit and really looked like much the better team.

Referee Quigley tossed the ball up at center, and with the blast of his whistle, the ballgame was on. [John] Wulf tipped to Frederick, who swooped upon the ball in midair and started a frantic swinging dribble circularly toward Kansas's basket. Big Herb Bunker, Missouri's bulldog of the basket, crowded him away from the coveted goal. Frederick quickly pivoted toward the sideline and rifled a back pass to the trailing Rody. Rody crouched and shot a long looping arch shot, dead into the basket. The score was Kansas 2, Missouri 0; and but six seconds of the ballgame gone. We needed the confidence this gave us. The strategy was working; Missouri was now surrendering her dominant position and was clearly on the defensive.

The mental lash of the Missouri crowds was showing in the Tiger play. The fury of the jungle was apparent to the Kansans, who were out in front by the slightest margin.

Frederick was slowing up, and immediately the Kansas offensive slackened. Missouri scored and the game was deadlocked.

Bowman, the diminutive Kansas firebrand, was shot into the fray, in the place of Frederick, to stem the Tiger onslaught.

Bowman did the superhuman thing. By dogging a ball destined for out-of-bounds and trapping it in its flight at the far corner of the court, he miraculously spun a one-hand, underarm shot for a bull's-eye, just as he and a Missourian sprawled headlong into the bleachers. The Kansas charge was still potent, and this score-adding punch was the ingredient needed to hold these Tigers at bay.

The half ended with the Kansans leading 10 to 6. "Certainly Missouri has not found herself," and "Doubtless Kansas is playing over her head," reasoned the Tiger followers as the teams left the court.

A long and lean sophomore Kansan—heretofore unmentioned in this story—Tusten Ackerman, before the half ended, was evincing a brand of basketball drive that, in this and the years to follow, was destined to write his name among the basketball immortals of the Middle West.

In another section of [*Better Basketball*], in a chapter on "Esprit de Corps," is told Ackerman's story of his pledge to avenge the death of his great athletic hero, Tommy Johnson, which he had erroneously supposed to have been caused by a Missouri football player many years before.

As the game went on it became clear that this was to be Tusten Ackerman's night. He was playing the game as if Tommy were watching him play it.

Spectators who watched Ackerman thrust through Missouri's defense like D'Artagnan's rapier, time and time again, commented that he played as if he were inspired. Ackerman was playing for Kansas as Tommy Johnson incarnate.

He did not miss a free throw, and his field goals were the balance of power in a smashing 26–15 upset victory for Kansas. So long as Tusten Ackerman played on a Kansas team, and even long after his graduation, Missouri did not win a basketball game from Kansas.

We are not dead so long as we live in the hearts and deeds of youth. Traditions are built by the continuity of youth's selfless acts in faithful emulation of the valorousness of the great who have lived before.

In the closing moments of this basketball drama, Woestemeyer, the obedient scorer but ineligible athlete, constantly kept urging me to put him in the ballgame. Our strategy as outlined had succeeded in keeping a Missouri star on the bench to match Woestemeyer's speed and skill, should he enter the game.

Just a minute or so before the game ended, we confided our coup d'état to the press reporters at the scorers' table, but too late for Missouri to pull the game out of the fire.

Perfect cooperation in game strategy and commendable team spirit in the face of adversity made this Kansas victory possible. The early-season defeat, the taunting alien challenge at the chocolate table while en route to Tigertown, the lost scorebook, the ineligibility of our star, and the season's hard grind were all forgotten in the glorious half hour in the dressing room after the game. The victory was worth the price we had to pay.

In the dressing-room celebration, the Kansans gave their world-famous battle cry, elongating, especially tonight, with abounding pride, the K and the U. Then they would give the three short staccato lines with an added victorious burst as they expressed the joy of conquest in their immortal yell:

> Ro-c-k ch-a-l-k, Ja-y Ha-w-k, K—U-oo-oo-oo
> Ro-c-k ch-a-l-k, Ja-y Ha-w-k, K—U-oo-oo-oo
> Rock chalk, Jayhawk, K-U
> Rock chalk, Jayhawk, K-U
> Rock chalk, Jayhawk, K-U

With this victory, Kansas won a conference co-championship with Missouri for the season of 1922. In an hour of commanding glory, she wrested from Missouri her right to share the crown.

Blair Kerkhoff, *The Kansas City Star*

AT 21–0, KU WANTED GOLD

As the Jayhawks started the 1996–97 season with a 21–0 record, people started talking about an undefeated season and reminiscing about other near-perfect seasons, in articles like this one by The Kansas City Star*'s Blair Kerkhoff, who was the KU beat writer for the paper. Incidentally, that '96–97 team went 34–2, losing in the Sweet 16 to eventual national champion Arizona.*

This Kansas team wants to become the best in the nation by winning the NCAA Tournament. The last time Kansas started a season this well, the Jayhawks were out to conquer the world.

Today against Nebraska, top-ranked Kansas, 21–0, can set the school record for the best start. Tip-off is 3:05 PM.

For the 1935–36 season, there were no weekly rankings or NCAA Tournament. But for the first time, there was a basketball competition in the Olympic Games, and the nation's top college team had an opportunity to supply the head coach and half of the team that was going to represent the United States in Berlin.

For most of 1936, that looked like Phog Allen and the Jayhawks.

They rolled through Big 6 competition at 10–0 and were 18–0 when a regional Olympic playoff was scheduled in brand-new Municipal Auditorium in Kansas City.

Kansas put away Washburn and Oklahoma A&M in regional competition. All that was left to qualify for the final eight-team Olympic playoff in New York was to win two of three from unheralded Utah State.

Again, the games were played at the Auditorium. Allen had the building dolled up in American flags and red, white, and blue streamers. Allen had been more responsible than anyone for getting basketball into the Olympics, and he wanted to display his patriotism in a first-class setting.

If only his team felt as strongly. The Jayhawks, behind all-conference stars Ray Ebling, Francis Kappelman, and Fred Pralle, won the opening game 39–37 in overtime.

10

There had been some controversy. Allen wanted his team to wear its white jerseys throughout the series. KU was the host, putting up the bucks, and had even paid Utah State's traveling expenses when the Aggies said they wouldn't come otherwise. Allen wanted to make a fashion statement.

Utah State coach Dick Romney told Allen that the Aggies had packed only their white jerseys. Allen called his bluff and had Kansas wear its white jerseys for the opener. Romney sent a manager back to the hotel for their blue tops.

That, and the opening game, were the only battles KU won against the Aggies. Utah State won the next two games and advanced to Madison Square Garden. The Aggies didn't get far there. The first Olympic team was made up of players from two [Amateur Athletic Union] teams: the McPherson, Kansas, Globe Oilers and the Universal Pictures from Los Angeles.

Kansas finished 21–2. Winning the last two games of the previous season gave the Jayhawks another school record, a 23-game winning streak.

As for the Olympics, Allen and the Jayhawks got another shot—26 years later. KU supplied half the team and Allen was the assistant at the 1952 Games in Helsinki, Finland, because the Jayhawks won the NCAA title and advanced to the finals of the Olympic playoff.

Dick Snider, *NCAA March Madness*

WHEN LOVELLETTE GOT CAUGHT

Clyde Lovellette, who led the nation in scoring in 1952, took the Jayhawks to college basketball's promised land that season for their first NCAA Tournament championship. Dick Snider, who was a sports editor at the Topeka Daily Capital, *penned the following article for the book* NCAA March Madness.

By the time the game ended and the Kansas Jayhawks had defeated St. John's of Brooklyn to win the 1952 NCAA basketball title, a sportswriter was standing on the court next to KU's legendary coach, Dr. Forrest C. "Phog" Allen.

The tournament was in Seattle, and it was well past deadline back at the writer's newspaper, the *Topeka* (Kansas) *Daily Capital.* He was in a hurry.

"Doc," the sportswriter yelled as the celebration started, "how about a quick quote for the folks back home?"

Allen, 66, who was in his 42nd year as a college head coach, and who had just won his first national championship, hesitated only a second.

"Tell them," he yelled back, "that we were just like Casey at the bat." With that Allen started to move into the crowd. The sportswriter grabbed his arm.

"But Doc," the writer yelled into his ear, "Casey struck out."

"Yeah," Allen thundered, "BUT WE DIDN'T."

That was that.

The sportswriter was hoping he would say something about Clyde Lovellette, his 6'9" senior center, who had played exceptionally well most of the season and who had been phenomenal in the final week and in the NCAA playoffs. The title was a personal triumph for the 245-pound Lovellette as much as it was for the controversial Allen.

In the last two games of the regular season, Clyde scored 33 points as Kansas defeated its top rival, Kansas State, to clinch a tie for the Big

7 title, and then scored 41 in a victory over Colorado that clinched both the title and the NCAA berth.

In regional play in Kansas City, he scored 31 in a 68–64 win over Texas Christian and 44 in a 74–55 bashing of St. Louis. Allen called the latter Clyde's best game ever.

In Seattle, he scored 33 as Kansas whipped Santa Clara, 74–55, in the Western final, and 33 more as the Jayhawks wiped out St. John's, 80–63, in the NCAA championship game.

And remember, folks, this was in the days when 30 points was a whole bunch, and 40 was a rare night to remember.

Kansas went on to play in the Olympic trials and defeated Southwest Missouri State and La Salle before losing to the Peoria Caterpillars of the AAU in the final. Lovellette scored 91 points in the three games but somehow missed a layup that could have been one of the biggest buckets of his career.

With 50 seconds to go against Peoria and the score tied, Lovellette stole the ball and dribbled the length of the court, escorted by two teammates. It was a three-on-nothing break. Incredibly, Clyde missed the layup. Peoria got the rebound and scored with eight seconds left to win, 62–60.

Clyde and four other Jayhawks made the Olympic squad that went to Helsinki and defeated Russia in the final.

Despite all this, *Look* magazine, headquartered in New York and one of the major sports voices of the day, didn't name Lovellette to its All-America first team. This caused Allen to dust off his old observation that "New Yorkers are taller and fairer than the Chinese, but not nearly as progressive."

Allen had a lot to say and made his usual headlines as Kansas ran out the season. First, Phog ripped the NCAA playoff system, saying Kansas was going only because the players wanted to go, and calling NCAA Tournament officials "as big a bunch of promoters as the AAU's quadrennial transoceanic hitchhikers."

After Kansas won the NCAA title and faced the Olympic trials in New York's Madison Square Garden, Allen threatened not to go unless he could have at least one Midwestern official work Jayhawk games. He didn't get the one he wanted, but he got one.

Phog had no reason to complain about the NCAA Final Four, particularly after St. John's upset Kentucky, which included the likes of Cliff Hagan and Frank Ramsey, in the Eastern final in Raleigh, North Carolina, and Santa Clara bounced UCLA in the Western final in Corvallis, Oregon.

Kansas won in Kansas City in a tournament that is memorable not only because of Lovellette, but also because a TCU player named George McLeod closed out a remarkable season there. In 24 games, he fouled out of 14 and had four fouls in nine of the other 10 (in all probability an NCAA record that still stands).

Big Ten champ Illinois won in Chicago to complete the Seattle field, and Lovellette took care of the rest. The toughest time Kansas had came the night before the tournament, when Clyde went out for the evening and was missing all night.

It wasn't his fault, and Allen knew where he was—or at least thought he did. Lovellette laughed about it later but admitted it was a matter of some concern at the time. Here's what happened:

A Sigma Chi fraternity brother of Clyde's from KU had become an ensign in the coast guard and was stationed on a cutter anchored in Puget Sound. He invited Lovellette out for dinner, and things went fine until they tried to return to shore in a small boat.

A dense fog had set in, and the two couldn't make it. After wandering around for a while, they wound up back on the cutter, and Clyde didn't get back to the hotel until after dawn.

"Phog had something to say to me," Clyde recalled, "but not too much. I think he was as glad to see me as I was to be back on dry land."

An early-rising radio man from Topeka, Gerry Barker, saw Clyde enter the hotel upon his return, but he never said anything and neither did the Jayhawks, so the rest of the media missed the story.

Compared to current Final Fours, the 1952 affair in Edmundson Pavilion on the University of Washington campus didn't amount to much. There was no television, so the teams traveled directly from the regionals to Seattle, and settled it all by playing Tuesday and Wednesday nights.

A few radio stations covered the tournament, but there probably were no more than a dozen newspapers from outside the area represented. Because it was an Olympic year, the Associated Press sent star writer Will Grimsley out from New York to cover it. It was the first time the Associated Press had invested that heavily in Final Four coverage.

Things were so slow that when the writers covering Santa Clara learned that Midwest writers called Lovellette "the Great White Whale," they looked over their roster and dubbed Kenny Sears, the lean, fairskinned Santa Clara star, "the Wan Worm from Watsonville."

Members of the Kansas supporting cast also deserved mention. Allen's assistant was Dick Harp, who was said by many to do most of the coaching while Phog did all the talking. Harp never dignified that observation with a reply.

On the squad with Lovellette was a fellow named Dean Smith, who didn't play much but who obviously learned a lot. There was Charlie Hoag, who also played football well enough to be ranked right up there with contemporaries Billy Vessels of Oklahoma and Bobby Reynolds of Nebraska.

There were the Kelly brothers, Dean and Allen; B. H. Born, who would lead the Jayhawks to the 1953 Final Four; Al Squires, the first black player ever at Kansas; and the rest—[Bob] Kenney, [Bill] Lienhard, [Bill] Hougland, [John] Keller, [Bill] Heitholt, and [Larry] Davenport.

Allen died in 1974 at age 88. Lovellette played professional basketball and was in law enforcement for a time before becoming a teacher at White's Institute in Wabash, Indiana.

Frank Deford, *NCAA March Madness*

WHEN THE FINAL FOUR CAME OF AGE

The 1957 NCAA championship game between Kansas and North Carolina is still maddening for KU fans, but it remains one of the best NCAA Tournament games of all time. Frank Deford, a longtime writer for Sports Illustrated, *as well as several other publications, wrote about the 1957 title contest for the book* NCAA March Madness.

The 1957 championship marked a watershed year for the NCAA and was, indisputably, one of the two or three most important tournaments. It was not just that North Carolina won in perhaps the most exciting final—before or since—in triple overtime; North Carolina also won its semifinal in triple overtime. North Carolina finished undefeated and became the first team from the old Confederacy to take the title.

In a sense, that was the last step in making college basketball truly national, for before that champions had come from the East, West, Midwest, and Southwest. Perhaps even more significant was where the personnel came from. Carolina, an essentially regional university in a Protestant state, fielded a team of Irish Catholic Yankees (and a Jew), while the team it beat in the final, Kansas, a rural state of down-home whites, featured a black sophomore seven-footer from Philadelphia, the fabled Wilt Chamberlain. College basketball was never the same again.

In point of fact, though, the 1957 championship did not have the immediate effect all of the foregoing would suggest. For purposes of comparison, recall that about a year and a half later the National Football League finally went on the map with an equivalent showcase—the overtime championship between the Baltimore Colts and the New York Giants. That changed the stature of the NFL literally overnight. But the greatest game ever played in college basketball, Carolina's 54–53 win over Kansas in triple overtime, was only the beginning of the process which made college basketball big-time.

There were simple reasons for this. In 1957, even though everyone in college basketball recognized that the NCAA Tournament had replaced the NIT as the official championship, the parochial *New York*

Press—and its first cousin, the *National Press* in New York—still looked down on the NCAA as a bush-town rival imitation. Even the presence of Chamberlain, who, it is safe to say, was the most ballyhooed athlete ever to enter college, wasn't enough to attract genuine national television coverage.

A few years ago, in searching for photographs to go with an article on the game, *Sports Illustrated* discovered, to its amazement, no more than three or four photographers on the floor. *Sports Illustrated* itself gave the game exactly one page—and no photograph—buried deep in the magazine back where there used to be bridge and food articles. Jerry Tax, who covered basketball for the magazine then, managed to get the article in only by pleading that it was, after all, three overtimes, Wilt the Stilt had been upset, and the kids who wore Carolina blue all came from New York.

Ironically, even though almost nobody saw the game—there was, evidently, only one television feed, back to North Carolina—the Kansas loss appears to be what is responsible for Chamberlain being tagged with a loser label. Chamberlain himself was convinced that was so. But in fact, he played a terrific game, and Carolina had to be almost picture-perfect to win by a point. In fact, in the last five seconds, Carolina botched defense on Chamberlain, and the teammate passing the ball to Chamberlain botched the pass. Chamberlain was the only one who did it right, but he didn't get the ball, and he got forever jacketed as a loser.

Actually, Carolina had no business even being in the final. Chamberlain had scored 32 to lead Kansas past San Francisco, 80–56, in its semi, but the only reason the Tar Heels got past Michigan State was because Bob Cunningham, the fifth man and a defensive specialist, scored a career-high 21 when the others went cold. Michigan State led, 64–62, and had Jumpin' Johnny Green on the free throw line with six seconds left in the first overtime. But Green missed, and Pete Brennan took the rebound, dribbled up the court, and fired up a 20-footer at the buzzer to stay alive. As Chamberlain told Tommy Kearns, the Carolina playmaker, years later after the old rivals became best friends, "Tommy, you were blessed."

Frank McGuire, the Tar Heels coach, sent Kearns to jump against Chamberlain at the tip-off. He wanted to rattle the giant; Kearns was the smallest Tar Heel, short of six feet. Chamberlain won the jump, of course, but Carolina won the rest of the half, going to the locker room on top, 29–22. Kansas coach Dick Harp elected to play a box-and-one, dogging the Carolina high scorer, Lennie Rosenbluth. It was not, it turned out, wise strategy. Carolina did better, sagging everybody onto Chamberlain.

But in the second half, Chamberlain brought Kansas back. Thirty-one minutes into the game, the Jayhawks finally took the lead, 36–35, and second-guessers still think they could have blown it open then—especially with two Carolina starters in deep foul trouble—but Harp elected to sit on the ball.

Still, it almost worked. Kansas led, 44–41, with 1:45 left, and when Chamberlain, moving up to high post, made a beautiful pass down into Gene Elstun, Rosenbluth had to foul Elstun—his fifth. When Elstun moved to the line, Chamberlain clearly remembers spotting a buddy in the stands and smiling at him, sure of victory. But Elstun missed and the moment was gone, and with seconds to go in regulation, Kearns tied it at 46–46 from the free throw line.

In the first overtime, each team scored one basket. In the second, nobody scored at all. The Tar Heels especially were exhausted, for their bench was thin, their high scorer was out of the game, and they were entering their sixth overtime—110 minutes of action—in barely 24 hours.

Kearns made a basket and then a one-and-one, but Chamberlain came back with a three-point play, and when Elstun sank two free throws, Kansas was up, 53–52. There were 10 seconds left when Joe Quigg, the center who had been playing with four fouls for almost half an hour's playing time, got the ball at the top of the key. Quigg pump-faked and drove against Chamberlain, but Maurice King reached in as Quigg put up the shot, and the foul was called. Six seconds remained on the clock.

Carolina called timeout, not Kansas. McGuire was renowned for knowing when to call time. Quigg was a 72 percent free throw shooter on the year, but he had missed his only foul shot in this game, so McGuire wanted to reassure him. "Now, Joe," he said, "as soon as you make 'em..." and then McGuire went on to discuss the defense.

Quigg swished twice, 54–53.

When Kansas threw in to Chamberlain, Quigg was also the one who batted the ball. Kearns picked it up, dribbled once, and then heaved the ball high in the air. He had seen "Hot Rod" Hundley do that once. By the time the ball came back down, North Carolina was the undefeated NCAA champion.

McGuire threw a victory party that night for all the Carolina people in Kansas City. The tab was $1,500, which the athletics director considered far too excessive just for winning a national basketball championship. So he made McGuire spring for the $58 extra for the Roquefort dressing.

The Tar Heels were celebrated in North Carolina, and then most of them returned home to New York, where, they assumed, more glory awaited them. Pete Brennan rushed to his home in Brooklyn. The Brennans shared a two-family house with the Cocoas next door. Mrs. Cocoa was coming out her side just as Brennan hurried up his steps. "Hey, Petey," Mrs. Cocoa said. "When did you get back from the soivice?" It would be a bit longer before what truly began in Kansas City in 1957 became the event it is today.

Bob Hurt, *The Topeka Daily Capital-Journal*

KANSAS FALLS IN TWO

There are very few games during KU's history that are as controversial as the 1966 Midwestern Regional loss against Texas Western, when star guard Jo Jo White was called out of bounds on a shot during the final minute of regulation. This is the game article written by longtime Topeka Daily Capital-Journal sports editor Bob Hurt.

Kansas stretched the season out by a couple of overtimes Saturday.

But the season ended Saturday. It ended as Texas Western defeated the Jayhawks 81–80 in the wonderfully weird and exciting finals of the NCAA Midwestern Regional.

Both teams oozed effort. Kansas could hardly be faulted. It lost only by a couple of inches—the inches by which Jo Jo White's foot was out of bounds as he shot in what appeared to be the winning bucket at the end of the first overtime.

Out of Bounds
Only two seconds showed on the clock as White let fire from 30 feet. But as the shot swished through the nets the official was pointing to the spot where White's foot had touched out-of-bounds on the sideline.

Kansas escaped lightning once, spurting through five points in a mere 38 seconds near the end of regulation time. This flurry, climaxed by White's steal for a three-pointer, sent the game into the first overtime at 69–69.

It was 71–71 at the end of the first overtime—after White's 30-footer was canceled. And the Jayhawks made another flurry at the end of the second overtime as Al Lopes scored seven points in the last 57 seconds. It was not enough.

Board strength, a factor for Western, was most evident at the start of the second overture. The Miners got the outer jump tip, missed four shots but retrieved the rebound each time. Finally, on try number five, sub Willie Cager tipped the ball in. With 3:50 left, Nevil Shed, who sat out the first half as a disciplinary measure for slugging a Cincinnati player Friday, hit two charities.

And the margin grew to 77–71 when Odsten Artis hit two more charities on Delvy Lewis's fifth foul. That proved insurmountable.

Lopes hit the free throw on the technical. Then, with two seconds left, he hit again from the field. It was too late.

The season was over for KU. It was a 23–4 season, fifth best in the school's history. For Western (26–1), the biggest part of the season lies ahead. The Miners, and three other regional survivors, go to Maryland for the national finals Friday.

The Jayhawks had fretted over Western's inside strength and aggressiveness, but they were killed, in the end, from the outside by Billy Joe Hill, a nifty southpaw who does everything with the basketball but lace it. He scooped, wheeled, drove, popped from outside, and hooked. The 8,000 fans kept waiting for him to bounce one in off some Jayhawk's head. He scored 22 points; David Lattin added 15 and Artis 12.

Walt Hits 24
Walter Wesley, although fouling out with 1:05 left in the second overtime, had game honors with 24. White scored 19, Lopes 17, and Franz 12.

Hill Stars
White's two free throws chopped it to four, but Western retaliated with its most awesome weapon of the game, 5'10" Billy Joe Hill. He hit two charities at 1:05.

Then Lopes took control of the game. He popped one in at 57 seconds, but Willie Cager, operating off a delay, got a layup for the Miners at 35 seconds.

Back bounced Lopes with 22 seconds. Now it was 81–77. Hope remained, thin though it was. The Jayhawks got a king-sized break when Western was called for traveling with six seconds left. Either in jubilation or in anger Western's 240-pound monster, David Lattin, took this occasion to hang from the rim. A technical foul was assessed.

The Jayhawks shot better from the field (45.5 percent to Western's 40.8) but were outrebounded by four (46–42) and outshot from the free throw line.

Bill Mohr, *The Topeka Daily Capital*

KANSAS BIDS BREWER NASTY FAREWELL, 71-69

Dave Robisch had some wonderful games for the Jayhawks during his career. But this one against Missouri, in the Tigers' final game at Brewer Fieldhouse, might have been the best, as Bill Mohr pointed out in his game story from March 9, 1971.

Dave Robisch has had better days, much better. But he might not savor them any more than his last minute of play against Missouri Monday night.

The Kansas senior's three free throws and two rebounds in the final minute of overtime carried KU to its second two-point, extra-period victory in the past three days, a 71–69 win over archrival Missouri in the final game ever in Mizzou's 42-year-old Brewer Fieldhouse.

The Tiger fans were up for this one. An overflow crowd of 6,000-plus kept the noise level high enough to split a truckload of crystal glass. And, the way KU played the first half, it appeared the crowd and an inspired Tiger quintet might hand the Jayhawks their first defeat in Big 8 play.

MU led by nine, 37–28 at the half, but the Hawks would not be denied, wiping out that lead in less than three minutes of the second half and going on to their 18th straight victory: 13th in the Big 8 and 24th against one loss for the season.

Missouri struck first in the overtime as 6'7" John Brown drove past Greg Douglas on the baseline for a layup and a 64–62 Missouri lead. Bud Stallworth countered for KU with a 15-foot jumper before Brown, driving on Douglas, again was fouled by Greg. The 6'7" Missouri sophomore hit one free throw for the final Tiger lead of the night.

Aubrey Nash, whose outside shooting was the only consistent KU weapon in the first half, wheeled around Mike Griffin and spun in a layup with 2:40 to play when KU went on top 66–65.

MU center Henry Smith, high for both teams for the night with 24, tried to slip past Douglas on a drive, but Greg intercepted and, after wiping 30 seconds off the clock, Pierre Russell fired in a wide open 10-footer with 1:52 to play for a 68–65 KU lead.

Smith gave Missouri partisans hope with a short hook 1:18 from the end and, when Nash missed both ends of a deliberate two-shot foul, the roar was deafening.

Robisch, however, shut down the volume considerably by rebounding Aubrey's second miss. He laid the ball in, but Mike Jeffries was detected fouling Dave and the bucket was not allowed.

Robisch got the two points anyway from the charity stripe with 44 seconds of play left. Missouri came down and lofted four shots goalward. None connected. The fourth miss was captured by Robisch, who was immediately decked.

He hit the first of two free throws with 11 seconds remaining to make it 71–67, and KU let Griffin drive the length of the court to score two seconds before the buzzer.

KU, four points down, 62–58, with 2:45 left in regulation, gained the deadlock on a layup by Douglas and two free throws by Stallworth. Mizzou tried to nurse the slim lead through the final two minutes with a stall, but two errant passes gave KU possession.

The Jayhawks were at their best in the early portion of the second half. Working mainly to Roger Brown inside, they outscored the Tigers 10–1 to draw even at 38–38 in a span of 2:56.

Brown got six of the points, then two minutes later picked up fouls four and five.

Douglas filled in capably, finishing with 11 points. The 6'8" senior has had his best efforts in Brewer Fieldhouse. Two years ago he scored his career high of 16 points here.

Nash led KU scorers for the first time in his two seasons at Lawrence with 16, going 7 for 15 from the field. Robisch was next with 15 but only connected on five of 19 tries.

Kansas will try to become the third team in the past 25 years to have a perfect conference record when it hosts Nebraska in the regular season finale Saturday night.

Dick Russell, *The Sporting News*

JAYHAWKS FANS HAIL STALLWORTH, AND NO WONDER!

The 1971–72 season was a disaster. A year removed from playing in the Final Four, the Jayhawks weren't going anywhere with their 10–13 record heading into the February 26 game at Allen Fieldhouse against Missouri. Bud Stallworth, who was an academic All-American at KU in 1971, played the game of his career that "Senior Day" afternoon against the Tigers. Dick Russell, who wrote this article for The Sporting News*'s March 18, 1972, issue, was a staff reporter for* Sports Illustrated *between 1969 and 1970 and later for* TV Guide Magazine, *before becoming an author and environmental journalist. He graduated from the University of Kansas in 1969.*

It was like the state had just repealed prohibition. In all of Kansas, from the capitol dome to the western wheatfields, the same sign flashed neon-red: BUD.

Inside Allen Fieldhouse, the University of Kansas band played the Bud commercial. Jayhawk partisans swayed in rhythm, arms above their heads, "waving the wheat."

And on the basketball court, a thousand jubilant fans jostled to touch just one man. A flowing sheet with red and blue lettering proclaimed: "When you say Bud Stallworth—you've said it all."

"I've never seen anything like this," shouted one Kansan to another. "You'd think we'd just won the national championship."

The Jayhawks' 11–13 record was a long way from championship caliber, but Bud Stallworth, the 6'5" senior forward, had just scored 50 points against Missouri, giving the Jayhawks a 93–80 victory.

The Big 8 conference scoring record toppled in typical Stallworth fashion. It happened in his last KU appearance, on a painful knee and before his mother, Ivy, who journeyed up from Hartselle, Alabama, for her one and only chance to see Bud play in Allen Fieldhouse.

That's the way Bud does things—with an unassuming manner, a perpetual "gee-whiz" grin, and a penchant for embodying the wildest Walter Mitty fantasies.

Bud was discovered at a high school music camp. He now becomes the first All-Star trumpet tooter to grace *The Sporting News*'s All-America team.

He's Already a Legend

The story of Stallworth's discovery now ranks with Quantrill's raid as a Kansas legend. After his junior year at Hartselle's Morgan County High, Bud journeyed to Lawrence for the university's annual six-week music camp. His sister, Harrietta, already was a math major at KU and had urged Bud to come to gain some trumpeting expertise.

One afternoon, Bud wandered over to Robinson Gymnasium for a pickup basketball game. Included among his opposition was Jo Jo White, the KU All-America guard and now a Boston Celtics star. Jo Jo liked what he saw and promptly gave the word to Jayhawks coach Ted Owens.

Journeying to Hartselle on a winter recruiting trip, Owens watched Stallworth score 45 points. Bud soon put away his trumpet to become the KU trump.

He will finish his college career as the number seven scorer in Big 8 history. The Missouri game sent him soaring past Wilt Chamberlain into the number three spot on Kansas's own list of marksmen. With two games remaining, his season clip of 24.9 would give him the fourth-ranked average in conference history.

Stallworth has been the neon rainbow in an otherwise dim Kansas season. Owens, whose teams have produced such pro stalwarts as Walt Wesley, Ron Franz, White, and Dave Robisch, rates Stallworth with the best of them.

"I think he compares with any of Kansas's great ones," said Owens. "I've never had a forward with that kind of offensive potential. And I've never seen a better offensive game than the one he had against Missouri."

Bud should be an even better pro, Owens continued. "He has almost classic form and hasn't even touched his potential. When he gets in a wide-open running game with a team that can dominate rebounding, you'll see the best Bud Stallworth has to offer."

It hasn't all been a fairy-tale road, despite Bud's ubiquitous smile. Even the smile got dented at the summer music camp, when he received a misplaced elbow in the mouth from 6'8", 260-pound Vernon Vanoy (now with the NFL Giants).

Following a prep career that saw him score 50 on five occasions, Bud outpointed Travis Grant in Alabama's prep All-Star game and was named the Most Valuable Player.

Turning down a chance to become the University of Alabama's first black athlete, he led the 1969 Jayhawk freshman squad in scoring and rebounding.

His sophomore varsity debut was 27 points—only Wilt had a better one. But by the end of the year, Bud had fallen into a drastic slump. Riding the bench the last four games, he averaged only 12.7.

Last year, when the Jayhawks took a 27–1 record into the NCAA final round against UCLA, Stallworth was all-conference with a 16.9 average. Then the Jayhawks had a pair of 6'10" stars, Robisch and Roger Brown.

Key Member of Cast

This season, Stallworth was one of the tallest men in the lineup. Very early, it was evident how important his shooting would be. This was a young Kansas team, with Stallworth and 6'1" guard Aubrey Nash the only returning starters.

The Jayhawks couldn't match many foes on the boards, and only inexperienced sophomore Dave Taynor and Stallworth possessed keen shooting eyes.

Most of Bud's shots came from the five- to 20-foot range. Opponents tried a variety of "stop Stallworth" defenses. After Colorado's box-and-one held Bud to 11 points, others tried to copy it, but Bud solves problems in a hurry.

One difficulty has been a lame right knee. On the day before the crucial Kansas State clash in mid-January, Stallworth collided with 6'9" center Randy Canfield in practice. Until just before game time, he seemed a doubtful starter. Hobbling out to warm up, he told a teammate, "It feels like it's coming off." Still, he insisted Owens keep him in the starting lineup.

"After he'd played five minutes, I thought it was very doubtful he could finish," said KU trainer Dean Naismith. "But he wouldn't ask to be taken out."

Owens rested Stallworth only once, for a three-minute stretch.

"When he put me back in the second time, I just put the pain out of my mind," Bud recalled.

The result was 28 points, a bundle of clutch defensive plays, and a double-overtime 66–63 victory over the Wildcats. The remainder of the season has been a daily round of weightlifting, whirlpool treatments, and taping.

Ice Pack for Knee

"I've been able to do everything I normally do," said Bud. "My knee is usually sore after games, so I just keep an ice pack on for a while."

Naismith sees a hidden design behind Bud's grin.

"He's like a grinning tiger. Sure he smiles when he fouls somebody, but that grin is saying, 'I did something wrong this time, but I'll get you next time.'"

When Owens talks about mental attitude, he can't resist drawing comparisons with White.

"Both have had great confidence in their shooting ability. Jo Jo had a different kind of facial expression, almost unemotional. He did smile some, but he was pretty cool and businesslike. Bud has a pleasant expression, but he's really an extremely intense competitor. Neither one loses his poise very easily."

The comparison with White may be more than coincidental. Bud worked out all last summer with the man who discovered him, in scrimmage games at East Topeka High.

Learned the Hard Way

"Jo Jo must have been playing over his head," Bud recalled, giving that sly grin again. "Either that, or I was wondering if I was really that bad."

Stallworth figures he learned the hard way. "Man, it's tough to compete in that summer heat. Jo Jo's kind of tough to handle in a one-on-one situation with no referees. He has a lot of little tricks."

Owens noticed improvement, particularly once the conference race began.

"Before, Bud had not used a good shot selection," said Owens. "Teams were learning to predict his moves. He's improved considerably in both areas.

"Bud never has been one of our defensive stoppers, mainly because I haven't wanted him to get in foul trouble. I haven't usually put him on our opponent's best offensive player. But against Oklahoma I had to use him against Bobby Jack, and he really responded."

That's the only way to describe Stallworth: he responds. Missouri came to Allen Fieldhouse February 26 with a 19–3 record and the conference lead. The Jayhawks, already out of the race, were cast in a spoiler's role.

Few ever have "spoiled" better than Stallworth. The Tigers tried three different defenders. Still the points kept swishing home. When Bud scored 24 of Kansas's first 30 points, every one of the 15,900 fans sensed something special brewing.

Lovellette Watches Show

Rallying the Jayhawks from a two-point halftime deficit, Stallworth kept the shots falling in. Clyde Lovellette, on hand for the 20th reunion of KU's 1952 NCAA champions, watched Bud surpass his own personal high of 44 with 6:16 remaining. Then with 20 seconds left, Owens got a call from the upper bleachers. It was freshman coach Bob Frederick, telling him Bud was close to 50.

"We were out of timeouts," said Owens. "We were screaming for them to try and get it to Bud. I motioned with my hands for him to shoot.

"I think," Owens added with a grin, "he knew what I meant."

While the crowd hushed, Bud calmly swished in two free throws (12 of 13 for the game) to reach the magic figure. Only Chamberlain, who scored 52 in his debut in a nonconference game in 1956, ever had more for Kansas.

Stallworth was carried off the floor by jubilant fans.

Meantime, down in Hartselle, Alabama, a high school junior named Jerry Stallworth had a prep game scheduled. After his ninth-grade year, he, too, had visited Kansas.

But that one had nothing to do with music. It was Ted Owens's annual basketball camp. Obviously, the Jayhawks coach is taking no chances that Bud's younger brother might prefer the trumpet.

Bob Hentzen, *The Topeka Capital-Journal*

GUY BRILLIANT IN JAYHAWKS' 88-71 WIN

It had been a long drought for the Jayhawks. They hadn't advanced in the NCAA Tournament since reaching the Final Four in 1973–74. But here they were in 1981, through the first two rounds (including an upset of Arizona State), as reported by Capital-Journal *sports editor Bob Hentzen on March 16.*

Considering the events of the weekend in the NCAA basketball tourney, it comes as no real surprise that Kansas defeated Arizona State—the highest-seeded team assigned to Henry Levitt Arena.

But, no, the Jayhawks didn't need a stirring comeback. No, they didn't need a last-second shot. No, they didn't need to hold the ball against the team that led the Pac-10 in scoring (79.5) and came here 24–3 and ranked number three in the AP poll.

At the finish, believe it or not, the non-scholarship players were on the floor for the Jayhawks.

What happened is that Kansas treated Arizona State as if it were a Rollins or a Morehead—you know, one of those ballclubs that appear on the December schedule to absorb a flogging.

The score was 88–71, and ASU collected the last seven points.

"This is the greatest moment in my life," said junior guard Tony Guy afterward.

Anybody who has ever laced up a sneaker can only dream about playing a basketball game like Guy did Sunday. He hit 13 of 15 from the field and 12 of 14 from the line for 36 points. When he wasn't filling the nets, he took time to gather five rebounds and make four steals.

"He's played a lot of great basketball for us, but that's his best," said coach Ted Owens, whose team is now one of only 16 left with a chance to win the national championship.

The Jayhawks move on to New Orleans's Superdome Friday night to meet Wichita State—the two schools haven't met since December 7, 1955—in the Midwest Regional semifinals.

Guy, who had an average 14-point game here Thursday night in the squeaker against Ole Miss, gave early evidence that this was going to be a special occasion.

He scored KU's first three buckets and four of their first five to give the Jayhawks the lead, momentum, and confidence.

As the capacity crowd of 10,666 buzzed, Kansas scored the last 10 points of the half to go up 45–29. Certainly a team the caliber of Arizona State wouldn't fold its tent, would it?

Well, ASU ripped in seven unanswered points to open the second half as KU missed four shots and committed two turnovers. But the rally was of short duration.

John Crawford banked one in off the glass, Guy hit a driving layup and another from the baseline, and David Magley followed with a spectacular layup on a fast break. KU was back up 53–38, and you could stick a fork in the Sun Devils.

Crawford was another big hero for the Jayhawks, scoring 18 points and embarrassing Arizona State's 7' center Alton Lister by stuffing over him and pinning an attempted Lister jam against his hand.

"I guess we weren't mentally prepared for them," said Sun Devil guard Byron Scott, who provided most of their offense with long swishers over the KU zone to finish with 32 points.

"We were definitely flat," said ASU coach Ned Wulk. "We simply did not play with much intensity at all. We just had a horrendous game, that's all, and it couldn't have happened at a worse time."

A coaching ploy—sending guards Darnell Valentine and Guy to the backboards—worked to perfection. Owens felt rebounding was the key going in, and the Jayhawks finished with a 38–33 edge.

"We had five people jumping on the boards," said Owens. "I talked to Tony and Darnell after the Mississippi game about adding their contribution." In all, three KU guards accounted for 12 boards—and this preoccupation with rebounds didn't prevent the Jayhawks from getting out on the fast break.

"We didn't have real intensity picking guys up," said the perplexed Wulk, "and we did nothing on the offensive boards at all."

Explained Crawford, "We just played fundamental basketball and blocked out on the boards. When you control the boards, you more or less control the tempo of the game."

Jackie MacMullan, *Boston Globe*

KANSAS IS THE BIG ONE

They say you always remember your first one and your last one. So, 1988 remains embedded in the minds of Jayhawks. Not just because it was the last one, but also because of "Danny and the Miracles." This piece was written by the Boston Globe's *Jackie MacMullan, one of the nation's best sportswriters.*

They said Oklahoma couldn't be beaten if you ran with them. They said Oklahoma couldn't be beaten if you crawled with them.

But no one ever said anything about doing both in the same game. Kansas, the master of momentum, ran at the Sooners for the first 20 minutes, then put Coach Billy Tubbs and his troops down for a nap in the final 20 to shock its heavily favored Big 8 counterpart, 83–79, to win the NCAA basketball championship last night in Kemper Arena.

A highly partisan Jayhawk crowd howled with delight as Kansas controlled the tempo from start to finish, leaving Oklahoma guessing at every turn.

Then, with the game on the line, Kansas counted on Danny Manning to put the game away with free throws. The All-America forward answered the call, hitting both ends of a one-and-one with 14 seconds to play (81–77, Kansas), then coaxing in two more with five seconds left to seal the 83–79 victory.

Oklahoma, which led for the last time with 9:42 to play (68–67), missed nine of its final 12 shots.

Oklahoma, down 78–77, fouled Scooter Barry with 0:16 on the clock, and he hit the front end. Barry fell short on the second, but Manning grabbed the rebound and was fouled by Stacey King. Manning hit both. Ricky Grace put in a 360-degree layup in the middle with 0:07 to play.

Oklahoma had missed seven shots in a row when Grace finally coaxed in a layup with 0:59 to play to pull his club within 78–75. Mookie Blaylock then picked off the inbounds pass by Chris Piper and relayed it to Grace.

Grace's three-pointer didn't fall, and Oklahoma quickly fouled Manning. Manning missed the front end of his one-and-one with 52 seconds to go, and Blaylock iced his perimeter jumper to make it 78–77 Kansas and just 41 ticks until it was all over.

Kansas was on top, 73–71, when Manning went hard to the hole. His shot bounced three times, then fell.

After Grace missed a three-pointer down the other end, Kansas took its sweet time before Piper nailed a short jumper just as the shot clock expired. With 3:05 to play, the deliberate Jayhawks were ahead, 77–71.

Kansas coach Larry Brown said he wanted to be close at halftime, since Oklahoma was 31–0 on the season after leading at the half. Knowing full well his club could not keep up the kamikaze pace of the first 20 minutes, the coach got his club back into his motion offense in the second half.

In fact, the Jayhawks built up a four-point lead (58–54) before a Grace three-pointer caused the momentum to swing back to the Sooners.

But even after the 11–2 run was complete and Oklahoma was on top, 65–60, the advantage was only safe for the moment.

Piper answered with a 15-footer, then Manning took King to school for the second time with a nifty three-point play that tied it 65–65 with 11:13 to go.

Then Kansas made the decision to take the air out of the ball. The Jayhawks taunted Oklahoma by holding the ball out until the shot clock wound down under 10, then went inside to Manning. On three straight possessions, Kansas slowed the pace to a crawl, and on three straight possessions, it scored a hoop. The last, a baseline jumper from Piper, kept the lead in Jayhawk hands, 71–68, with 7:22 to play.

Seconds before that, Grace picked up his fourth foul, and Tubbs made only his second substitution of the game. At that juncture, Kansas had already made 26.

It was no surprise that Oklahoma would try to run away with this national championship, but Kansas beat it to the track in the opening minutes.

The two teams geared into a suicidal pace in the first six minutes, a pace that was set by the Jayhawks the first time they touched the ball. On that play, Kevin Pritchard made a beeline to the hole. He was whistled for traveling, but it didn't matter. The Jayhawks kept coming and coming and coming and, in the process, one of the most exciting halves in college basketball history ended in a 50–50 deadlock.

No team had ever scored 100 points in the title game, yet both teams seemed quite committed to being the first.

Kansas pushed it up when Oklahoma missed, and pushed it up with long inbounds lobs even if the Sooners scored.

By the time the first official break came at 14:02, Kansas was on top, 16–13, and had scored 10 of those points on transition. The

Sooners, meanwhile, the team that likes to break, had scored only one basket on transition.

The obvious question was, how could the Jayhawks keep up the pace? Brown's answer was to sub in a new body on almost every whistle. As it was, Oklahoma did not make its first (and only) substitution of the half until there was 7:16 left before intermission.

By then, a small semblance of order had been established, mainly because the key to the Jayhawks' game plan, Manning, was forced to the sidelines with 10:44 until the half with two fouls.

As a result, Kansas actually let the shot clock click below 20 for the first time. No matter. Pritchard nailed a three-pointer and the Jayhawks were on top, 31–25.

That advantage stood for precisely eight seconds before Dave Sieger countered with one of his six three-pointers of the half. Without Sieger's bombardments, Oklahoma could have been in serious trouble. He added a seventh in the second half to tie Steve Alford's record for a championship game set last year with Indiana.

For one thing, Kansas had a white-hot shooting touch (it checked in at 71 percent on 22 of 31 attempts at halftime) and, for another, it was doing an admirable job of neutralizing the duo of King and Grant off the glass (Oklahoma held a slim 17–15 edge).

And, third, there was Manning. He checked back in with 7:16 left and, after Grant led his club on a quick 6–0 run (39–36, Oklahoma), Manning went to work again.

With the game knotted, 48–48, and less than a minute to play, Manning leaped in front of Sieger's entry pass to King. He then ambled down the floor, ball in tow, with King charging fast. Manning waited until the defender committed, then scooped an over-the-shoulder hoop that fell through with 0:44 on the clock.

Manning (14 at the half) missed the free throw, and Grace knocked in a hoop on a broken play with 22 seconds to go to tie it 50–50, but none of that detracted from the electricity generated by both teams.

Skip Myslenski, *Chicago Tribune*

KANSAS IS NO PIECE OF ART; IT'S JUST A NICE PIECE OF WORK

After the setback of probation during the 1989 season, which left KU as the only team not to be allowed to defend its championship, the Jayhawks made their move the next year under second-year coach Roy Williams. Basketball writer Skip Myslenski showed how the Jayhawks climbed from the ashes so quickly in 1990. Incidentally, KU lost in the second round of the NCAA Tournament to UCLA, but the groundwork had been laid for the Jayhawks' success for the rest of the decade.

Kevin Pritchard, the Kansas guard (and, parenthetically, a Cubs and Ryne Sandberg fan), remembers the predictions well. Fourth, sixth, even eighth, for heaven's sake: that is where the preseason prophets saw the Jayhawks finishing in the Big 8. "It was almost kind of a joke to us," he also remembers. "But, maybe, in the back of our minds, it made us question ourselves. It sent some fear into our hearts, and made us work as hard as we could."

Roy Williams, the Kansas coach (who, parenthetically, was introduced as Ron Williams at an NIT banquet), remembers that time as well. "I didn't have a feel for this team until we started practice," is what he remembers. "But after we started and I saw how everyone was meshing—that word *chemistry*—I felt pretty good."

Then, independently, both player and coach remember that preseason NIT, the tournament the Jayhawks used to announce themselves to an ignorant world. First, at home, they easily defeated Alabama-Birmingham, and then they set off for Baton Rouge and a meeting with highly heralded LSU. "Boy, you guys can spoil [the NIT's] party," TV analyst Dick Vitale told Williams as his players shot around hours before that game. "They really want LSU and Vegas [the preseason top pick] up there bad."

"Let's go spoil their party," Williams told his players just before they left their locker room to play that game.

They did just that with their surprising victory over the Tigers, and with that they were off to New York, where they routed Vegas and St. John's and grabbed a tourney title all thought beyond their grasp. "That," Williams now remembers, "gave us a great deal of confidence. Then the kids believed we could be pretty good. So it kinda snuck up on everybody—and, I can say, it snuck up on me, too."

"At the beginning of a season," remembers Pritchard, "there are always question marks, so I thought LSU was a stepping stone for us. More than anything, it gave us confidence. Then we beat UNLV and, well, any time you beat the number one and number two teams in the nation, you know you can't be too shabby."

Shabby is hardly the adjective to describe these Kansas Jayhawks, who entered their 77–71 loss Tuesday night to second-ranked Missouri atop the polls and sporting a garish 24–1 record. They are, instead, one of this college basketball season's certified success stories, a collection of diverse talents who operate together with the cool precision of a watchmaker.

They are, as a whole, better than any of their individual parts and in action are able to breathe life into all those Xs and Os that normally exist only on a blackboard. They may not be an All-Airport team, as Syracuse is, and they may resemble a YMCA team, as Pritchard himself once described them, yet they operate always with full-blooded will-fulness and an unerring sense of purpose.

"Poetry in motion" is what Miami coach Bill Foster called them.

"I really enjoyed watching Kansas play. They're a team. I'd like to see more teams like that," said former UCLA coach John Wooden.

"It's seldom you run against a team that plays with such good chemistry and feel. It's like no one plays with any ego," said Oklahoma State coach Leonard Hamilton.

"I give them a 'thought of the day' every day," says Williams himself, "and the first one I gave them this season was this: it's amazing how much can be accomplished when no one cares who gets the credit."

But credit for much of their success must go to the 39-year-old Williams, who was hired by Kansas shortly after it won the 1988 NCAA title and Larry Brown defected to the NBA Spurs. Williams was then an unknown—nothing more than a longtime assistant (10 years) to Dean Smith at North Carolina—and his selection distressed those Jayhawk fans who favored a coach with a higher profile (Maryland's Gary Williams was another candidate).

Their reservations put immediate pressure on the newcomer, and then the NCAA added to the weight when it slapped the school with probation on Halloween night. No postseason play in 1989, that was one of the sanctions then imposed, and when Williams heard the news, he recalls, "It was shock, disbelief. I felt a little bit sorry for myself. I didn't know what I was going to say to the kids."

That sense of self-pity cloaked him through the next morning's press conference and as he boarded a bus with his team for a trip to nearby Salina. They were scheduled to scrimmage there that evening, and as they traveled, Williams mused. "If I lay my head down on the desk and cry, I'm not going to help anyone," he thought.

"I knew the kids were going to look at me, so by 3:00 it was over," he says now. "Then it was, 'Let's go to work and play ball.'"

His Jayhawks played well enough to open that season 13–1, but then injuries struck; they stumbled badly and finished at only 19–12. That poor finish, their tourney absence, and the lack of a marquee name were the reasons they were disregarded and relegated to the wings before this current year opened.

But, lurking unnoticed, were all the ingredients necessary for success. There were Pritchard and Jeff Gueldner, the starting backcourt on their championship team. There was transfer Rick Calloway, who had started for Indiana's 1987 national champions. There were Mike Maddox, a sub in 1988; Mark Randall, an injury redshirt in 1988; and newcomer Pekka Markkanen, a member of Finland's national team.

There was, simply, a plethora of experience, a bevy of battle-tested veterans; and they coalesced and easily handled Williams's strict demands. *Work hard* was one of them and *be smart* was another. [The team had to] apply those two principles while playing belly-up defense and a sophisticated offense that depended on numerous passes, crunching screens, and moving without the ball.

"I can't remember the last time I saw anyone cut someone up like that," marveled St. John's Lou Carnesecca after Kansas did just that to his Redmen. "They've got more moves than the Three Musketeers."

"They're running our stuff," Carolina's Smith once exclaimed. "What bugs me is they're executing it better than we are."

"Our kids," says Williams, "take a lot of pride in doing it this way."

"I think we show that you don't need great talent all the time," says Pritchard. "You need some, but if you like to play together, if you have that buzzword *chemistry*, you can do all right."

All right is hardly the adjective to describe these Jayhawks' accomplishments, yet that question still buzzes around them. Just how talented are these guys, that is the question. It is prompted by their looks (unimposing), their style (subtle), and their lack of an All-American (though five of them average in double figures). And it has led to comments like this, from a Miami writer: "They would have trouble jumping over a telephone directory."

"I believe," Williams said to that, "that we can jump over two telephone directories."

"These kids are talented, and that [question] bothers us a little bit," he says now. "But we laugh at it and preach that talent is more than running and jumping. We preach that your brain is part of your talent, and so, yes, we want to play smart basketball. A lot of people talk about talent and forget about heart, but we preach that your heart is part of your talent too, and we take pride in working harder than anybody."

"Being smart is a talent. Playing smart is a talent," echoes Pritchard. He is the catalyst of these Jayhawks, and—as an underrated and unappreciated point guard—a symbol as well. So now he is asked if they're feeling any satisfaction, any special sense of satisfaction in proving the experts wrong.

He bounces the ball he is holding, then smiles softly. "Ask me at the end of the year. Call me then," he finally says. "I don't want to go off saying yes or no now. You know, there's that saying about success not being an end but a journey. Right now, we're still in the middle of our journey."

Gib Twyman, *The Kansas City Star*

KU WAS TEAM LEFT STANDING

As many of this book's stories show, the University of Kansas and the University of North Carolina have had this long-shared bloodline, which may have ended for the most part when Roy Williams left KU to become the Tar Heels' head coach. But in 1991, there was one matchup that the coaches dreaded, the players didn't mind, and the fans loved: Kansas against North Carolina for a chance to go to the national championship game. The late Gib Twyman offered this assessment of the game.

If you put it in fighters' terms—and nothing could be more apt when defining the Kansas basketball team—you'd say that, above all, it has a great chin.

This battle with North Carolina, which the Jayhawks won 79–73 Saturday in a semifinal game of the Final Four at the Hoosier Dome, was theorized to coming down to some exotic abstract called "the [North Carolina] system." It was the maharishi, Dean Smith, versus the grasshopper, the student, Roy Williams. The teams would cut and pass and execute and one team would surgically excise the other from the tournament.

Instead, the game was as subtle as a wrecking ball. The teams wound up forgoing such niceties as shooting touch or passing fancy or nifty moves that diagram neatly on the telestrator. They stood toe to toe—Heel to Heel, if you will, because they were supposed to be playing Carolina basketball—and simply flogged each other.

When it was over, KU was more able to eat leather, to play Smokin' Joe basketball, to keep taking two or three punches to deliver one. Instead of the Jayhawks wearing down, it was KU that made Carolina buckle to a knee and exit this tournament on a TKO.

"The single best way I can describe this team is that we compete," Williams said, answering for the thousandth time whether his team was "athletic" enough to be a national champion. "If you had a running, jumping, dunking contest, we'd finish down the line. But we kept our poise. Even when we made mistakes down the stretch, they weren't panic mistakes.

"Competitiveness goes a long way to make up for who wins dunk contests. I'm not saying either team played pretty today. This team looks ugly and wins ugly at times. But it plays its tail off. We withstood every run they took at us and we won."

Ugly is almost too kind of a word for this game. North Carolina shot 38.4 percent from the field and KU 40.9. The turnover-assist ratios were beer-league, rather than Final Four, quality: 17 assists, 18 turnovers for Kansas; 16 and 15 for the Tar Heels.

North Carolina's seniors simply seemed to conclude their uniforms made nice swimming trunks and went into the tank. Rick Fox hit five of 22 shots, King Rice one of six, Pete Chilcutt two of eight. KU had to weather a poor night by Terry Brown: one of 10.

In a scenario like that, it might be assumed that the Dean Machine would grind KU under. It had too many bodies, too talented a bench for Royball to survive. But it was KU's subs who torpedoed North Carolina. Freshman forward Richard Scott had 14 points in 16 minutes, and KU got 25 bench points to the Tar Heels' 13.

KU also won this game because Williams outcoached—and eventually outclassed—his mentor, Smith. It was Williams who got his team back to playing the game Phog Allen taught Dean and Dean taught Roy: easy hoops win games. KU got 49 frontcourt points to North Carolina's 36.

"Eight minutes into the game we were too tentative, shooting too much outside," Williams said. "I had to chew them out: 'Let's not give them too much respect. Don't give in to fatigue. Challenge the lanes, get on the boards, take it to their big men.'" When Smith got the third ejection of his career, after his second technical, KU was up 76–71 with 35 seconds left.

"I screamed at them, 'Let's play! The game's 40 minutes, not 39 minutes, 25 seconds. Keep the pressure on to the horn,'" Williams said.

KU did. It took one more punch in the mouth and landed one more haymaker than North Carolina, and now the Jayhawks are in the title bout.

Kevin Haskin, *The Topeka Capital-Journal*

KANSAS EXTENDS STREAK, CLINCHES SHARE OF CROWN

Going into the 2005–06 season, no one really knew what to expect out of the Jayhawks, including head coach Bill Self. Sure, it was obvious they'd be young, with a freshman class that included Mario Chalmers, Brandon Rush, and Julian Wright. The team struggled throughout much of the season's first half. And, after beating Colorado in the Big 12 opener, KU lost at home to Kansas State, ending a 31-game streak, and at Missouri during consecutive games. After those games, though, the team matured, started playing together, and won all but one of the rest of their conference games that season, culminating with the Big 12 conference championship title. The following game served two purposes: it closed out the regular season with a win, ensuring at least a share of the Big 12 conference championship, and it avenged the earlier season loss to the Wildcats. The Capital-Journal's *Kevin Haskin filed the following story for March 5, 2006, which shows just how much this Jayhawks team changed during the season—and why KU fans could be optimistic heading into the 2006–07 campaign.*

The flailing arms exhorting fans to cheer, as well as the smiles beaming from the faces, said it all in the final seconds Saturday in Bramlage Coliseum.

But, as is customary whenever Kansas visits Kansas State, most of the fans weren't smiling.

Not when Russell Robinson was waving his arms, Jeff Hawkins was dribbling out the clock with a wide grin, and KU was doing all the celebrating.

With a 23rd consecutive road victory at K-State, the number-18-seeded Jayhawks also claimed a stake of the Big 12 championship, outlasting the Wildcats 66–52 before a sellout crowd of 13,340.

"From my standpoint, this was sweeter than any of the other [league titles] I've had, because we started 1–2," KU coach Bill Self said.

"We were 1–2, we weren't very good, and guys got confidence, guys grew up, and we got good late. So with me, I have more pride with a team that's not expected to do it."

At 22–7 overall and 13–3 in the Big 12, the only question for the Jayhawks is whether they must share the crown with Texas, which plays today against Oklahoma.

The Jayhawks can sit back and prop up their feet watching that one.

Anything subdued, however, will be a stark contrast to their exultation inside the tiny visitors' locker room in Bramlage.

"Nobody got hurt," reported freshman forward Julian Wright. "Everybody was laughing, jumping around. You wouldn't think we'd have that kind of energy, but everybody was into it and it was good to see all the seniors with smiles on their faces. This is going to be a nice ride home for an hour and a half."

Somewhere along I-70, as much as no one at KU or K-State wanted to talk about it before the game, the Jayhawks probably mentioned the streak in Manhattan, which also includes an 18–0 mark in Bramlage.

"It was pretty good, because they [won] on our home court," Hawkins said. "We knew that if they'd beat us, they'd have stormed the court, and we didn't want that."

"It's good to keep [the Manhattan streak] going," added KU freshman Mario Chalmers. "Maybe now we can start a new 31-game streak."

That was the number of overall victories, remember, that KU owned against K-State before the Wildcats' upset in Lawrence on January 14.

This time, the Jayhawks trailed once, at the very outset, before their 23–6 barrage opened a 25–12 advantage midway through the first half.

The flurry included a 5-for-6 start by KU from three-point range, a technical foul on K-State coach Jim Wooldridge, and halfcourt recognition for retiring KU broadcaster Max Falkenstien.

Moreover, it was the spurt the Jayhawks needed to gain a 39–24 halftime advantage.

Just one problem remained.

"We knew they were going to make a run," Robinson said. "Coach just told us to go out there and stay aggressive."

Easier said than done after a three-pointer by K-State's Cartier Martin sliced the margin to 49–46 with 10:57 remaining and had the place rocking.

But that would be the Wildcats' last field goal.

They missed their last seven attempts and mixed in eight turnovers, while scoring just six more points, all off free throws. K-State (15–12, 6–10) shot just 37.5 percent from the floor and committed 21 turnovers. Martin was the only Wildcat to score in double figures with 17 points.

"We self-inflicted ourselves too many times offensively," Wooldridge said. "A three-point ballgame, and we turned it over in the backcourt off a rebound. Those kind of things are just uncalled for. You can't beat people in our league doing that."

Not even an opponent that starts the youngest lineup in its history and lost two of its first three league games. But then, this KU team is considerably different than it was in mid-January when the three initials a perennial power never wants to hear—N-I-T—were muttered far too often.

"It really pumps energy in your blood when people doubt you and say you can't win big games," said Brandon Rush, who tied a season high by leading all scorers with 24 points.

Chalmers added 14, and Robinson scored 11 while adding a team-high five assists. Wright led KU with four steals and also grabbed six rebounds to share team-high honors with Chalmers and Rush as the Jayhawks held a slim 35–34 edge on the boards.

Yet on Saturday, it was the overall achievement Self marveled at most—the sixth Big 12 title for KU in the 10-year history of the conference.

"This team was 13–3, and last year we were a veteran team struggling to go 12–4," said Self, who earned his sixth league title in eight years dating to stints at Illinois and Tulsa. "To think we have a better record than last year is unbelievable."

Wilt Chamberlain's Kansas debut was a highly anticipated event throughout the entire country, and he did not disappoint. Photo courtesy of AP/Wide World Photos.

Section II
THE PLAYERS

F. C. "Phog" Allen, *Better Basketball*

LISTENING FOR A DRONING PLANE

One of the more remarkable stories from KU's history is this tale about star player Bill Johnson, from the 1932 season. Utilizing his well-known wit and storytelling ability, Phog Allen wrote about Johnson and the event in his 1937 book, Better Basketball.

For I dipt into the future, far as
Human eye could see,
Saw the Vision of the world, and all
The wonder that would be;
Saw the heavens fill with commerce,
Argosies of magic sails,
Pilots of the purple twilight dropping
Down with costly bales;

Heard the heavens fill with shouting,
And there rained a ghastly dew
From the nation's airy navies grappling
In the central blue.

—Tennyson

In his lone flight from America to France, Charles A. Lindbergh, in 1927, hooked up the Statue of Liberty and the Eiffel Tower, and thus further materialized this poet's prophetic dream of almost a century before.

In lesser degree, in his own smaller world in the middle west, Bill Johnson, phenomenal Kansas center of 1932, electrified basketball followers by a heroic flight from his family's grave lot in the cemetery at Oklahoma City, Oklahoma, to the basketball court on Mount Oread at the University of Kansas.

On this particular Saturday night, the Universities of Missouri, Oklahoma, and Kansas were facing their final games in the Big 6 conference championship race, with possibilities of a triple tie for honors.

Kansas was scheduled to meet Oklahoma at Lawrence, Kansas, and on the same night Missouri was to meet Kansas State at Manhattan, Kansas. Should Oklahoma defeat Kansas and should Missouri win from Kansas State, the Big 6 would be deadlocked with the three state universities in a dogfight.

Kansas had lost her first two conference games of the season, but after the loss of these games had remained undefeated. Oklahoma was cruising along at a terrific rate, and Missouri was looked upon as a most dangerous contender. The Kansas team seemed to pick up increasing power with each victory.

Upon Bill Johnson, a senior and an elongated and versatile rapier of the basketball court, Kansas pinned her chiefest hopes. For two years, Bill had shown the way to all Big 6 centers. He had no peers in his position. And since Kansas had held the Big 6 conference championship for the two preceding years, the race took on a Kansas hue.

As the season advanced, the Kansas Jayhawkers were moving in high gear—mowing down all opposition with relentless and ruthless regularity. This hectic struggle for the championship had gripped the imagination of the entire region of the Great Plains states. Column after column of newspaper space was devoted to this unusual race, and everybody was on edge over the outcome.

But, as is so often the case in man's best-laid schemes, something happened. On Wednesday afternoon, the Kansans had their last grueling workout. We had planned to polish off during the remaining three days. Our scrimmage was most satisfying. In fact, too satisfying. Everything clicked. The machine glided with no lost motion. Johnson and the rest of his teammates were superb, shooting, passing, and hitting with uncanny skill. Surely if they could function like this on their game night, just three days away, no Oklahoma team could stop them.

But, even then, I had a premonition that everything was too perfect. After practice, press correspondents queried me as to the probable outcome of the game. A strange foreboding gripped me. I seemed to feel that something would happen to my ace Bill Johnson. The bugaboo of injuries haunted me. I told them "If Bill Johnson doesn't break a leg, Oklahoma will be in for a busy Saturday night."

On that same Wednesday night, while I was at dinner, the telephone rang and a friend informed me that Bill Johnson's father had died suddenly in his home in Oklahoma City, 400 miles away.

Bill left on the night train and with him, so it seemed, went Kansas's chances for its third consecutive Big 6 championship.

Norman, the home of the University of Oklahoma, is just 18 miles from Oklahoma City, the home of the Johnsons. The athletic authorities at the University of Oklahoma were besieged by the press throughout this conference area to postpone the game until the following week, so that the two teams could meet at full strength. But the Oklahomans wanted to play the game on schedule.

The funeral hour of Bill Johnson's pioneer father, originally set for Friday, was changed to Saturday at 2:30 PM, in order to accommodate relatives from a distance.

All Kansas home games were scheduled at 7:30 PM. Apparently there was no way for Bill Johnson to travel 400 miles after his father's funeral and play the game. Certain defeat faced Kansas. Oklahoma had been the runner-up to Kansas in the two previous conference races, and now in this third year fate seemed to decree an Oklahoma victory.

Swan Johnson, a one-time Swedish immigrant boy and father of Bill, had blazed the hot and dusty trail from Iowa to Oklahoma in 1889 to homestead much of the land that he possessed at the time of his death. He had, at all times, evinced an intense pride and interest in Bill's basketball achievements. On the day of his death, a half-page picture of Bill was printed on the sports page of his local paper. With justifiable pride he had commented to Bill's mother, "I hope Bill plays the game of his life Saturday night."

This significant statement proved to be the real challenge in Bill's final decision to try to get back to play. Close friends of the family had counseled with his mother and had urged that, if at all possible for Bill to reach Lawrence, he should play in this, his final game, and thus fulfill the last wish of his father.

C. O. "Cob" Burnside, residing in Bill's hometown, a fraternity brother of Bill's and a loyal alumnus of Kansas, through his intimate friendship for the Johnson family, convinced Mrs. Johnson to send her boy by airplane to answer the call of Kansas.

Already the morning and the afternoon newspapers had announced that Kansas would play without her superstar, Bill Johnson.

During the day, many offers from businessmen and from university groups to sponsor a flight to Oklahoma to get Johnson came to me. But all such proposals [fell on] a deaf ear. Strong headwinds and air pockets aplenty made a 400-mile hop under adverse weather conditions seem too perilous to consider.

However, during the afternoon, another fraternity brother of Bill's, Maurice L. Breidenthal of Kansas City and a most loyal alumnus of Kansas, telephoned to me that he and Cob Burnside of Oklahoma City had arranged for a commercial plane to attempt the flight to bring Bill Johnson from Oklahoma City in time for the game.

The possible danger of a forced landing or a crack-up precluded the wisdom of informing the Kansas team of this contemplated air trip. The group reaction might have been most detrimental should the plan have failed.

The game between Missouri and Kansas State at Manhattan, Kansas, was to be called for 7:30 PM, the same time as was the Kansas-Oklahoma game to be called at Lawrence. After the information concerning Johnson was received, and since the home teams are responsible for setting the starting time of the games, we changed our starting time to 8:00 PM.

Immediately bulletins were published in the press and broadcast by radio that the Kansas-Oklahoma game would be called at 8:00 PM, instead of 7:30 PM as usual. On account of the possible effect upon the team, we were forced to keep our primary reason for this change of time a secret, giving as a reason for the postponement our desire to have Kansas followers listen in on the first half of the important Missouri–Kansas State game being played at Manhattan.

We installed loudspeakers in the Kansas field house for these radio reports of the first half of the Missouri–Kansas State game. If Missouri should win their game, then the winner of the Kansas-Oklahoma game would be tied with Missouri for the title. But if Missouri should lose and Kansas should win, Kansas would be the undisputed champion of the Big 6 conference for the third consecutive time. We were hoping that this additional 30 minutes would land Bill Johnson in our dressing rooms in time for the game.

Our team's pregame meal was a tense though drab affair. The group was on edge. The air was charged with mental static. Not one player mentioned the probability of Bill's coming. All day the press had announced for a certainty that Johnson was definitely out of the game. When I excused myself, presumably to step out for an instant, anxious and startled looks swept from one player to another. Actually, I had left them intending to accompany Dr. A. J. Anderson, our medical adviser, to the local airport to meet and, if necessary, to administer to our expected and most welcome air passenger.

At the airport, minutes flew. Soon darkness came on and made a landing at our unlighted airport impossible. So anxious was our vigil and so intense our watch that at twilight I called to Dr. Anderson, "Here comes Bill from the southwest!"

Fervently desiring his arrival, I had peered so intensely into the far-distant horizon that a piece of waving heavy tape had created an optical illusion which made me see the thing that I most desired to see—an airplane with Bill Johnson in it.

With pitch dark upon us, nonplussed and confused and disappointed and minus our prized cargo, we hastily drove the three miles back to the gymnasium. I entered the team's quarters and found the boys, outwardly quiet, dressing for the game.

Minutes were precious now. Less than an hour remained. Eyes were anxious, muscles taut. My untimely absence was still a mystery to them. Yet I had not a word nor a sign from our precious argosy of the air!

Serious business, this. All minds and hearts on the game just ahead. Suddenly, this ominous silence proved too much for one of our players. He rushed up and challenged me with a shout, "You know where Bill Johnson is! You *know* where he is! Even if he doesn't show up, I'll win that damn game myself."

"Quiet, you," I shouted. I did not know where Bill was and so stated in emphatic terms and ordered him to restrain and calm himself.

Suddenly, a summons came from the outside: "Telephone for you, Coach Allen." I rushed upstairs to the telephone and to my unrestrained delight, over the wires came the voice of the Argonaut of Kansas's hopes.

Long past nightfall, the ship had landed at a lighted airport some 30 miles away. Bill Johnson had taxied from there to our own city limits and had telephoned me to ask if he should eat before coming to the gymnasium.

Three hours and a half by air and 30 minutes overland by taxi had left Bill groggy. He had but 30 minutes to come the remaining five miles, to dress, and to warm up before the whistle blasted the start of the game.

"Eat nothing," I shouted. "For heaven's sake jump in that taxi and tear up here with all your might."

Back downstairs I lunged. I fairly flew into the dressing room. I was treading on thin air. I whispered the good news to my assistant coach and told him to stay behind and help Bill and bring him to the field house as soon as possible. We had but 25 minutes left.

"Come on, gang!" I shouted. "Over and after those Oklahoma Sooners!" And we swung away with a mixed joy and fear such as I never before had known in my 30 years of coaching.

The Kansas field house was packed. Already the radio reports were giving Kansas State a lead of eight points over Missouri. Surely the outcome of the local struggle would determine the championship.

As the Kansas varsity swarmed on the floor, the partisan rooters gave them a great ovation. Oklahoma had arrived early. They drove through their warm-up drills with skill and confidence. Keyed to the minute, these Sooners from Oklahoma looked formidable. Without Johnson, Kansas partisans still hoped that some magic power would aid the stricken Kansans.

The Oklahomans scanned the personnel of the alert Kansans to make sure that Johnson was not among them. Just 12 minutes before game time! Feverish excitement everywhere. Sweaters flung aside. Timers, scorers, and officials hurrying to their places for a final checkup. Oklahoma's coach was still wary, as if fearing an unseen phantom.

Bedlam broke loose! Look! Kansas rooters went wild. Standing, cheering, shouting like maniacs, they beheld a sight that brought tears to their eyes. Was that Bill Johnson's ghost? No! It was Kansas's own Bill Johnson in the flesh!

Pale and wan, even thinner than usual, Bill strode into the arena just six minutes before 8:00. Joan of Arc's spirit rekindled.

The roof fairly blew off. Kansas players, stunned for the moment, suddenly recovered their equilibrium and showered their haggard teammate with ecstatic adulations of joy. Kansas rushed into a huddle in her dressing room, just off the arena.

But four minutes remained before the game. Kansas now had more than her own strength. She had something indefinable. One could not measure it accurately but could feel it in the air. A positive psychic force!

I shouted, "All right, boys, sit here on this bench—Bill, Ted, Lee, Elmer, and Dick.

"Boys, words must be few. I merely want to remind you that 43 years ago a young man challenged the dangers of the great southwest and carved a home out of it for Bill Johnson to grow up in. Bill's father was a daring and courageous pioneer.

"Tonight, over exactly that same trail, came the same conquering spirit to answer the call of duty. Churning his lonely way over 400 miles of dangerous terrain through strong headwinds and treacherous air pockets in a small droning plane, Bill Johnson has fought his way to you. It was his father's last wish. His mother sent him.

"Ted, Lee, Elmer, and Dick, go out there and fight your hearts out for this cause that Bill represents.

"Bill, God bless you, my boy. You are wonderful."

We flung ourselves together in determined embrace. For a brief moment, the iron bands of love held us together. Then we tore apart for the business at hand. But the bond of our singleness of purpose still held.

Referee Ernie Quigley's whistle started the game and with it he introduced a Kansas tornado that, in the first few minutes of the game, fairly swept the Oklahomans off their feet. Kansas's attack was devastating. She was playing far over her head. There was fury in her charge, and it seemed that she was fast-paving her road to glory and to another Big 6 crown. Bill Johnson, Ted O'Leary, Lee Page, Elmer Schaake, and Dick Wells ripped and crashed through the Oklahoma defense, which was giving all it had to stem this withering assault that had piled up a 20–6 lead at the half.

At the end of the half, radio reports announced that Missouri had won at Manhattan. So the next 30 minutes would see Kansas and Oklahoma fighting for an undisputed crown—with Kansas enjoying a 14-point lead.

So long as there are playing minutes left, Oklahoma is never defeated. Undaunted by their handicap, the Oklahoma Sooners swore that they would still make a game out of it. As Oklahoma unleashed an attack which whittled down the one-sided Kansas advantage, silence fell over the confident Kansas crowd. Oklahoma had scored 10 points in the first four minutes of the last half, without Kansas's tallying. Score, Kansas 20—Oklahoma 16.

So the championship still remained disputed. But the tornado which struck in those early minutes of the game had devastated too much territory to be regained quickly. It was only the psychic stimulus generated by the rare circumstances preceding this game that stayed the desperate assaults of these superb and fighting Oklahomans. Unfortunately for them, they met Kansas on a night when a sensational climax to a season's play heightened Kansas's fighting morale.

Kansas won in a driving finish, 31–27. After the game, Bill said, "Doc, I can still hear the droning of that plane in my ears." To this I replied, "Is there any wonder, Bill? After your two charging rides? One into the clouds and the other to victory."

I was wondering, too, although I didn't say it, if, over and above all the din and confusion of that great crowd and over and above that persistent droning of the plane in his ears, Bill, at times during the game, had not seen a stalwart though aged pioneer moving with him from place to place and whispering that all was well.

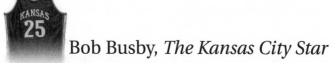

Bob Busby, *The Kansas City Star*

CLYDE'S TOUCH WITH THE BALL MAKES HIM A GREAT AMONG GIANTS

As was Charlie Black in 1943 and '46, Clyde Lovellette was a first-team All-American during 1951 and '52. More importantly, however, he led the Jayhawks to their first NCAA national championship in 1952. To this day, Lovellette remains the only player in NCAA history to lead the nation in scoring the same year that his team won the national title.

Even though Lovellette became a national star for the Jayhawks, this hometown piece by Bob Busby of The Kansas City Star *offers the best look at Lovellette on and off the court.*

Since the NCAA triumph, there is no question that his record-shattering feats have put him in a place never before occupied by a Big 7 player—personally he is a jovial person who eats so much that he takes his meals in the kitchen to be closest to the source of supply.

Clyde Lovellette, 6'9" All-America center at the University of Kansas, has finally convinced almost every skeptic in the country that he is head and shoulders above the other giants of basketball.

The Jayhawk skyscraper, who reached a new high in smashing school and conference records, finished the season with the best scoring average in the nation, and he moved into the NCAA playoffs.

Now, his critics said, we'll see just how good he is. Lovellette obliged by scorching the hoops for 31 points against Texas Christian, 44 against St. Louis, 33 against Santa Clara, and 33 against St. John's of Brooklyn, the team that KU downed to win the National Collegiate Athletic Association title.

When he left Seattle after the NCAA Tournament last week there were few who would deny that the big boy had what it took—and more, too—as a basketball player, not as a giant.

Concentrate on Him

Being of such tremendous size and bulk, Lovellette has naturally been the subject of considerable pressure during games, both from his foes and from the fans. His opponents usually deal him a bad time within—and sometimes outside—the rules. Once a tiny foe was seen almost chinning himself from one of Clyde's outstretched arms. Normally he has to operate with two or three men guarding him.

Upon first seeing him fans usually cheer when he misses a shot or is called for a foul. But invariably, as he proceeds to pour in points with graceful motion, his normally unsympathetic followers swing to his aid. They decide he's good, and they like perfection.

His record, speaking conservatively, is for the books. When he finished at Seattle, he owned virtually every collegiate basketball mark that amounted to anything in the conference and on the national scene.

In the four NCAA games at Kansas City and Seattle, he scored 141 points for an average per game of 35.2.

During his three years at Kansas, he gradually has stepped up the pace, each time leading the conference. As a sophomore in 1950, he tallied 545 points in 25 games, and as a junior last year he bagged 548.

In his second year at Lawrence, he surpassed the school record for total points made by any player in all years of competition—in other words, this season's addition only pushed the KU mark to more inaccessible heights. By the end of his junior year, he had stacked up 1,093 points in 49 games. This year he boosted that to 1,888, an average of 24.5 for 77 games. That's the way he stood going into last night's first round of the Olympic playoffs.

To Second-Highest Average

His season average goes on the books as the second highest in NCAA major college history. Only Bill Mlkvy, Temple's "owl without a vowel," posted a better pace last season, 29.2 for 25 games.

In the career category, Lovellette has the best average ever recorded. He has the fifth-highest total ever registered. The men who top him played many more games.

Lovellette has made shambles of the school and conference record books. In addition, he hogs most of the marks in the Big 7 preseason tournament and the NCAA Tournament competition.

In the Big 7 tourney he had a record of 222 points in nine appearances. Through Kansas City and Seattle, he obliterated seven of the NCAA marks, no mean task considering the great parade of Kentuckians who preceded him as the Wildcats annexed three straight titles.

Better Than 40 Three Times

Consider that, in three years at Kansas, he has scored 20 or more points 56 times. He has topped 30 on 20 occasions, and three times he has bettered the 40 mark.

His all-time high was 44 points in the finals of the Western regional NCAA at Kansas City against St. Louis. He holds the Big 7 peak with 41 points against Colorado in the final conference game of the season.

In the conference play last season, he pegged his average at 28 points for 12 games. In 1950 he set the mark at 23 and pushed it to 23.8 in 1951.

Lovellette's conference mark may stand for quite a spell, under the present league membership in which 12 games are played by each team. To accomplish what he did, he had to score 30 points in half of the games played—and six of these were away from home.

Many observers are convinced that the colossal Jayhawk has just reached his peak in the last month of play, when he began his terrific spree of scoring, and believe that he will become even better. Some venture the opinion that he is "two years away from his peak."

Lovellette not only passes the ball as well as or better than many, but he is making more plays off the post.

While there has never been much question of his ability in scoring, even that phase is improved.

His Technique

Significant late improvements by the big boy have been: a fake hook followed by one dribble and subsequent hook; much better tipping technique, which allows him to collect the easy ones that fall to most similar mastodons; a fake right then a cut back to the left and layup with his left hand. He drives exceptionally well for a big man on this one.

When Lovellette showed up at Kansas he was good. There was no question about that, but he didn't have his now-famous hook shot. That formidable weapon he uncorks from 10, 15, or even 18 feet out. Usually it is with his right hand, but he can also produce with his left.

He has a beautifully soft touch on the ball. When it seems that it might bounce away, the ball becomes a feather and floats in, so precise is the English. He puts terrific reverse spin on his free throws and aims for the back of the rim.

He credits Dick Harp, assistant coach, as well as Coach Phog Allen, with the development of his hook.

There is a lot of conversation about whether he looks at the basket when he shoots a hooker, or whether he just knows by practice and instinct where the hoop is. Lovellette explains this: "When turning, I look toward the goal just as the ball is leaving my hands."

In the early stages of his career, he did a lot of rope skipping, a practice suggested by his mother when she realized that Clyde was destined to be a big boy. She wanted to help him avoid awkwardness. It worked and he also developed his legs into remarkably agile and efficient supports for his 6'9", 244-pound frame.

Special Attention to Rebounds

Now, the only special routine practice that he works on is jumping for and tipping rebounds, one of the deadly phases of his game. With B. H. Born, his 6'8" alternate, Clyde works under the basket. One hand throws the ball up to the hoop while the other goes after it for the tip.

It takes a lot of food to keep the big boy going. He still retains the appetite that was the topic of the Sigma Chi fraternity house before he was married eight months ago.

"If I had my choice," explains Clyde, "I'd rather eat steak than anything. I don't ask for anything extra when we eat in a restaurant, but the waitresses usually see me coming and put something extra on the plate."

One of his fraternity brothers recalls, "Clyde usually ate in the kitchen, because if he ate in the dining room, he kept everybody busy passing food to him. Besides, he would eat about two ordinary meals at a sitting, and if he started in the dining room, he would wind up in the kitchen eventually."

It always has been this way. Lovellette says that when he was born he was the biggest baby ever born in Pike County, Indiana, which includes his hometown of Terre Haute. So he started setting records from the start.

His father is a 6'3" locomotive engineer for the New York Central, and his mother is 5'8", and she is part Irish and part Indian. He is the youngest of five children. His brothers are 6'5½" and 6'6", and his sisters are 5'7" and 5'9".

Clyde's wife, the former Sally Wheeler, his sweetheart at Garfield High School in Terre Haute, is 5'8". They live in a white duplex on Vermont Street in Lawrence.

His mother was his first "coach," he explains: "I was so awkward in high school; Mom got me a skipping rope and told me to go to it."

Practiced at Night

The neighborhood kids stared and laughed, so lanky Clyde did his rope skipping at night.

The Kansas All-American receives $75 a month on his athletic scholarship. He works during football season as an usher and cleanup boy at the stadium. Last summer he did "heavy lifting" as a contractor's laborer in construction of the addition to the KU union building on the campus.

Beds and clothes are a constant problem. On his income, $90 suits are the cheapest he can get—and $25 shoes, size 14, are bothersome items. His shirts must be made to order—16-inch neck and 37½-inch sleeves.

Sought by about 50 colleges, Lovellette went to Kansas. The reason, as devised by Coach Allen, now goes down with such fables as Babe Ruth's called-shot home run in a World Series.

When asked why Lovellette wound up at Kansas, the wily Phog, a fast man with a phrase, explained, "One big reason Clyde enrolled here was because the altitude helps his asthma." From Terre Haute (high ground in French) to Mount Oread was certainly a logical climb.

That started a wave of joking, which even to this day rises on occasion. Lawrence is only 825 feet above sea level, and Mount Oread, the site of the KU campus, rises only 180 feet above downtown Lawrence.

On the serious side, he was subjected to frequent sieges with colds because of a slightly asthmatic condition. He said sometime after his enrollment at Lawrence that he noticed he had fewer colds and was free from coughing spells.

Amused by Gags

But this was a fitting introduction to the big boy, who is by nature a jovial character and is frequently said to be remindful of a "big St. Bernard dog."

Clyde himself can go with a gag. On the recent trip to Seattle, when the plane was stacked up in bad weather outside the Washington city and all was tense aboard, he obtained a small bunch of flowers. He approached Coach Allen, seated with his hands clasped, attempting to relax, and planted the flowers between Phog's fingers.

"Now there, Coach," Clyde said to Allen, "if anything happens, you'll be ready to go."

That put the gang at ease for some time.

On a trip east by train, the Pullman company fixed him up with two upper berths, taking out the headboard divider. Upon retiring, he admonished an amazed porter, saying, "Be sure to wake up both berths at the same time."

After enrolling at Kansas, he returned to Terre Haute for summer vacation, and that was the basis for the famous "I'm him" story.

Clyde went into a drugstore, went up to the counter, and ordered a soda. In conversation with the girl behind the counter, it came out that he was a student at Kansas.

She Had Heard of Him

"Oh," exclaimed the waitress, "that's a coincidence. We have a boy from here who is a great basketball player and he goes to Kansas. Maybe you know him."

Clyde stopped gulping momentarily to reply, "I'm him."

As a boy Clyde didn't experience the thrill of shooting firecrackers because of Indiana state law. When he first visited Lawrence in July before his freshman year, he went out to follow Dr. Allen around the golf course. After a few holes, Clyde grew restless. He said he thought he'd go back to the clubhouse and shoot firecrackers. It was then, according to the story, that the resourceful Allen said, "Why, Clyde, you needn't go that far. I just happen to have a package of firecrackers here in my bag."

Phog produced them, and he finished the round amid the sporadic roar of giant salutes set off by his prize prospect.

Out for a Boat Ride

One of his big thrills in Seattle was what happened when he met Ensign George Newton of the coast guard, a fraternity brother, who took him for a cruise on Lake Washington. During the two-and-a-half-hour junket, Clyde wheeled the cutter.

Now 22 years of age, he will be 23 on September 27. When he receives his diploma, he says that he would like to play AAU ball for a while. It is almost a foregone conclusion that he will join the Phillips Oilers, where many of the basketball greats have collected to gain further athletic fame and continue in good jobs with the petroleum company when their years of athletic competition end.

As of now, however, Clyde says that the Phillips matter is merely in the talking stage.

In school he is an average student. His course is in physical education where, for instance, this semester he is required to take a course in anatomy.

Clyde says he studies hard before basketball season to get ahead so that he will not be in trouble when the hoop sport cuts into his classwork.

Radio work is attractive to the big blond-haired star, although his voice belies his size and is on the high-pitched side of the register. Until recently he appeared on WREN out of Topeka, Kansas, as a disc jockey, playing hillbilly tunes. He was introduced as "Hillbilly Clyde coming in on his mount, Cannonball, with his hound dog, Lester."

Remembers His Friends

In bidding his audience goodnight, Lovellette always added, "And you, too, Skippy." That was a special salute to Skippy Franks, a Lawrence boy who is an invalid. Skippy is a basketball follower who is a great fan of Lovellette's.

Probably no athlete in the country, and surely not in the Big 7, has ever been the inspiration for more nicknames. Don Pierce, the Kansas publicity man, has dreamed up many of them, but writers about the circuit have contributed their share. Not all are widely used, but all are known in conversation.

"Foothills" stuck with the 7' Bob Kurland of Oklahoma A&M, and Bill Spivey of Kentucky was usually tagged the "Lonesome Pine." But with Lovellette, only time will settle his eventual tag. Some of the nicknames: the Ponderous Pachyderm of the Planks, Colossal Clyde, Cumulus Clyde, the Terre Haute Terror, Jumbo, the Monster, Cloudburst Clyde, the Fabulous Frenchman, the Splendid Spike, the Terre Haute Tower, and so on.

But call him what you will, he is admired by friend and foe alike on the court, and he'll go down in the books as the greatest figure so far in Big 7 basketball and possibly one of the all-time greats in the game.

Jimmy Breslin, *The Saturday Evening Post*

CAN BASKETBALL SURVIVE CHAMBERLAIN?

That probably was the best question leading up to Wilt Chamberlain's first varsity season at Kansas in 1956–57. Chamberlain, who was a two-time All-American, was one of the most mysterious Jayhawks ever. Even though he left after his junior year, he's still considered one of KU's greatest athletes and one of the best basketball players in the history of the game.

Jimmy Breslin, one of the country's most well-known columnists, won a Pulitzer Prize in 1986. This article, which Breslin authored for The Saturday Evening Post, *appeared on December 1, 1956.*

Wilton Chamberlain, a 7' basketball player with the catchy nickname of Wilt the Stilt, is only a sophomore at the University of Kansas. His intercollegiate playing career doesn't start until next week. Yet because of this 20-year-old Negro athlete, many basketball authorities have already conceded the next three years to Kansas. They expect Chamberlain to be even more dominant than Bill Russell, the 6'10" Negro ace of San Francisco's two-time national champions.

There was a brief flurry of speculation that the advent of the Chamberlain era might be delayed when Wilt underwent a throat operation in October. However, the surgery was described as minor and his recuperation as excellent. He was back in action by the time basketball practice started on November first.

Wilt the Stilt has had an advance buildup to compare with that of Clint Hartung—remember him?—who was hailed at the New York Giants' training camp in 1947 as the greatest all-round phenom ever to put on a baseball glove. The Hartung fanfare reached such proportions that veteran scribe Tom Meany observed dryly, "Hartung shouldn't even bother to play. He should report directly to the Hall of Fame at Cooperstown."

In the case of Hartung, whose superman reputation sprang up in Army baseball, it was all an illusion. He turned out to be a performer of limited talents. This won't happen with Wilt Chamberlain. There is no real question about his ability. Along with his height he has the speed, grace, and shooting eye of players a foot shorter. The only thing that might conceivably hold him back—aside from unexpected complications arising from his throat trouble—is the abnormal amount of pressure and controversy that has focused upon him.

Up to now this hasn't affected his playing. Rival coaches got a frightening demonstration back in November 1955, when Kansas put the Stilt on public display for the first time as a member of the freshman team in its annual preseason game with the varsity.

Chamberlain had come to Kansas after averaging 37 points a game in three seasons at Overbrook High School, in Philadelphia. During his last year he had averaged 45 points, although he frequently played only half the time because of the lopsided leads he ran up.

So when Wilt took the floor in that freshman-varsity game at Kansas, the whole college basketball world figuratively was watching. Some of the coaches from other Big 7 conference schools were there in person, including Jerry Bush of Nebraska. Coach Bush took a seat in the field house at Lawrence, Kansas, intending to memorize every move Chamberlain made.

The Stilt, plainly nervous because of the 14,000 people who came out to this normally meaningless game, scored 42 points against double- and triple-teaming defenses. It didn't take Bush long to decide that this was only a sample of what was going to happen when Chamberlain became a varsity player. In fact, a single characteristic play was enough to shape his opinion. The Stilt drove to the top of the keyhole—or foul circle—and went up for what appeared to be a one-handed jump shot. But he didn't come down. He kept floating through the air, did a complete twist, so that his back was to the basket, shoved his arm behind him, rotated it in helicopter style, and dunked the ball in the net. He landed somewhere behind the basket.

Bush turned to the fellow next to him. "I feel sick," he said.

In addition to his incredible basketball skills, Wilt has other natural advantages. Scholastically, Chamberlain is no freak getting by through grace of a D in basket weaving. He has shown he can master business-administration courses at Kansas, earning a shade better than a C average for his freshman year. Unless his celebrity status becomes unduly distracting—photographers and writers have already made him a national sports figure—Chamberlain's instructors see no reason why his classroom performance shouldn't remain satisfactory on through to graduation.

Furthermore, his future looks most inviting. The Philadelphia Warriors, current champions of the National Basketball Association, already have claimed draft rights to him after his college time is up. Owner Eddie Gottlieb probably will be forced to pay an all-time high to sign Chamberlain. And a part-owner of the Warriors, Abe

Saperstein, says he wants to keep the Stilt making money in the off-season via tours with Saperstein's Harlem Globetrotters. Chamberlain probably will have contracts worth close to $30,000 during his first year as a pro.

It's quite a setup for a youngster and, on the surface, the Stilt seems to reflect the glee that goes with success at an early age. A jazz-talking, automobile-loving youth, he is a popular figure around both the Kansas campus and his neighborhood in Philadelphia. Chamberlain plainly likes the fact that people know him wherever he goes. His only complaint with his public is that the nickname "the Stilt" has firmly stuck. He prefers "the Dipper," which he has printed in bold red letters across the rear bumper of his antenna-studded 1953 automobile.

But there is another side to the story of Wilton Chamberlain, and when you look at this side you see a different fellow. This one is a moody, reticent youth who is conscious of his height, his race—and the fact that many people have been critical of his career in basketball.

"I'm not as lucky as everybody says," Wilt has observed. "That's for sure. A lot of people tell me how easy I got it. Well, I think there's a little more than luck involved. I've had problems."

The problems center around his enrollment at Kansas last year. This created a tempest which, a year later, still gives hints of erupting again. In the whole disorderly history of college recruiting, the Chamberlain case was one of the most contentious. Alumni from other colleges still grouse over their failure to land him. Newspapers, particularly in the East, openly question the manner in which colleges wooed Chamberlain. Throughout his high school career, Chamberlain was constantly badgered by college alumni, some of whom seemed willing to violate the Lindbergh Kidnapping Law to grab the Stilt for their alma mater. Usually, a high school athlete is courted chiefly when a senior. With Chamberlain, the rush was on when he was a sophomore. He was 6'11" then, and already a standout performer.

As a result of all this, with strangers he changed from a carefree, where-we-going-tonight type of boy to a cold and peevish youth who balked at anything that was not exactly as he wanted it. The more recruiting attention he got, the harder the Stilt grew to deal with.

"Nobody gave me time to think," he has said since. "Every day when I'd come home from school, somebody would be in my living room, there would be four or five letters on the bureau, and my mother would tell me at least two people called long-distance and would call back later."

By the spring of 1955, the competition for Wilt had turned into a national sports-page story. When he finally picked Kansas that May, he knew it would be a long while before he heard the last of it. "They'll say things no matter where I go," he snapped. "It could be anywhere. They'll all say, 'You must have got a mint.'"

Several sportswriters were quick to prove his estimate correct. Harry Grayson, veteran NEA Service sports editor, wrote, "Why does a Philadelphia boy have to travel halfway across the country to attend college?"

Max Kase, *New York Journal-American* sports editor, said, "Isn't the NCAA investigating reports of a special trust fund due to mature on Wilt the Stilt Chamberlain's graduation?"

Leonard Lewin, in a *New York Daily Mirror* column, cracked, "I feel sorry for the Stilt when he enters the NBA four years from now. He'll have to take a cut in salary."

Even after he entered Kansas, Chamberlain could not slip into the comfortable obscurity usually surrounding a college freshman. Too much had been written and said about the recruiting race for the atmosphere to clear abruptly. The NCAA, in fact, having heard some of the rumors, had investigators speak to the Stilt before he left Philadelphia for Kansas.

During his freshman year new storms broke out. In March, Colonel Harry Henshel of the Olympic Basketball Committee asked, "Why isn't Chamberlain a candidate for the Olympic team? Is Kansas afraid to let him get around? Are they trying to hide something?"

This started a heated series of verbal exchanges between Henshel and Dr. Forrest C. "Phog" Allen, the Kansas coach who won the Chamberlain chase. Ironically, Allen never got to use Wilt; he reached the university's compulsory retirement age of 70 and was obliged to turn over the coaching job this year to his longtime assistant, Dick Harp. Anyway, nobody ever accused Phog Allen of having a speech impediment. With his usual bluntness, he launched a personal counterattack on Henshel that prompted the latter to file a libel suit, which is still pending.

In April, the Stilt found his name back in the headlines again. J. Suter Kegg, sports editor of the *Evening Times* in Cumberland, Maryland, did a column stating that Chamberlain was no stranger to local basketball fans. "He played here under the name of George Marcus in a professional game," Kegg wrote. Henshel sent Kegg a letter asking for more details; NEA's Grayson broke the story nationally. Phog Allen screamed rebuttals—and another rumpus was on.

"I never was there," Chamberlain said, in a brief departure from the firm no-comment policy he has adopted for such situations.

Because of the continuing rhubarbs in the East, Chamberlain stayed in Kansas City last summer. "I thought it would be good to meet the people out here," he said, "and at the same time we agreed it would be better to stay here because of all that stuff in the East."

As recently as September, the NCAA had investigators speaking to complaining Indiana alumni, but nothing was expected to come of this. Meanwhile, the Cumberland story seemed at least temporarily forgotten. Sports editor Kegg had not been approached by anybody seeking additional information or documentation of his column. A rumor that one Big 7 school, Missouri, would challenge the Stilt's amateur standing was denied by its coach, Wilbur Stalcup.

In Kansas last summer the only difficulty the Stilt experienced came on his job as a salesman for the McDowell Tire Agency in Kansas City, Missouri. "His sales weren't tremendous, but that was because we didn't have time to teach him," Dick Utterback, the sales manager, says.

Also contributing to his low sales volume was the fact that the first eight customers Wilt brought around were turned down by the company's credit department. Another time he brought in Vic Power, the Kansas City A's first baseman, but Power was with a girl and "wouldn't stand still long enough even to look at the stock," Utterback recalls.

Now that he is back in his basketball element, the Stilt is entirely capable of hitting close to 50 points a game this winter for Kansas. "It's a tougher game in college and there's a lot more big men," he says, "but I've matured right along with the step-up in caliber. I don't think it will be too much different."

Most college coaches ruefully agree with him. Coach Stalcup, of Missouri, tried to read some hope into the situation when asked for an opinion. "He has a lot to learn. After all, he's only a sophomore," Stalcup said. Then he grew realistic for a bleak moment. "But I guess I've got to say he's the best I've seen."

Frank McGuire, the University of North Carolina coach, doesn't beat around the bush. "I told Phog that he was trying to kill basketball by bringing that kid into school," McGuire says. "Chamberlain will score about 130 points one night and the other coach will lose his job. There might be somebody in the penitentiary who can handle him, but I guarantee you there is nobody in college."

Fear of the Stilt is so widespread that college basketball's rule makers have already put in several changes which are aimed at all big men, but at Chamberlain in particular. Among other things, it now is illegal for a player to jump and guide a teammate's shot into the basket—he can't touch the ball until it hits the backboard or rim. Nor can a man shooting a foul cross the foul line until the ball reaches the basket; Wilt used to shoot fouls while springing into the air so as to arrive about the same time as the ball. Another change copies the professional rule which places defensive men at both sides nearest the basket on foul shots. This reduces the easy rebound baskets a player of Chamberlain's height usually gets.

However, Chamberlain feels he won't lose many points because of the new legislation. "Instead of guiding a shot, I'll just have to get it on the rebound, then go up again," he says. "It'll lead to a lot more fouling.

On the foul shots, it looks impossible to get a tap-in. Now I'm talkin' about the average cat. Me, I might get a chance here or there. And I'll sure get us more defensive rebounds."

There have been other 7' boys in college basketball. Rosters this season list numerous men only an inch or two shorter. But the college basketball player over 6'6" normally leaves much to be desired in the way of coordination, speed, and stamina. He stations himself primarily in the pivot post and stays there as much as possible.

Chamberlain, however, is no cement-footed goon. The Stilt has as many maneuvers as the game calls for. From the outside, his graceful jump shot is dangerous. In the pivot, he disdains the usual sweeping hook shot and relies instead on a turnaround jump shot and that back-handed affair that made Coach Bush feel ill. Close-up shots he usually dunks in.

The Stilt weighs 231 pounds, with most of it seemingly concentrated in the well-developed neck, chest, and shoulders of an athlete. His waistline is only 31 inches. Standing, he can reach up to a height of 9'6". A leap carries him to 12'6". The basket, at 10 feet, doesn't have a chance against him. Nor can defenders place much hope in the time-honored treatment for a big man—a good bang in the back when the referee is occupied elsewhere. "They shove," Wilt says, "and I use my elbows." His elbows, which move like the driving rods of a locomotive, should be classified as dangerous weapons.

One thing Wilt can't control, however, is the muttering of disappointed recruiters. There were so many who thought they had a chance. During high school Wilt really got around. He liked the idea of sightseeing—and having people make a fuss over him. He and Cecil Mosenson, Wilt's coach for his last two years at Overbrook High, put in a great many of their weekends on junkets to various colleges.

Wilt visited so many campuses that he is hazy on numbers and places, but a sample list includes Washington (of Seattle), Oregon, Dayton, Denver, Cincinnati, Illinois, Indiana, Michigan, Michigan State, Iowa, and Northwestern—along with Kansas, of course.

"I got a kick out of it," he says. "Got to be known as a regular down at Philadelphia International Airport. The alumni would send the tickets, and the coach would show us around the school and take us to dinner and all that. The first trip I made? That was to Dayton in 1952."

Jim Enright, the *Chicago American* sportswriter who doubles as a basketball official, recalls working four straight college games—and seeing Wilt at each of them. "I thought he was a fan of mine," Jim says. "I worked Dayton, Cincinnati, Illinois, and Indiana. Chamberlain was there every time."

Chamberlain outwardly was the fun-loving kid on these visits. Inwardly he was wary. "When I went to Dayton," he recalls, "they had me eat my meals in a hotel room. When I figured out why later on, I crossed them off my list. The first time I went to Kansas, the Missouri coach [Wilbur Stalcup] met me at the airport—he was kind of cutting in—and asked me if I wanted to be the first Negro to play at his school. I told him no. Same as I told Oklahoma A&M. And I crossed off a lot of other schools because they never had gone in for colored athletes.

"A couple of schools in Florida made a mistake and wrote me. South Carolina too. They didn't know I was colored. I let 'em find out themselves. But I know that Everett Case, of North Carolina State, was thinking about me. He came to see me play and said something to a friend of mine about trying with me."

Many of the recruiters antagonized him. "I didn't like a lot of 'em," he says. "They would try and take advantage of my age by flattering me with all kinds of talk. Then they'd start in building up their own importance in business, telling me how big they were. Like they owned the school as a sideline. Seems they all had the same phrases—'Make it worth your while,' or 'We can afford'—you know, leading up to some offer if I promised to come to the school."

At the start of his last term in high school, Indiana seemed to be Wilt's favorite. By now, everybody trying for him began to realize an important truth: the disgraceful bargaining which had gone on was going to leave the winner an open target for finger-pointing. Branch McCracken, the Indiana coach, kept warning alumni about breaking NCAA rules. When Jerry Ford, the University of Pennsylvania's athletics director, heard that some of his alumni were working to get Chamberlain, he noted, "Nobody will believe he 'just came here.'"

At this point Phog Allen stepped in with a late but carefully planned campaign. "I played every angle I could think of to get Chamberlain," Allen says frankly. A key part of his strategy was to have "the Negro talking to the Negro." Allen interested a group of prominent Negro alumni in getting Chamberlain to come to Kansas.

Phog's main allies were Dowdal Davis, personable editor of the *Kansas City Call*, an influential Negro newspaper; Etta Moten, a concert singer; and Lloyd Kerford, a chubby little man who has a large quarry business in Atchison, Kansas, and also receives considerable income from the government for the rental of caves he owns. The government stores equipment in them.

As Allen explains it, "They wanted another Jackie Robinson out here." The university's campus at Lawrence is in an area which has been steadily improving as far as racial tolerance is concerned. Movies and hotels in Kansas City, Missouri, restricted until a few years ago, now are open to all.

"One good push," Dowdal Davis says, "will bring things to where they should be. I think Wilt can help us accomplish this simply by playing basketball and conducting himself the same as any other undergraduate. He doesn't have to do anything special—just be himself. That will do a lot. People will get used to him."

Kansas athletic officials started thinking of the Stilt back in 1952, when Don Pierce, the sports publicity director, spotted a photo of Chamberlain in an out-of-town newspaper and ripped it out. He circled it in red, marked it "Doc"—an Allen nickname—and passed it along. Allen promptly tacked the picture on his office door so he wouldn't forget it.

"I didn't think it was any good rushing to him then," Phog says. "He was only a sophomore in high school. But in February of 1955 I thought it was time to move. I made my contacts with the alumni, and then went to Philadelphia with Lloyd Kerford. We didn't announce ourselves. We went to a game he played against Germantown High, and attended a YMCA banquet afterward.

"I talked to the boy's mother more than I did to the boy himself. I wanted to convince her that Kansas is a sane place for a youngster to get an education and play basketball." Allen may have clinched his case here. He has a reputation as "the champion recruiter of mammas."

Wilt made two trips to Lawrence, along with young coach Mosenson, and was entertained royally. "Indiana," Allen declares, "never showed him the time we did." A Cadillac-equipped reception committee was on hand to meet him at the Kansas City airport. A Negro fraternity leader loaned the cause his girlfriend for a dance date with Chamberlain.

It was after his second tour of the school, in May, that Chamberlain had Mosenson tell Kansas authorities he would enroll. "I want to do my race some good," he said. This is a heartfelt matter with the Stilt. "If I get Jim Crowed, I'll pack my bags and leave," he often told Kansas officials.

Testing points this year will be the Kansas away games with Missouri and Oklahoma—both in sectors where the prevailing attitude on the race question differs considerably from the Eastern outlook to which Wilt is accustomed. But Chamberlain has established the position that "I'm part of the Kansas team, and I go wherever it goes. They agree with me. That's why we don't make a Texas trip this year."

Haskell Cohen, of the National Basketball Association, who got Chamberlain summer jobs as a bellhop during Wilt's high school days, says, "He can become impossible to handle if any racial trouble comes up. This I know."

In the Lawrence area, the Stilt has been more than merely accepted. At the school, he and Charley Tidwell, a low hurdler on the track team, share a modern dormitory room. Wilt has been supplied a special seven-and-a-half-foot bed. His big frame is a familiar sight around the campus and in the first row in classrooms—he invariably sits up front so that he can stretch out his legs.

He likes bowling and movies. Wilt has no steady girl, although he squires quite a few to dances. His habit of driving fast—he was in two smashups during high school days—brought Chamberlain a speeding fine last summer. This was front-page news in Kansas.

The Stilt also goes in for track. At the Kansas Relays last April, he entered as an unattached contestant, decked out in a uniform of his own design—plaid cap, green shirt, and black trunks with an orange stripe. He tied for second in the high jump behind Charley Dumas, the world-record holder from California's Compton Junior College. Wilt has ambitions of becoming a varsity track man in both the high jump and the shot put.

By now Kansas athletic officials are weary of being asked what they did to land Chamberlain. From the day Wilt's enrollment was announced, Phog Allen was ready for all questioners. "There wasn't one cent involved in bringing Chamberlain to Kansas," he declared firmly. Later he answered one persistent reporter by saying, "I don't know how much he got. I never asked him."

Cecil Mosenson, Wilt's coach at Overbrook High, was watched carefully during this period, too. Many predicted he would ride along with the Stilt and become an assistant coach at Kansas.

"There was talk of it," Mosenson says, "but it never developed. I was more interested in seeing that Wilton was happy at Kansas. He always wanted to get away from Philadelphia. He said that from the start." Mosenson gave up his Overbrook High job last summer and went into his father's bread business.

Dick Harp, the 39-year-old Kansas coach who stepped into Phog Allen's job this year, feels understandably that he is on a spot with Chamberlain. "Here it is my first year as varsity coach, and everybody expects me to go through three years unbeaten," he says. "But it's a nice spot. I like it. Who wouldn't?"

Harp says Wilt is easy to work with on the basketball court. Much of Chamberlain's basketball education came from summer play. He was in leagues around Philadelphia with older boys, like Jackie Moore and Tom Gola, who advanced from LaSalle College to the pro Warriors. Wilt also was at Kutsher's Country Club, a Catskill Mountain luxury resort, where he benefited from working out one summer with Neil Johnston, the Warriors' 6'8" scoring star.

But Wilt does not feel he knows it all. "He does just what you tell him," Harp says. "For example, we think he shoots too hard. And he doesn't shoot enough. When we told him these things he started working on them immediately."

Chamberlain had no organized freshman schedule last year—the Big 7 doesn't allow this—but he played intra-squad games before varsity home contests. The Stilt averaged 35 points in these pickup affairs. Harp wants him to go for more points, now that it counts.

The Stilt is in talented company on the Kansas varsity this season. Last year's center, Lew Johnson, has been placed at forward. With his 6'9" frame he can give Wilt plenty of help. And Ron Loneski, a 6'5" scholastic crackerjack from Hammond, Indiana, is rated only a shade behind Chamberlain in ability.

With Chamberlain in the lineup, Kansas has a player capable of matching the shot-blocking techniques for which San Francisco's Bill Russell became famous. Some experts believe that the Stilt is much better. "Chamberlain," said Tom Gola last year, "would kill Russell."

Chamberlain will have people talking as much about the way he scores his baskets as about the number he rings up. His style of shooting a one-hander is a good example. The Stilt usually goes up at the foul line and fires a line drive at the backboard, a few inches to the right of the basket. Then he flies through the air after the ball, grabs it with both hands as it comes off the backboard, and fires it downward through the net. After this, he ducks his head so it won't bang into the backboard.

Head-ducking has become a conditioned reflex for Chamberlain. Walking from room to room, he automatically dips his head as he reaches a doorway. He used to be sensitive about his height, but when the college rush started, Wilt began to see that there definitely were compensations. The realization that he is in for a lot of money someday has helped to end any possible psychiatric problems.

He did need medical help this fall, however. For some months his throat had irritated him. Doctors at the University of Kansas Medical Center diagnosed the trouble as nodes on his vocal cords—comparable to the "singer's nodes" of Bing Crosby. In the Crosby case, nothing was ever done for fear of altering his singing voice. But Chamberlain is not a singer, and the doctors thought it advisable to operate. As has been said, the surgery was pronounced a success.

For Chamberlain, the outwardly easy but often rocky road he is now taking started when he was a fourteen-year-old boy. He was one of three sons and six daughters raised by William and Olivia Chamberlain in a pleasant eight-room row house at 401 North Salford Street in Philadelphia.

"I grew four inches in two months that summer," Wilt recalls. "It was only natural for the junior-high-school coach to start me takin' up basketball. I played a lot around the neighborhood. It was a little tough keeping me in clothes, though. I needed a new pair of pants every month or so. The cuffs always were at my ankles."

His father is only 5'8½", and his mother is 5'9". Wilt has one brother who is 6'5". Wilt's father works as a porter for the Curtis Publishing Company. His mother still goes out and does housework two or three days a week.

His roommate, Charley Tidwell, has seen only one side of the Chamberlain picture. "You read the headlines and then look across the room at him trying to study, and it doesn't seem like the same guy," Tidwell says. "He's just another kid to us. We play pranks on him, stealing his dinner plate and all that. Sometimes I wake him up in the morning by pouring a glass of water on his head."

Tidwell likes the idea of rooming with the Stilt for a variety of reasons, including a special one. With Chamberlain, there is no cause for worry about one deep-seated cause of friction which so often crops up between two strangers placed together in a college room.

"My clothes," the 5'6" Tidwell explains, "are always in the closet. Wilt just isn't the clothes-borrowing kind."

Dick Russell, *The Sporting News*

JAYHAWKS BID SAD SO-LONG TO JO JO AS PROS SAY HELLO

Coach Ted Owens just couldn't wait to get Jo Jo White on the court with the varsity. So, as soon as White became eligible midway through the 1965–66 season, Owens suited up the guard. Dick Russell wrote this piece for The Sporting News *the week after White's final game at KU, which was an 80–70 win over Colorado on February 1, 1969.*

For three years now, he has floated through pressure defenses like an evasive helium balloon. Perhaps you could hold him momentarily, but at the precise moment of release, he was gone—synchronizing his way downcourt with the precision and grace of a Balanchine dancer.

For three years, he has been the adhesive tape of the Kansas defense. He made the spectacular seem almost commonplace, stealing passes so often that his mere presence provided psychological traumas to opposing guards.

And as Jo Jo White leaves the Jayhawks lineup, appreciative fans note the tremendous contribution he has made to Kansas basketball. His kind come by but once.

Master in Backcourt
Rarely has anyone dominated a collegiate backcourt like the 6'3" St. Louis native. White came to Kansas as a highly sought midsemester high school graduate, best known for his scoring talents and surprising durability in summer pickup games against fellows like pros Lenny Wilkens and Chico Vaughn.

Adjusting rapidly to Ted Owens's ball-control system, he became the type of guard that coaches only dream about—a staunch defender, devastating outside shooter, and soloist on breaking down the opposition. In short, he could do it all, and Kansas won 80 percent of its games (67 of 83) with him in the lineup.

His international record was even more impressive. White was America's number two scorer at Mexico City as the United States won a seventh consecutive Olympic title. In the 1967 Pan-American Games, he topped everybody with 125 points in nine games, then sparked a U.S. victory in the World University Games at Tokyo.

"He probably is as complete a player as you would want to run into in a university class," said Henry Iba, the veteran Oklahoma State coach who tutored White in the Olympics.

All-America Choice

Other experts agree. Despite a 15.3 scoring mark, relatively low compared with the Alcindors, Maraviches, and Murphys, White received numerous All-America honors last season (including *The Sporting News's* first unit). This year, he was basketball's nominee for the coveted AAU Sullivan Award, given annually to the nation's outstanding amateur athlete.

White's college eligibility ran out on February 1, when Big 8 leader Colorado met Lawrence. Now Jo Jo's thoughts will turn to fresh horizons—and a professional career.

Indeed, Jo Jo cannot conceal his enthusiasm about pro basketball. When he talks about the future, he flashes his gentle smile, and his round, almost doll-like countenance brims with anticipation. For Joseph Henry White is a cool, confident individual, aware of his vast capabilities and aware that, on the basketball court, he has few peers.

"His greatest assets are directing plays and an ability to shoot out on the floor," said Henry Iba. "But he's still a tremendous driver without the ball. In fact, he will play better when he moves more without the ball inside the defense. He is a great pro prospect."

Since the National Basketball Association won't draft until March, White is expected to spend another semester finishing up at Kansas. He's already been drafted as a future by Dallas of the ABA, but admittedly prefers the more established league. And reports have him being a high choice in the NBA draft.

He Likes Pro Viewpoint

"I just like the way the pros go one-on-one," says Jo Jo. "A height advantage seems to make no difference because they don't look for just one thing. Here, you may have a height advantage over your man, but everybody still thinks 'big man,' that you have to get the ball inside."

White also sees a chance to drive more. Kansas plays a tight, controlled game, and most of White's shots come from 20 or 25 feet away. This philosophy is understandable, since the Jayhawks boast 6'10" Roger Brown and 6'9" Dave Robisch underneath. White's greatest effectiveness thus lies outside the free throw circle. But, personally, Jo

Jo always has preferred a more wide-open game and should find it in the pros.

For example, in high school, he averaged nearly 30 points a game and connected on 53 percent of his shots. Most of his scoring came on drives or short jumpers around the free throw line. At Kansas, his three-year totals show a 15.1 average and .417 percentage.

Of course, added versatility on defense and handling the ball have been White's primary assets at Kansas; Owens always has had good height inside. But the scoring potential is there if the pros desire it.

"In the pros, you really get to show what you can do," said White. "With the freedom to move like that, I feel you can make better plays. You get to really move, like on the playgrounds."

Learned Against Hawks

White's first feeling for competition came on the playgrounds. He spent his prep summers scrimmaging against several St. Louis Hawks stars, learning the ropes early against rugged pros. Actually, his organized basketball career began in the fourth grade, when Jo Jo became so captivated by the sport that he's missed only 10 days of practice since.

It wasn't always easy to make his parents understand. His dad was sure his nights weren't always being spent at the recreation center, and White recalls many a time he had to invent an excuse to get away for a while.

While attending McKinley High School, White acquired the nickname that has stayed with him ever since. It seems the youngster had a tendency to doze off while Coach Jodie Bailey was giving chalk talk sessions. And it always took two calls ("Jo! Jo!") to bring him back to life.

White didn't do any dozing on the court. His pulverizing moves brought 63 colleges rushing to his door. First, he leaned to Cincinnati, but shied away because "they were having some kind of racial problem." Then he decided on Kansas.

Near Miss on Tide

When White became eligible for the varsity at midsemester of 1966, he nearly sparked the Jayhawks to the NCAA championship. Kansas was tied with Texas Western in the Midwest Regional finals when White's last-second shot creased the cords. The officials ruled he was inches out of bounds, and the Miners went on to win in overtime, ultimately downing Kentucky for the NCAA title.

Assuming the leadership role his next season, White helped Kansas to a 23–4 record. Last year, the Jayhawks finished 22–8 and runner-up to Dayton in the National Invitation Tournament. This winter, the young club has spurted to a 14–3 start.

Jo Jo's career highlight didn't occur on a college court, though. "My biggest thrill came in the Olympics," he said. "Just winning it made you feel so good because so many sportswriters had said we weren't a strong team."

Though he was approached several times, White never considered joining the boycott of [the Olympics by] black athletes. Neither did he understand the disruptive attempts of some of the trackmen.

"I talked with Tommie Smith [the suspended sprinter] about it," White recalled. "I didn't really understand some of the things that were going on, though. We didn't get too deep.

"I felt that going to the Olympics couldn't hurt the Negro athlete, but it could help him if he went and did well. It was something I'd looked forward to since I was a kid, hoping someday I would be good enough to play in the Olympics.

"Yeah, I was approached to join the boycott. It didn't make any difference."

Key Man in Olympics

The day after he returned from Mexico City, where he scored 105 points and was called "instrumental in every victory" by Iba, Jo Jo was back on the Kansas court. A new double-post offense awaited him.

White now took on the responsibilities as the "point" man, bringing the ball downcourt by himself and setting up a somewhat looser offense.

"This year, we got a chance to loosen up a little bit," noted White. "We got to drive a little, come off a screen. If I drove last year, I'd run right into my own players because they were all stacked up. Now I've been working more on shooting, releasing it quicker and getting up."

What Kansas will do for court leadership down the stretch is questionable. Owens hasn't tipped his hand on the new point man and, with defenses expectedly employing more pressure than ever, may go with two men to get the ball across midcourt. Rich Bradshaw, a 6'3" junior from Chicago, or 6'5" Bruce Sloan, a consistent Kansas Citian, would expectedly step in, gaining support from zone-breaker Phil Harmon.

But certainly there will be no replacing White, whose leadership qualities extend beyond his basketball ability. Consider this statement made prior to the recent pivotal contest at Kansas State. The Jayhawks had just dropped consecutive road games to Missouri and Iowa State. A loss at Manhattan would have been fatal to the Jayhawks' Big 8 chances.

More Determined

"I think the fellows are a little more determined now," said White, dressing casually for morning classes in his dormitory room. "I have been trying to get everybody up. I still think it's my duty, even if I do have just two games left here."

The following Saturday, Kansas put together its most consistent effort of the season, jumping to a 17–4 lead and averting a fast-closing Kansas State team for a 73–67 victory. To no avail, the Wildcats employed four different men on White.

He scored 21 points himself and led Dave Robisch for many of his 28.

Wildcat fans offered no ovations. Many simply shook their heads. Others smiled in the happy realization that Jo Jo would haunt them no longer. And, amidst the hubbub of the Jayhawks dressing room, White was smiling, too. For he would bow out the way that he came in—a winner.

Mal Elliott, *The Sporting News*

VALENTINE GREETING FROM KANSAS SHAKES UP FOES

Darnell Valentine, a two-time academic All-American, helped lead the Jayhawks back to the NCAA Tournament during his freshman and senior seasons, 1977–78 and 1980–81. He became the standard for KU guards during the 1980s, which was unfair to anyone who followed in his footsteps. Valentine, featured in this article written during his sophomore season, remains a fan favorite.

The thighs of his powerful legs are as big as a couple of 100-pound watermelons. His 6'2", 180-pound body looks more like that of a weight lifter or a football player than a basketball player.

Kansas University's teenage whiz, Darnell Valentine, is not slowed by all the muscle. The quick are usually as slender as a whippet. But by any standard, Valentine is among the quickest.

He flits. He darts. He leaps. And his physique gives him strength and power when he gets where he is going.

Valentine's teen years are almost at an end. They have been filled with heady stuff. Athletic honors began to come his way even before he was a high school All-American and led his Wichita Heights team to a perfect season.

As a freshman, Valentine led Kansas to the Big 8 conference championship and a spot in the NCAA playoffs. He was conceded All-America status in many quarters even before this season began.

He'll become 20 on February 3, just 11 days before the date celebrated by lovers in honor of the Christian martyr St. Valentine. Darnell is the darling of the KU faithful, and he exemplifies the true meaning of his last name, which comes from a Latin root word meaning "to be strong or healthy."

"He is an enormous worker," said Ted Owens, his coach. "I never have seen an athlete keep himself in better condition."

The Kansas team the sophomore leads is not as powerful as the one of last season, but Valentine's presence has made the Jayhawkers the unanimous favorite to win the league title, although they were 1–2 after being upset by Missouri, 58–55, January 17.

The KU star has not acquired one of those flamboyant nicknames normally attached to standout athletes. The backs of KU's warm-ups carry the nicknames of the players. There is "Big Mo" for 7'1" Paul Mokeski, "Little Mo" for guard Wilmore Fowler, and so on.

Valentine's warmup simply reads "The DV."

Rival coaches call him "the Penetrator." So do Owens and Red Auerbach, president of the Boston Celtics.

The comparison that is sometimes made for Valentine is with Jo Jo White, the former KU All-American who went on to become a pro star with the Celtics.

"Darnell and Jo Jo have a lot of likenesses," said Owens, who also coached White. "Both have a great attitude toward work and both are complete players.

"But Jo Jo never penetrated like Darnell does. He does that better than anybody I've ever seen."

Auerbach agreed. "Valentine is quicker than Jo Jo and he penetrates better," said Auerbach after watching the KU ace win MVP honors in the Big 8 Holiday Tournament in Kansas City.

Valentine leads Kansas in scoring with a 20-point average. That would be the top credential for most players. But not for Valentine.

"His scoring is just a plus," said Owens.

He leads the league in steals with an average of three per game and is second in assists with an average of six.

Nor is he found lacking in the clutch. He scored 27 points at Kentucky and 28 against the host Southern Cal.

It was discovered before this season that Valentine is nearsighted. Some speculate that may be why he is not a great outside shooter. Soft contact lenses were prepared for him, and he has played some games with them but says they do not seem to affect his play. He is shooting 48 percent, just as he did last year.

Many wondered if Valentine could improve on a freshman season in which he led the league champions in scoring and took them to a 24–5 season. But he has. He is scoring more and rebounding right up there with the frontliners.

"He is penetrating and staying down better," said Owens. "He is aggressive on defense without fouling and he is running the club better than a year ago."

Fouling was a big problem for Valentine last year, as it was for Mokeski. This year, Owens has used more zone defense in an attempt to keep them in the game.

But Valentine is at his best in a harassing, full-court pressure defense. With quick hands, he can strip a ball handler in a wink and is nearly impossible to stop from driving to the basket in a fast-break situation.

Stopping the running game has been a priority item for KU foes. Colorado did a good job of it and narrowly lost in the Holiday Tournament title game. Oklahoma did it recently in a resounding 68–45 upset win. In that one, Valentine got only eight points.

"When he doesn't have his sharpness, it has a 'down' effect on our performance," said Owens. "It happens so seldom, our other players just don't adjust.

"It's not fair to him to expect him to be letter-perfect every time he goes out on the floor."

Oklahoma Coach Dave Bliss praised his sophomore guard Ray Whitley for the defensive job he did on Valentine. But he said:

"Valentine is a great player. We didn't stop him. He just had an off night."

John Feinstein, *Washington Post*

MANNING: A TOPSY-TURVY FINALE

There have been only a few players throughout the history of KU bas-ketball who affected the program as much as Danny Manning. In fact, a case could be made that since Clyde Lovellette and Wilt Chamberlain 30 years earlier, no player impacted the school as much as Manning. Best-selling writer John Feinstein realized early that Manning was going to be quite a player, and he wrote about Manning during his freshman year. This feature, however, which shows a more mature Manning, was written less than three months before Manning's domi-nation through the NCAA Tournament in 1988. Manning became one of the features in Feinstein's book, A Season Inside.

The look on his face was blank, his eyes fixed on the people standing in front of him even though he didn't really see them. The answers came easily, a drill in rote rather than thought because the questions never seem to change.

"Danny, is it tough being triple-teamed all the time?"

"Danny, how difficult is it to play here?"

"Danny, what's the matter with the Jayhawks?"

"Danny, do you think you guys can bounce back?"

Answers: Yes. Very. I don't know. Sure.

But Danny Manning stretched those answers, giving the TV man tape, the radio guy audio, and the newspaper reporter a paragraph. He is 21 now, a professional at this, just as he will be a highly paid profes-sional basketball player a year from now.

Finally, he stood to leave. His teammates were long gone. Only the stars have to stay to answer the last question, and Manning is the star. So he stayed—wishing he wasn't the star.

"If Danny had his way, he would be able to play the way he does but no one but the other guys [players] would know about it," his father, Ed Manning, said. "But that's not the way life is. Being the best isn't always easy and it isn't just playing the game. Danny has to learn that."

Manning is learning. But it hasn't been easy. And in this, his final winter as a kid, it has been harder than ever. Manning came back to Kansas because he wanted to play one last season with his close friend, Archive Marshall, because he wanted to win a national championship, and because he wanted to get his degree.

Marshall tore up his knee December 30 in New York and is out for the season. Last Tuesday, starting center Marvin Branch was declared academically ineligible. Suddenly, the Jayhawks are young and thin up front. Their guards were suspect from the start.

"At least," Manning said with a smile, "I think I'll get my degree."

The season—for Manning, for Coach Larry Brown, and for Kansas—is hanging on the edge of a cliff. It is Manning who holds the rope, and everyone at Kansas knows it.

"Danny is the best player in the country; it's very simple," Brown said. "But it's hard for him to go out and dominate because that just isn't his nature. When he first got here, we had older kids he deferred to and most of the time that was okay because they wanted to be the leaders. But starting last year, he's had to be the guy; not just playing, but everything else.

"It was hard for him last year, being surrounded every time he touched the ball. He thought that was all over this year because we had Archie back and we were going to be deeper. Now, he feels like he's back on square one and he's frustrated."

Manning isn't the only one feeling that way. Branch's ineligibility was close enough that Brown hoped the junior college transfer might survive. When he didn't, Brown publicly criticized the faculty and once again fueled the ever-present rumors that his time is up at Kansas.

Brown has been there five years and is very happy in Lawrence—he even owns part of a local Mexican restaurant—but with Manning graduating, recruiting difficult, and many other opportunities available, Brown may well be elsewhere next reason.

Manning and Brown both had the chance to move to the NBA last spring. Brown was offered the New York Knicks job, and Manning seriously considered passing up his last year of eligibility.

"It was close," Manning said. "I knew my parents wanted me to stay, but the thought of not having to go to class, of just playing basketball and getting paid to do it, was tempting. Very tempting. In the end, I came back because of Archie and because I wanted to spend one more year with the guys."

Manning, his father, and Brown have been one of the most studied triumvirates in college basketball ever since Brown, in one of his first acts as Kansas coach, hired the father as an assistant coach. Danny Manning was completing his junior year at Page High School in Greensboro, North Carolina, at the time and was already considered a guaranteed college superstar. He was 6'10", could run, shoot, and pass, and was being compared with Magic Johnson.

A Howl Went Up

Earlier that year, Ed Manning had undergone heart bypass surgery. He had played pro basketball for nine years, including a stint with the Carolina Cougars, coached at the time by Larry Brown. After retiring, Manning coached for several years, but in 1983 he was looking for a coaching job and driving a truck to make ends meet.

When Brown hired him, a howl went up among those recruiting his son, especially at North Carolina and North Carolina State, considered the favorites to win the Manning derby. Brown, they said, had hired a truck driver to sign his son.

"They completely ignored the fact that he had coached or that he was my friend and had played for me," Brown said. "Did I think about Danny when I hired him? Of course. But if I didn't think Ed could do a job for me, I'd have been stupid to hire him."

Both Mannings have heard the jokes and learned to shrug them off. For one thing, working together every day has brought them closer.

"When I was little, my dad was away so much that my mom had to explain to me all the time that he was doing it for us, not because he didn't love me," Manning said. "He never really got to see me play that much. Now, we see each other every day. Sometimes he gets on me, but that's okay. I like having him around."

Marshall's importance to Manning and to Kansas cannot be underplayed. He was a key player two seasons ago when Kansas was 35–4 and went to the Final Four. In the semifinal against Duke, the Jayhawks had a four-point lead with seven minutes left when Marshall stole the ball and went flying toward the basket. When he came down, his knee crumpled. He was helped off, clearly hurt, but no one dreamed at the time that he had suffered ligament damage that would keep him out for all of last season.

"Seeing Archie come back meant a lot to everyone on the team," Brown said. "No one ever worked harder than he did. Having him back at the start of the season gave everyone a boost, especially Danny. He was just starting to really feel comfortable again when he got hurt."

Marshall went down again in the ECAC Holiday Festival final against St. John's in New York. There was a scramble under the basket and Marshall fell, screaming in pain right at Manning's feet. "I looked down at him and I said to myself, 'No way, not again,'" Manning remembered. "I just knew it couldn't be another blown knee. I refused to believe it."

Marshall was helped to the locker room. A couple of minutes later, the report came back: just a sprained knee. "I think they told us that to try to keep us from getting too upset," Manning said.

But during the next timeout, Brown talked to the doctor for a moment. When he came back into the huddle, he was crying. "That was when we knew," Manning said. It was ligament damage—this time in the other knee.

Since then, Manning has worn Marshall's No. 23 on his wristbands and even shaved the number onto the side of his head before the Jayhawks' victory over Missouri. "Every time things get tough from now on," he said, "I'm just going to look down at my wristbands."

Even before Marshall was hurt, the season had not been easy. The Jayhawks had started in Hawaii, losing two of three games, one of the losses a 100–81 embarrassment against Iowa.

Brown was not happy. Ever since Manning's arrival at Kansas, Brown has pushed him to turn up his intensity level. Brown was a 5'9" guard who succeeded because he played harder than other people, and he coaches that way, too. Manning, blessed with so many skills, is more laid-back than Brown—and his father for that matter—and is constantly being pushed by both coaches to be intense all the time rather than some of the time.

"Sometimes, we just get ticked off at him," Ed Manning said. "I try to tell him how hard I had to work to become a good player. I grew up in Mississippi. I never went to a basketball camp or had any real coaching when I was a kid. Danny's been very lucky. He's got great ability—much more than Larry or I ever dreamed of having—and he's had good coaching. Maybe we get on him too much sometimes, but it's only because we know how good he can be."

Most NBA scouts have little doubt about how good Manning can be. He will be one of the first three players chosen in the draft this June and might be the first.

Changed in Four Years

Manning is looking forward to pro basketball. The last four years have been a learning experience for him, and he is very different than the 18-year-old freshman of 1984. Then, he took his laundry home and, when he got hungry, didn't hesitate to let his mother cook for him. Now, he does his own laundry and his own cooking. He is still most comfortable around his teammates but deals with the public pressures of stardom smoothly.

In October, during the annual midnight practice that begins the season at Kansas, Manning led his teammates in a rendition of "My Girl." It was awful, but Manning belted it out with 16,000 people listening.

That was in the fall, however, before the leaves had turned and before Marshall went down and Branch went out. Everyone at Kansas was upbeat, and when the band played "Kansas City" as the final number of the evening (the Final Four is in Kansas City), everyone joined in and Allen Fieldhouse rocked with enthusiasm.

It is always that way when Kansas plays. Manning has not lost a home game—55 straight—in his four seasons at Kansas. "My goal," he said half-jokingly before the season began, "is to not lose at home and win once at Iowa State."

In Manning's four years (and Brown's five) at Kansas, the Jayhawks have not won in Ames. Last week, Manning was brilliant with 32 points and eight rebounds, but it wasn't enough.

Brown had tried desperately before the game to build up his sagging team. "Even without Archie and Marvin, we're a better team than last year and we won 25 games last year," he told his players. "Just play with confidence and rebound and we'll win."

The Jayhawks rebounded, but they also turned over the ball 25 times. They didn't win and, when it was over, Manning sat in front of his locker, his voice soft.

"What now, Danny?"

"Get on the plane and go home."

Manning is the leading scorer in Kansas history and probably will be the leading scorer in Big 8 history before he is through. His teams have a four-year record of 98–27, two Big 8 tournament titles, and a trip to the Final Four. Yet, unless the Jayhawks find a way to get the ball to Manning even more often and reach another Final Four, many—Manning included—will judge his Kansas career a disappointment.

"I still think we can win the Big 8," he said softly, munching on a pizza in his apartment last week. "We're going through an adjustment period, but we'll be okay. Coach Brown may be tough on us some-times, but he's a great coach. If there's a way to get it done, he'll find it.

"This team has gone through a lot together. Who knows? Maybe it will make us better in the long run. You never know." He paused. "In the end, though, the responsibility gets back to the best player. I'm supposed to be the best player. If we lose, it's my fault. My job, from here on in, is to keep us from losing."

Pressure is nothing new to Manning. It has always been part of his life. His family, his coaches, his teammates, his friends, his fans have always expected miracles from him. Now, the pressure is coming from a different source.

It is coming from within. It may be the most pressure Danny Manning has ever faced.

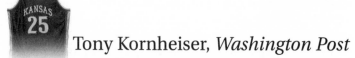

Tony Kornheiser, *Washington Post*

MARSHALL'S ROLE IS SUPPORTING FACTOR

There likely has been no player that has inspired his Jayhawks team more than Archie Marshall did during 1986 and '88. Both seasons—both Final Four seasons—Marshall went down with a knee injury. This article by Tony Kornheiser, who is one of the nation's best-known sports columnists, appeared in the Washington Post *the day of KU's national championship game against Oklahoma in April 1988.*

Some of you with particularly keen eyesight may have noticed that the wristbands Danny Manning wears are numbered differently than his jersey. Across Manning's chest is a 25; around his wrists, a 23. The 23 is actually Archive Marshall's number. Marshall is the senior forward whose collegiate career ended for all practical purposes in Madison Square Garden December 30 when he blew out his left knee in the final of the Holiday Festival against St. John's. So severe was Marshall's injury that he needed to be carried off the floor.

In Kansas's next game, to honor his friend and teammate, Manning took the court with "23" on his wrists. "Because Archie couldn't be out there physically," Manning explained, "and I wanted to have him there with me."

To this day, Marshall never has spoken to Manning about his gesture. "And I don't plan to," Marshall said. "But I see it. I think it's wonderful." Rubbing his eyes to keep from crying, Marshall said, "I love Danny. I love my teammates."

What made Manning so sensitive to Marshall's plight, and indeed what made Marshall's injury so heartrending, was that it had happened once before. Two seasons previous, in the Final Four semifinal against Duke, Marshall went down with a wrecked right knee. That cost him a season. After what was described as "major reconstructive surgery," Marshall spent a year rehabilitating the knee and returned to the Jayhawks' starting lineup for his final season of eligibility. "I never saw a kid work this hard to come back from an injury in my entire life," said Larry Brown, who named Marshall a cocaptain of the team.

Eleven games later, Marshall was writhing on the Garden floor, screaming in pain. Kneeling at his side, Brown openly wept.

"Two years ago I didn't know what was going on," recalled the soft-spoken Marshall. "I felt the pain, but I got up, walked back to the locker room, and even jogged a bit. I knew I couldn't play any more that game, but I thought it was just a bad sprain. I wasn't able to walk off from this one. This time I knew it was over, I knew I couldn't continue the season. I was devastated. I'll be honest with you, I was ready to totally give it up—school, everything. But the support of my teammates made it impossible to do that. I mean, everybody was there for me. They had half the season to go, but it seemed like all they cared about was me."

Rather than distance himself, Marshall stayed in school and tried to stay involved with the team. Emotionally it's too painful for him to go to all the practices and meetings, but he's there for some. And he's been on the bench in a jacket and tie—sort of like a coach, except he admits he doesn't know "half the stuff we're doing out there"—for all the games. All but one, that is. In the last home game of the season Marshall sat on the bench in uniform, which felt "so strange" to him after all that time, "like I'd never worn a uniform before."

It was assistant coach Mark Turgeon's idea to put Marshall in the game against Oklahoma State. Just for a moment, mind you, and with Brown's blessing, so the home folks could give him a friendly hand for his years at Kansas. "Coach said he was going to try," Marshall said.

The plan was for Marshall to go in on a safe inbounds situation. After the pass was made, Kansas would call time and get Marshall back out. It was designed to be a gesture of appreciation, not unlike the wristbands. With a minute and change to go and Kansas comfortably ahead, Brown sent Marshall in, and the crowd roared such a tumult, chanting "Ar-chie! Ar-chie!"—that Marshall felt warm tears well in his eyes.

Marshall stood near midcourt, some 45 feet from the basket. "Once I got a spot on the court I wasn't supposed to move," Marshall said, recalling Brown's instructions. "Coach told me to stay there." Marshall was a mile away from everybody, nowhere near harm's way. The ball went in to Manning, but instead of calling time, Manning dribbled over to Marshall, handed him the ball and urged him, "Shoot! Shoot!"

Manning grinned at the mention of the incident. Yes, he'd disobeyed the instructions by involving Marshall in the play. "But I knew he'd like to take a shot," giggled Manning. "I just assumed he'd move in a lot."

He didn't.

Coach told him, stay in one spot.

So he launched it from 45.

"Air ball," Marshall sheepishly admitted, "way short, and off to the right about five feet from the goal." He shrugged good-naturedly. "It had no chance."

This Kansas team has suffered through so much upheaval, so many personnel changes—injuries, academic probations, disciplinary suspensions—that Brown has become fond of quoting the adage that good can sometimes come out of bad. Marshall believes it. He remains optimistic he isn't done with basketball yet. And he swears that no matter how unfortunate his denouement appears, he wouldn't change a thing.

What's more, he says even if he was declared healthy enough to play in tonight's national title game, the only one he'll ever be eligible for, he'd decline. "My job is support now. That's why I'm here," he said. "I couldn't play. I haven't played in months. I'd look like a total fool."

Marshall drew in a deep breath and let it out slowly as he considered every word he was about to utter. He knew his injury had opened the door for Milton Newton, and who's to say that hasn't been a good deal for Kansas? "Physically I'm not a player on this team, but I think of myself as a part of it. I'll tell you, maybe if I'd still been playing it wouldn't have come out like this. I'd go through all of it again to see us in this position." And smiling, his smooth face as guileless as the first crocus of spring, Archie Marshall said, "I'm having the best time of my life. Look at us. *We're* playing for the national championship."

Harvey Araton, *The New York Times*

VAUGHN HAS LEARNED ALL THE RIGHT LESSONS

Despite missing several games during his KU career because of injuries, one of the most exciting players ever to wear crimson and blue was guard Jacque Vaughn, who was a two-time academic All-American. Harvey Araton tried to get to the bottom of Vaughn's success in 1997.

Though it lacked the incredulity that would surely greet the Loch Ness monster or a UFO, there was nonetheless a rare and distinguished sighting here yesterday afternoon at the Hartford Civic Center: a senior All-America college basketball player.

An academic All-American at that. Jacque Vaughn, poetry-writing point guard with a grade-point average climbing toward 4.0, represents something of a serious anomaly in the sport of federations and regulations, a throwback to when freshmen were freshmen and sophomores were sophomores and stars such as Vaughn and Wake Forest's Tim Duncan (my e-mail buddy during a self-imposed five-month exile from the newspaper wars to first-grade soccer league games and other Rodman-free zones) weren't on the endangered-seniors list.

"A lot of the kids just don't understand that the next level is not just about the game," mused Vaughn, who stayed behind and helped unbeaten and top-ranked Kansas weather another numbing, cross-country winter excursion, a wild Civic Center crowd, and a 23–7 Connecticut lead that eventually became a 73–65 KU victory. "They never think about the business and social aspects of it and, unfortunately, I guess many times it shows."

Vaughn said he returned this season not so much for the glory of the institution or the benefit of his championship-less coach, Roy Williams, but for a bachelor's degree and one underrated amenity not often considered during the ongoing soap opera "As the Underclassmen Turn."

"There's so many things I've gained already from still being here," Vaughn said. "Another year of growing up socially, another year of games like these in places like this, of getting the chance to go to the free throw line and make four free throws in the last minute, of feeling better about myself and being more of a leader every year."

This concept is as elementary as grammar school, where any know-it-all parent will tell you it is far better for a boy to begin late, to become a leader. But the sad truth is that more and more of the dreamers down on the basketball food chain view the Division I colleges not as a means to an education, or even improved skills, but as a place for television exposure and enhanced National Basketball Association draft status. The result is that the sport is dominated by Dick Vitale's diaper dandies, and we all know the problem with that. Diapers invariably get dirty.

The sight of two UConn starters, Kirk King and Ricky Moore, cheering from the bench yesterday in street clothes, was yet another reminder. Both allegedly accepted plane tickets from an agent named John Lounsbury back in October 1995 and are under suspension by the school while the matter is investigated by the National Collegiate Athletic Association.

King and Moore reportedly took the tickets to visit their families, no egregious violation in a sport that dispatches its so-called student-athletes all over North America in search of a game and completely ignores ethically questionable relationships, such as the one between Georgetown coach John Thompson and the agent David Falk. [Falk represents Thompson as well as many of Thompson's high-profile players from Georgetown.] The problem, of course, is what occurs when the gifts become more extravagant, with strings attached to them—as they did with Marcus Camby of Massachusetts. [Camby received payments from an agent with the expectation that Camby would sign with that agent after college.]

There are no easy answers, certainly not last week's NCAA legislation that will allow players to take part-time jobs for about $2,000 per school year.

"I think the NCAA is trying, but for a kid to go to school, go to practice, and have a normal social life is hard enough," Vaughn said. "I don't worry about the University of Kansas being honest, but it's going to be tough to enforce a standard. It may create more problems than it solves."

Vaughn paused a second and offered his heartfelt advice to America's coaches. "I think," he said, "the best situation is to look for kids who want to be in college and play college ball, who enjoy all this."

As for himself, he has had better days than yesterday, when he waited until 10 minutes before tip-off before deciding to play. His left knee, sprained Friday night in practice, was heavily wrapped. His right wrist remains tender from the ligament damage that sidelined him for the Jayhawks' first 10 games. Early in the game, while UConn was hitting seven of its first nine shots, he took an elbow to his lower forehead and needed a butterfly stitch that oozed blood the rest of the game.

Vaughn played 30 minutes, hit the three-point shot that awakened the Jayhawks when they trailed by 16, scored nine points, had five assists, passed Cedric Hunter to become Kansas's career assist leader, and played his typically dogged defense. Nothing special, unless you were out there with him.

"You'll never fully appreciate Jacque by looking at his statistics," said Scot Pollard, the Kansas center.

Given his spotty jumper, there has been some debate over how much of an NBA prospect Vaughn actually is, but we may safely assume he won't be kicking any courtside photographers in the groin, throwing towels in his coach's face, or feuding with his backcourt partners over dates with pop stars. Some of that's just Kidd stuff.

"I know a knee is nothing for a basketball player to fool around with, but I've gotten a lot of support from people on the East Coast," he said. "I felt like I owed it to them to play."

Owed it to the fans. Imagine that.

Bob Dutton, *The Sporting News*

JAYHAWK JESTER

In 1998, the same year that this piece appeared in The Sporting News, *Paul Pierce and Raef LaFrentz were selected as first-team All-Americans. It was the first, and so far only, time the Jayhawks have had two players on the list in the same season. Pierce has gone on to a great career in the NBA. Bob Dutton was the KU beat writer for* The Kansas City Star, *where he now covers the Kansas City Royals.*

That other preseason All-American at Kansas, Paul Pierce, has had quite an enjoyable season, even in the absence of Raef LaFrentz.

The moment captured everything there is to know about Paul Pierce, the Kansas junior elevated to a solo starring role because of the recent injury to All-America forward Raef LaFrentz.

Through the courtesy of CBS, a national audience had just witnessed Pierce generate 31 points and 10 rebounds in leading the Jayhawks to a 102–72 victory at Texas.

He had done so despite a twisted right ankle and a poke to the eye, all of which came three days after a slight sprain to his right knee in the previous game against Colorado.

What the cameras didn't catch January 10 was Pierce's act in the locker room at Erwin Center in Austin, Texas. There, he arched his neck in full concentration before responding to the question:

"So, can you go through a game without getting hurt?"

Pierce replied: "They felt if they could get me out of the game, they had a chance. They were trying to hurt me. I saw my man look over, and he said, 'Let's get Pierce.' He stuck his foot under there, and I twisted my ankle."

Then, a baleful look from Pierce, a prototype 6'7" small forward who weighs 220 pounds. Finally, a smile.

Yes, he was kidding. But he was enjoying himself, and so are the Jayhawks, which didn't seem possible when LaFrentz suffered a broken bone in his right hand in a freak practice injury December 26 in Honolulu.

After struggling initially to adjust to LaFrentz's absence, Kansas again looks the part of a serious contender for the national title. The

Jayhawks managed to go 7–2 without LaFrentz, including 5–1 in the Big 12, where their average victory margin was 25 points.

And Pierce was the chief reason, averaging 21.2 points a game after shedding his role as the junior partner in Kansas's two-man attack of preseason All-Americans.

"One of your All-Americans goes down," coach Roy Williams says, "the other one had better step up. Paul has done that."

Pierce's recent scoring surge pushed his season average to 20.2 a game. No player in Williams's previous nine seasons at KU averaged more than 18.5 for a full season, although LaFrentz, who had a stunning 31 points and 15 rebounds in his return last Saturday against Texas Tech, is at 21.8.

"I think it's hard for other teams to play me because I can go outside and inside," says Pierce, who answered Williams's call. Pierce averaged 22.5 points and 50.8 percent from the field in eight of the nine games LaFrentz missed. In the one game Pierce struggled (3-for-13, 11 points), so did Kansas in its seven-point win at home over Kansas State.

When paired, LaFrentz and Pierce offer an intriguing contrast. LaFrentz, a 6'11" senior, is the perfect system player at Kansas, which preaches balance and precision as its foundation.

LaFrentz seldom performs the spectacular except in the context of playing a complete game. Before his injury, he was college basketball's most bankable performer at 21.2 points and 11.4 rebounds a game. But good as he has been, it's debatable whether he's the best player on his team.

That's how good Pierce can be. NBA scouts privately gush over his potential while maintaining the discipline of not commenting on underclassmen as prospects.

Others aren't as reticent.

"Paul Pierce is like a silent assassin out there," Texas A&M coach Tony Barone says. "He hangs around, gets an offensive rebound. All of a sudden he steals the ball and gets a dunk. Then he hits a three-pointer."

Specifically, Pierce is a terrific open-court performer capable of taking over a game, which, to some, makes him an odd fit at Kansas. Williams is forever fighting the notion that his system, a modified North Carolina approach, inhibits a player's individual style—much the way, supposedly, the Tar Heels' version under former coach Dean Smith once kept Michael Jordan under wraps.

"The other schools use that against us in recruiting," Williams says. "And I just say one thing—the early [NBA] draft report says Raef is number one and Paul is number two. How are we hurting them?"

In any event, Pierce says he knew what to expect in coming to Kansas after a standout prep career in Inglewood, California, and that he signed with the Jayhawks precisely because of those expectations.

"I wanted to go somewhere where someone would push me," he says. "If I went to a team where everything was built around me, I'd probably get lazy and spoiled.

"I wanted to go to a team that also had a chance to win a national championship, where I'd get good exposure and have a good head coach—somewhere where I could learn."

So, he picked Kansas, which already had a strong, veteran nucleus of Jacque Vaughn, Jerod Haase, Scot Pollard, and LaFrentz. The first three departed after last season.

"It helped me to develop slowly," says Pierce, whose measured emergence as a go-to player may be the difference for the Jayhawks come March. "My first year, I couldn't do the things that I do today. We had other great players and there was no need. But I developed because there was a process of learning—learning the system and learning the things I could do.

"If I had gone to a program where I was 'the man' right away, I think it would have hurt me in the long run. Coming here, I felt, would help the other side of my game and make me a better team player."

Williams contends that is exactly what has happened.

"Maybe he could average eight to 10 more points a game [somewhere else]," he says, "but his field-goal percentage would probably be down in the low 40s (vs. his current percentage of .497, .391 from three-point range). Instead, he's taking good shots. He's getting people involved. He's a far better player.

"He's a complete player."

If there is a weakness, it's turnovers, in which Pierce led the team last year with 108 and is on pace to break 100 again this season. But in the nine games without LaFrentz, in which Pierce not only got more attention from the defense but also had to handle the ball more, his average per 30 minutes dropped from 2.94 to 2.57.

As LaFrentz says, "There's not much that can stop him. He can really do some great things."

Unlike LaFrentz, Pierce openly embraces the Jayhawks' quest for the NCAA title and shows no hesitation in discussing the disappointment of last March, when Kansas stumbled in the tournament after reigning as number one in the polls for the final 15 weeks of the regular season.

"I've always wanted to win the national championship," he says. "In school, I'd look at the national championship game every year, and I'd tape it. I'd see the guys celebrating, and I've always said to myself that I want to be in that game.

"Last year's game, over the summer, I watched that game almost every day. I saw the adrenaline that flowed through the guys and the whole atmosphere. It's tops. I want to experience that."

That's one reason Pierce didn't enter the NBA draft last spring, when he was projected as a mid-first-round pick.

"That did play a role," he says. "I knew with the [roster] additions and the players coming back, that we would have a shot at [the title]."

Even so, Pierce came close to leaving last season, which he ended with a rush, burning with motivation after the media and the coaches placed him on the All–Big 12 third team.

"I've actually kept the clipping that said I was an AP third-team All–Big 12," he says. "I taped it to my closet in my room. Every day when I wake up, that's the first thing that I see, that third-team All–Big 12 selection.

"On top of it, I've written, 'This is what they think of you. Prove them wrong.' That's motivation for me. Every day."

Pierce led Kansas in scoring in all six postseason games. He was a runaway choice as Most Valuable Player in the Big 12 Tournament, and he scored 27 in almost single-handedly rescuing the Jayhawks in their Sweet 16 loss to Arizona.

It was enough to catch everyone's attention, including NBA scouts. Buoyed by the prospect of realizing a lifelong dream, Pierce nearly left KU.

"It got pretty close at times," he says, "but I reevaluated, and I didn't think I was quite ready, physically or mentally. I thought there were things that I still needed to work on and improve on. I felt I needed to get a lot stronger, too, to match up with some of the guys at that level."

Pierce hedges when asked if he'll return for his senior season but disputes, with a laugh, the belief that he's certain to turn pro.

"I'm human," he says. "I've thought about the money. I've looked at guys' salaries. It's definitely tempting, but I love the game of basketball. And if I was just in it for the money, I would have left last year.

"At this point in my career, I'm right where I want to be. I'm playing on one of the best teams in the country, and I'm considered one of the best players in the country. That's been one of my goals ever since I came to college."

Although he admits that he, like his teammates, was thrown for a loop when he first learned LaFrentz would miss up to six weeks, Pierce said he was comfortable with the added weight of being the Jayhawks' undisputed go-to guy.

"A lot of guys look to me for leadership," he says, "and I feel like I can provide some of that. When times get tough, I feel like I can be the guy who helps us out, whether it means getting the big rebound or taking a big shot.

"Now, we have other good players, and they're stepping up—Billy Thomas, Ryan Robertson, Lester Earl, and even [Eric] Chenowith is coming along."

Cautiously, he says LaFrentz's injury could be a blessing for Kansas, which last reached the Final Four in 1993.

"Now, understand, I didn't like it that he was out," Pierce says. "But the other guys are stepping up. So, with him back, they'll be ready for big-time action."

With LaFrentz's return coming in the middle of the conference season, [he] should [have] plenty of time to fine-tune his game before March Madness begins. But Pierce alone has proven to be a handful for any opponent

And as he has become more comfortable in the spotlight, Pierce increasingly has allowed the public to glimpse a playful personality his teammates maintain has been there all along.

Mat Edelson, *Sport Magazine*

DELAY OF GAME

Raef LaFrentz shocked most in college basketball when, after being selected as a first-team All-American in 1997, he decided to stay in school and play his senior year. He had his reasons, as Mat Edelson learned for this Sport Magazine *article from April 1998. Besides, it wasn't a completely bad move, as LaFrentz became KU's fifth two-time All-American, joining Charlie Black, Clyde Lovellette, Wilt Chamberlain, and Danny Manning.*

When you tower 6'11" over terra firma the way Kansas University's Raef LaFrentz does, owning an unusual perspective may just come with the stratospheric territory. That said, the man-child touted as a potential top-three NBA draft pick for the second year running really does have a refreshing take on Life, The Universe, and Everything. Mustering the guts to tell his home state, and later the NBA, that he was looking out for number one is merely the most public tip of Mount LaFrentz, who at age 21 is mature beyond his years yet still very much a little boy.

That's not hyperbole. Consider the reaction LaFrentz has to the hoopla that's followed him since he was a high school junior in Iowa. "So what, I play basketball," he says, leaning his long frame across several rows of bleachers in an empty Allen Fieldhouse. "That's not really that big a deal, contrary to what a lot of people think. It's my gift. I'm just fortunate that my gift is basketball rather than tiddlywinks. I could be the best tiddlywinks player in the world and I wouldn't get this much attention."

As for every hoop kid's nirvana, turning pro, here's why he sacrificed bucks for books: "I live a sheltered life right now," says LaFrentz, whose retired parents reside in Lawrence, Kansas, during the school year to lend support and a touch of home. "I wanted to continue to live a sheltered life for one more year rather than get out in the real world and have to make a living. Whether or not the NBA is the real world, I wanted to enjoy one more year being carefree and having fun."

If LaFrentz has his head screwed on straight, maybe it's because nature and nurture give him little choice. His take on the world was formed 450 miles away from Lawrence, in a remote northeastern Iowa hamlet. Monona, Iowa (pop. 1,500), is hard-core farm country that lends itself to proper perspective; it's hard for a boy—even a tall, talented one—to feel as if he stands out in rolling country so vast that cows look like raisins as they dot the distant horizon.

Most Mononans work the land, a humbling lifestyle that leads them not to get too excited about anything, even the town's greatest sports legend. Pride, sí. Bragging, no. Although school was closed and the entire town took off to attend Raef's high school tournaments, there's no LaFrentz Street in Monona, they haven't renamed MFL MarMac High School after him, nor have they even retired LaFrentz's jersey. A snub? Hardly. Just the Mononan way. As proof, school superintendent Dr. Lee Wise points to several small, unobtrusive blue banners around the gym chronicling MarMac teams. This is the first year the banners were allowed up. "Some of the old-timers didn't want it," says Wise. "They think it's a little gaudy."

Raef understands Monona's self-effacing mentality: it was drilled into him as a kid. So was the ability to think for himself.

"We're GDIs," says LaFrentz's mom, Ellen.

GDIs?

"God-Damned Independents!" roars Ron LaFrentz from across the Lawrence house the couple rents from former Jayhawk Rex Walters. At 6'5", Ron was quite the hoopster in his day, earning a scholarship to the University of Northern Iowa. Teaching and coaching at MarMac followed, and he soon found himself with a budding phenom in the family—no, not Raef, but rather older sister Ann. Raef calls 6'5" Ann a phenomenal shooter. "From 18 feet on in, there was a period where she wouldn't miss," he says. Especially during one memorable high school contest when she hit 25 for 25 from the field and 10 for 10 from the line.

Ann did more than play little brother one-on-one. Seven years older than Raef, her presence allowed him to sit behind the girls' bench during games and absorb Dad's coaching wisdom. By osmosis Raef was indoctrinated into sacrificing self for team. "Don't get a big head...we can't afford new hats!" was a typical Coach Ron response to ego-oriented court behavior.

The lessons took hold early. Joe Dotzler coached LaFrentz in junior high and in junior-varsity ball, but he first hooked up with Raef during fifth-grade peewee games. LaFrentz was already a standout but far from a ball hog. "He played with everybody," recalls Dotzler. "We had this one kid who loved the game but was just terrible. [Raef] would pass him the ball, it didn't matter to him. This kid loved to cast from 30 feet out. Raef would never say anything to him, just 'nice try.' Even at that age, I always thought he was something special."

It soon became apparent to everyone just how special LaFrentz was—everyone, that is, except Ron. As an assistant coach throughout Raef's high school career, Dad knew Raef was good. Still, he needed an old friend to put his son's ability into perspective. Northern Iowa coach Eldon Miller watched LaFrentz in a camp following Raef's sophomore season. LaFrentz was only 6'4" at the time, but swimming and steady growth had given his body a fluidity he'd never lose. Ron asked Miller for a realistic evaluation of Raef's college potential.

"Are you kidding?" wondered Miller.

"Well...where could he play? What's realistic?" asked Ron, straight-faced.

Miller shook his head in amazement. "You really don't know, do you?" said the UNI coach. "He can play anywhere he wants."

By his junior year, 50 recruiting letters a day were pouring into the LaFrentz household. "Everybody loves attention," says Raef of the recruiters. "But you quickly learn there's a fine line between attention and invasion. After a while, it got old, and then it got to be just a pain in the butt."

Kansas Coach Roy Williams was one of the many paying attention. Sure, LaFrentz's physical abilities and numerous on-court honors had Williams drooling, but there was something more. A kid without attitude, patient to a fault, with a genuine, infectious smile. Says Williams: "I watched every move he made, every person's reaction to him, and what I saw was, here's a kid who, wherever he goes to school, this entire town will favor that school. Everybody thinks this kid is theirs. That's a very positive statement about a kid."

Williams maniacally recruited LaFrentz, which included three consecutive red-eye flights between Kansas and Phoenix to watch Raef in a tournament. That devotion, along with Williams's Carolina-bred, aw-shucks charm and a top-flight program, slowly won over Raef and family. Each Sunday at 9:00 PM, coach and player talked by phone. Sometimes they chatted about KU's century-old basketball heritage. Often they talked about life. During one call, Williams admitted he'd wanted to coach since the summer after ninth grade.

"What do you want to be doing 20 years from now?" Williams asked the Midwest's top recruit.

"Chiropractor," answered Raef.

Eventually the two found themselves sitting in Williams's office during a campus visit. LaFrentz's moment of truth was at hand. Williams had scheduled a visit to see another recruit, a fallback if LaFrentz nixed Kansas. "I said, 'Raef, I really don't want to go visit him; I'd rather spend all my time on you,'" says Williams. "He said: 'Coach, just cancel that visit.'"

"The bottom line was, I couldn't say no to Coach Williams," says LaFrentz. "The kind of relationship we have is something that I thought was special, even in high school."

LaFrentz's decision reverberated far beyond Monona. It's worth noting that to get from Monona to Lawrence, one passes the birthplace of both John Wayne and Jesse James. The LaFrentzes should have considered that an omen. For if Kansans saw LaFrentz as The Duke, coming to save Jayhawks basketball, fanatic Iowans viewed him as the Hawkeye State's most wanted *hombre*.

Twenty-one hundred mostly outraged Iowans called the *Des Moines Register* the day LaFrentz chose Kansas. Threatening letters soon appeared at the family's Monona home. Iowa football coach Hayden Fry wondered publicly how any kid could desert his home state. (Obviously Fry hadn't checked his own recruiting roster.) Fry's remarks earned him a 40-minute phone call and tongue-lashing from Ron LaFrentz. "I'm prouder of that call than anything I've done in my life," says Ron.

During Raef's first KU road trip to Iowa State, he was raucously booed—vicious signs were even hung in the team's hotel—and scored but five rattled points for the night. LaFrentz and dozens of Mononans who trekked to Ames were stunned.

"There were a lot of people who were ticked off at me, thought I was a traitor, thought I had betrayed the state of Iowa and wanted to make life as difficult as possible on me," says LaFrentz. "I remember asking Dad: 'Why are these people doing this? What do they get out of this, what's the big deal?'"

Ron anticipated that the college game would rough up Raef. "We've raised a good boy, now I want you to make a man out of him," was Ron's message to Coach Williams, who promised he would. "I told Raef, 'He [Williams] didn't get where he was by being a goody-two-shoes. He's gonna rip you a new [orifice] in practice.' Raef said, 'Oh, noooo, not Coachie.' You ask him now about that."

Three years later, the work of Williams and his assistants is visible every time LaFrentz takes the court, most notably in his bulk, balance, and leadership. Though far from a Shaquille O'Neal, LaFrentz no longer resembles a Ping-Pong ball caught in a Kansas twister each time he defends the lane. Balance-beam exercises have helped. So has adding 20 pounds of much-needed muscle to his 235-pound frame. "He has a much greater understanding now of how important [weights are]," says Williams. "It's not that he was lazy by any means, but he just didn't understand the value of that as much as he does now. He didn't push himself three years ago as much as he does now in the off-season."

The numbers speak for themselves. Until recently breaking his non-shooting hand, LaFrentz never missed a college start. Every year, his rebounds, scoring average, field-goal percentage, and blocks increased, a pace he maintained this year before his injury. By the end of his junior campaign, LaFrentz was averaging 18.5 points and 9.3 rebounds for a Jayhawks team expected to capture the national title. When Kansas lost an 85–82 heartbreaker to Arizona in the not-so-Sweet 16 round of the NCAA Tournament, many Kansans thought LaFrentz and sophomore teammate Paul Pierce would turn pro.

"He came home before the decision was made," says Monona neighbor Bonnie Hains, once Raef's babysitter. "I said, 'You got a big decision coming up,' and he said: 'Yes, I do. I just wanted to come home and be on solid ground.'"

To LaFrentz, the dollars seemed almost unreal. Depending on where he was drafted, a $6- to $8-million rookie contract appeared assured.

"Do you know how much a million is?" asked his mother one day, seeking to enlighten her son.

"No," said Raef hesitantly, sensing a lesson.

"If Christ spent $1.30 a day, every day of his life, through the year 2000, he wouldn't have spent a million," concluded Ellen.

LaFrentz put that lecture in the bank, talked with Dad and Coach Williams...then ultimately passed on the pros. "I figured that once you get to that stage, it's a job, and the money will be there next year, and I have one more year of enjoyment as far as just being a college student. That's not so bad, taking a final," says Raef.

He's not the only one who gave up millions for now. So did Roy Williams, sought after as an NBA coach. "I had one team say several million, another team say 40 million...and I'm telling you, as soon as [LaFrentz and Pierce] gave me the word, I said no and never thought about it again," says Williams, adding: "There's no way I could have ever, ever gone to the NBA while Raef LaFrentz was here...because that youngster had belief in Roy Williams four years ago against a lot of pressure. And there is no way, no way."

With a $2.7 million insurance policy (for which his family pays a $22,600 premium), LaFrentz should eventually cash in one way or another on his pro dream. NBA experts say his soft turnaround jumper and rebounding skills could net a 10- to 12-year career. But that can wait. "I wanted to complete my college, and I wanted to get a degree," says LaFrentz.

He may get more. A national championship. A retired jersey, finally. And maybe, if his hand heals quickly, the honor of being the top pick in the NBA draft. But should none of those things come to pass, don't mourn a moment for Raef LaFrentz. He's allowed himself something that most of us in our zeal shed too quickly. One more year of childhood, one more season to be adored, one more chance to run through the tunnel at musky Allen Fieldhouse and inhale the essence of college basketball.

"There's definitely one same smell every time I walk into Allen Fieldhouse on a game night," says LaFrentz, staring across the same court where Manning, Chamberlain, and even a young Dean Smith once thrilled the faithful. "It's a mixture of popcorn, perfume, cologne, and a basketball which has a certain salty smell about it. It's a whole mixture, a unique smell, and I think if you talk to anyone on the team, you can smell it on game night. That's the smell that sticks in my mind."

For LaFrentz, it's a scent that's literally priceless.

Ron Kroichick, *San Francisco Chronicle*

ZERO HOUR FOR GOODEN

Drew Gooden, a 2002 All-American, came to Kansas from the San Francisco area. Over time he became known as one of the greatest rebounders in school history. His 423 rebounds during 2002 place him second behind only Wilt Chamberlain, who hauled in 510 in 1957. During 2002, Gooden also accumulated 25 double-doubles (double-digit points and rebounds in this case), including a streak in which he accomplished the feat in seven straight games. This article by the Chronicle's *Ron Kroichick appeared toward the end of the season, on March 12. It was Gooden's final season at Kentucky.*

Calvin Andrews took many phone calls from Lawrence, Kansas, that first season, calls resonating with the sound of an angry young man. Drew Gooden was playing barely 20 minutes a game despite leading Kansas in rebounding, despite averaging more than 10 points, despite his obvious talent.

The conversations had a distinct pattern: Gooden vented and Andrews, his AAU coach and mentor, listened. After hearing the threats of transferring to a Pac-10 school or even a junior college, Andrews would say, "Drew, you're not going anywhere. When you leave Kansas, you're going to the NBA."

Two years later, as Gooden leads the Jayhawks into the NCAA Tournament, it can be said: Andrews was right. Gooden, the once-slender, once-soft kid from El Cerrito High School, embraces Kansas as his college home and launching pad to untold riches.

Gooden and the Jayhawks are the number one seed in the Midwest Regional, with a first-round game Thursday against Holy Cross. The main reason Kansas envisions a trip to the Final Four is No. 0 himself, a player not especially slender or soft anymore.

Gooden is all the rage these days—first-team All-American, national Player of the Year candidate, on the cover of *The Sporting News*. Only three years removed from playing in Bay Area high school gyms, Gooden floats in an altogether different realm. "I kind of always wanted to be in the limelight," he said last week.

Still, the path from his hometown of Richmond to national acclaim was hardly a straight line. Before he played the piano with Tom Arnold on *Fox Sports Net*, before Dick Vitale showered him with breathless praise, there were moments when Gooden wondered if he had made a mistake in choosing Kansas.

He chafed at his reserve role as a freshman, bristled at all the criticism from Jayhawks coach Roy Williams. It was nothing personal, because Williams often lit into his entire team during that 1999–2000 season.

Even so, Gooden was not prepared for the structure and discipline at Kansas. He was not mature enough to see how his basketball knowledge was growing. In retrospect, he never really came close to leaving, even if Williams once offered to pay for a bus ticket home.

"Drew was just frustrated and angry," Andrews said. "Roy was trying to break him in, and Drew wasn't trying to be broken in."

They eventually found common ground after Gooden tried a novel approach: he started listening to Williams. Gooden still drifts into his bad habits every now and then—Williams chastised him Sunday for his, well, *curious* shot selection.

At the same time, Gooden has bought into the Kansas system and Williams has pulled back. Hence, this Jayhawks team runs with controlled abandon, if that's possible, leading the nation in scoring (92 points per game) after ranking among the leaders in field-goal percentage (now 51.1) all season.

The explanation rests partly with the departure of lumbering 7'1" center Eric Chenowith, who prevented Kansas from becoming a fast-break team in Gooden's first two seasons. The explanation also rests partly with the play of two other juniors, guard Kirk Hinrich and forward Nick Collison.

And do not dismiss this: Gooden would not be leading the way, averaging more than 20 points and 11 rebounds per game, unless he learned from his freshman frustration.

"I found out you have to pay your dues first," he said. "You can't come in and play right away and take all the shots, especially at a place like Kansas. I understand now that I had to take it a step at a time before Coach Williams gave me that freedom."

One example of Gooden's growth occurred February 27, Senior Night against Kansas State. Gooden's likely departure for the NBA meant this might have been his final game at historic Allen Fieldhouse. He wanted to make it special.

Still, when Gooden toyed with taking an outside shot on one possession, he instead passed the ball, established position on the low post, got the ball back, and scored. Williams said Gooden would not have done that as a freshman, when he tended to shoot first and think later.

These three years at Kansas have clearly turned him into a more well-rounded player, even if he might have put up bigger numbers at another school.

"In some ways, Kansas has accelerated his growth, and in some ways it's stunted his growth," Andrews said, "but it will help him in the long run, no question."

It also will help in the long run if Gooden maintains some of his father's toughness. Andrew Gooden Sr. played high school basketball in San Francisco, then later in college at Central Washington and professionally in Finland.

Gooden Sr. was a rugged 6'3" player known for his rebounding and his ferocity. Drew's mother, Ulla Lear—she and Gooden Sr. divorced when Drew was a child—recalls her former husband as a vocal player who occasionally got into confrontations as the only American on his Finnish team.

There was little evidence of this combativeness in Drew Gooden's game at El Cerrito. He dominated with his height, grace, and agility, not by outmuscling opponents near the basket.

Now, at Kansas, Gooden is still long and agile, still quicker than most 6'10" players. He also rebounds with vigor, as though his father had given him a transfusion.

"I guess you could say I added my dad's personality to my game," Gooden said, "but I'm not 6'3". That's good if you can be 6'10" and still be scrappy."

Or, as Andrews said, "More of his dad is coming out in him every day. His dad is a very tough, aggressive man."

Gooden Sr. is also brutally honest. He charged onto the court during one of Drew's high school games, angry with the referees for letting opposing players hammer his son. This year, at the Maui Invitational, Gooden Sr. made an impromptu dash around the gym during a timeout to energize Kansas fans and, he later acknowledged, to bring attention to himself.

So it follows that Gooden Sr., in speaking proudly of his son's bright future, reflected on his own lack of education and lifetime of modest jobs and said, "I didn't want him to be another me." And it follows that when considering Drew's NBA prospects, Gooden Sr. holds nothing back.

"By 2006, he'll be a household name," Gooden Sr. said. "He'll be one of the best players in the NBA."

It is certainly realistic to picture Drew Gooden as another quick, long-armed forward who can play both on the low post and the perimeter. That's almost the prototype in the NBA these days, from

Kevin Garnett and Rasheed Wallace to Dirk Nowitzki and Shareef Abdur-Rahim.

Gooden insists he will decide whether to turn pro after the season, but it's difficult to envision him returning to Kansas, given widespread projections that he would be a top five pick in the NBA draft.

One scout says Gooden could go as high as third, though the scout wondered if he has the "edge" to play power forward in the NBA. A mock draft on www.nbadraft.net taps Gooden as the fifth overall choice.

"If someone wants to give me millions of dollars, I'm gone," Gooden said.

It all seems a long way from 1998, when Gooden burst onto the national recruiting scene at a summer camp in New Jersey. Last summer, Gooden went to Michael Jordan's camp in Santa Barbara and played ball with the Man himself. Gooden thought Jordan shot too much; Jordan thought the same of Gooden.

Do not expect him to stop shooting anytime soon, but Gooden is no longer the stubborn, restless freshman pouting about playing time. Far from it.

Wright Thompson, *The Kansas City Star*

END GAME

For four years, Kirk Hinrich carried on the tradition of excellent guards for the Jayhawks. In 2003, along with fellow Iowan Nick Collison, Hinrich helped the Jayhawks reach the national championship game against Syracuse. Wright Thompson's look at Hinrich ran on the day of the Syracuse game. Just a few months removed from the pageantry of Kansas basketball, Hinrich quickly became a fan favorite with the NBA's Chicago Bulls.

Their phone rang, after the game and the shower and the team meal. It was Kirk Hinrich, calling his parents' hotel room, and he wanted to come down to talk.

He had just led Kansas to a romping win over Marquette, and now he had one game left in a Jayhawks uniform. So much had changed for the player since his freshman year.

"This is the last shot for me," he said. "I've never been the oldest kid on the team."

In his fantastic four-year career, he had done everything coach Roy Williams asked of him. He switched positions to help the team. He spent hours in the gym, alone, working on his shot. He became a more vocal leader as a senior because the team needed leaders.

Now, Williams needs one more thing. The Syracuse Orangemen stifle opponents with their zone; because the inside is clogged, a good way to win is to shoot over it. Some teams trot out two or three gunners. In crunch time, Kansas has Hinrich.

In the championship game, with a chance to finally win the big one, Roy Williams needs his star guard to be on.

With a break in the schedule, Hinrich—who said he feels "overwhelmed" at this opportunity—sat down for a while with his parents. Mostly chitchat, with ESPN playing in the background. His dad did have some advice—the same thing he'd told Kirk before his last high school game, a state-title matchup that the father-coach and son-player had won.

"Enjoy it" was the message.

"I think," Jim Hinrich said, "you've got to look at it like a reward for all the time and effort you've put in."

Hard Worker

Hinrich's first word, his dad has said, was *ball*. Always, it seems, he has chased basketball dreams, initially with his father as coach, then with Williams. He always has done what was needed.

"He'll do anything for this team to win," said close friend and former teammate Brett Ballard.

This road to the championship game really started when, unlike teammate Drew Gooden, Hinrich decided to return for his senior year—skipping the NBA for one more shot at cutting down the nets. People around KU hoops said he has been smiling more lately, clearly enjoying this senior year and all it means.

"I think Kirk has tried to soak it up a little more," Ballard said. "I think he realized from talking to Drew that college is really special. Especially at KU."

He had always worked hard to be a better shooter, seemingly preparing for the day when he would be called upon to shoot his team to a national championship. Leading up to this season, that work intensified.

During that summer, freshman reserve Christian Moody came to the gym one night on an errand. It was around 11:00 PM. The gym was quiet, save for a few noises. A passing machine popped out balls, while a team manager helped out.

"Kirk was in there, in the dark," Moody said. "The field house lights were off. You hear passes going, and then you can hear the swishing. That's Kirk Hinrich. You almost wanted to stand there and watch."

Even though he'd been projected as a first-round draft pick, Hinrich wasn't satisfied. The coming year was so important to him. Moody realized at that moment exactly what a senior season meant.

"I knew," he said.

Hinrich didn't always go to work alone. Before the season, he called Ballard.

"Wanna go shoot?" Hinrich asked.

They got to the gym and started messing around. Soon, a game of one-on-one, first man to seven, was under way. Ballard shot lights out and won. Oops. He had sparked something in Hinrich, who won the next two games 7–0, 7–0.

"Which is pretty humbling," Ballard said, laughing.

Speaking Out

Despite the hard work, the season didn't start off the way he had hoped. The team, ranked number two in the preseason, played poorly. Hinrich, whose back was bothering him, couldn't understand what was going wrong. He felt frustrated. He felt bad. He took an injection before the Florida game, wanting to be on the court. The team still lost.

After talking with the coaches, he sat out the Central Missouri State game, hoping to heal. Next up was Oregon, and despite [Hinrich's] playing, the Jayhawks lost again, pushing their record to 3–3. Four days later, before the Tulsa game, a newspaper headline read: "Jayhawks Exposed?" The questions were everywhere.

His senior year was falling apart, and he needed to turn it up a notch.

"I think that's what happened this year at times," Ballard said. "He knows when he needs to turn it on."

The team always needed Kirk the shooter. Now, it needed Kirk to be a more vocal leader as well.

The leader part came naturally. The vocal part was another matter entirely.

At Kansas, Hinrich initially came off as aloof until teammates and friends realized he was focused only on basketball. Before Senior Day this year, his mother found Ballard. She knew how much her son disliked speaking in front of people, and she was concerned.

"I wish all he had to do was go out and shoot free throws in front of everybody," she said, "but I don't know how he's going to do with this speech."

Even the promise of the title game—the chance at a championship—is hard for Hinrich to articulate.

"To explain what it would mean in words, to be able to accomplish this, I don't think I could do that," he said. "You know, it's something we've been working on for four years now."

Helping Out

With the season still young, Hinrich did one of the many behind-the-scenes things that make his teammates love him and want to play that much harder. Freshman forward Moulaye Niang was having a hard time learning the plays. He was getting frustrated, his confidence flagging.

Hinrich found him.

"Come to my room tonight," he told him.

Niang sat down with Hinrich—being the typical coach's son—while Hinrich pulled out a notebook. He drew a basketball court, filling in the positions. He showed Niang how the Jayhawks' system worked.

"That guy," Niang says, "is a great man."

And Hinrich wasn't afraid to help his teammates in other situations, either. Halfway through the season, after the team had rebounded from its poor start and climbed higher and higher in the polls, it hit a snag.

First, an embarrassing loss to Colorado. Then, at home on national television, the Jayhawks collapsed in the second half and lost to Arizona. The year, saved once already, was dying again.

Kansas's next game was against Texas—the third-ranked team in the country. Another loss was unthinkable. With the first half whittling away, a Longhorn jacked up a wild, long-range three-pointer.

It looked as if Kansas would go into the locker room down only three, except Jayhawks forward Bryant Nash didn't block out. Texas's Jason Klotz slammed home the rebound: Texas 48, KU 43.

Hinrich was absolutely furious. One of the maybe five times he did it all season, he ripped into his teammates in the locker room. He got in people's faces.

He told them, "We need to block out!" and "We're playing scared!"

"When he's outspoken, everybody listens," freshman guard Steve Vinson said. "When he gets on somebody, it's pretty rare. When he does something like that, you're like, 'Wow.'"

Kansas came back and prevailed 90–87. The Jayhawks would go on to win 11 of their next 12 games. The season was back on track as Kansas and Hinrich aimed their sights on March.

Dream in Sight

In the NCAA's Sweet 16, the season began to come full circle. Although Hinrich played poorly—scoring only two points—he stayed behind his teammates in the huddles and on the court.

Having beaten Duke, it was time for a rematch with Arizona. Kansas controlled the game, behind Hinrich's 28 points, and beat the Wildcats. With about six minutes left, Moody remembers Hinrich nailing a big three-pointer. He can still see Hinrich throwing his arm in the air and pumping his fist. The Jayhawks were going back to the Final Four.

Staying for his senior season now made total sense.

"The moment I realized this is why I came back is when we beat Arizona," Hinrich said. "We'd been working for it all year. We believed in ourselves when not many people believed in us."

On the plane after the game, Hinrich and teammate Nick Collison sat next to each other in the second row of first class. They joked and cut up all the way home.

Now, after blowing out Marquette 94–61, Hinrich is one game away from a national championship—and from the end of his career.

"It's kind of crazy knowing I'm going into my last game, and it's the national championship game," he says. "You dream about that kind of stuff."

It's also a dream come true to be this close to taking Williams to his first title as a head coach. The player and coach have formed a special bond over the last four years; on Sunday, they walked together deep inside the Superdome, sharing a laugh, and it seemed as right as rain.

His teammates sometimes call Hinrich "Jerod Junior" because he shares a relationship with Williams much like the lovey-dovey one the coach had with former star Jerod Haase.

"We always give Kirk a hard time," Ballard said. "Instead of Jerod, all the stories are gonna be about Kirk and how hard he worked."

All that hard work has brought him here, to the Louisiana Superdome, for a shot at Final Four redemption. He's ready for it, been preparing his entire life.

"Just cutting down the nets," he says. "That's all we want."

Jay Mariotti, *Chicago Sun-Times*

COLLISON A KANSAS CLASSIC

Nick Collison, a 2003 first-team All-American, had several memorable games at KU, including his 23-rebound game against Texas in 2003 at Allen Fieldhouse, but his 33-point, 19-rebound performance against Duke in the 2003 NCAA Tournament is one of the reasons the Jayhawks eventually advanced to the Final Four that year. Chicago Sun-Times *columnist Jay Mariotti is known by many for his work on ESPN's afternoon show,* Around the Horn.

Even if he liked the swarms of praise, which he could do without, Nick Collison would correct us on one description. Never, ever call him a warrior on a basketball court, much as the term fits down to the nubs of his buzz cut. Warriors fight real wars, and in his world, no one is a mightier hero than his late grandfather, Arden Collison, an Army air fighter whose plane was gunned down during World War II.

Somehow surviving the crash when his colleagues did not, the soldier easily could have fled the wreckage and said his prayers. Instead, he decided to be an incredible teammate, rushing through the flames and debris in a final attempt to save lives. He didn't succeed, and for his valor, he suffered near-fatal facial burns that haunted him until his death two years ago. But a proud grandson won't let his memory fade in this new era of wartime, scribbling the initials "AC" on his sneakers.

"The way he fought for his country puts basketball in its proper place," Collison said. "He gave up part of himself helping others."

It's easy to see in the NCAA Tournament why Collison, the Kansas power forward, has the lineage of a war hero. He is playing merely a game, yet the inner will of the 6'9", 255-pound rock has become a predominant story line of March. He was such an unstoppable force in the comeback victory over Duke, producing a career-high 33 points and 19 rebounds while playing the entire game, that championship-favorite Arizona is sure to collapse on him and leave outside shooters open in tonight's West Regional final. If Collison could be so brutish on a night when his partner in Rock Chalk Jayhawk karma, guard Kirk Hinrich, was shooting one of nine and nearly fouling out, what happens if all Kansas players are purring in tandem?

Another classic game in a month of masterpieces, that's what. I still like Arizona to win it all, but if anyone is capable of turning off the faucet for the annual Roy Williams Tear-a-Thon, it's Collison arriving in the Nick of time. "The game Nick had against us is one of the great performances you can have in a tournament," said Duke's Mike Krzyzewski, who earlier had called Collison the premier player in the college game. "Nick played like a champion."

As for Collison's lungs and legs, don't worry about fatigue. "I feel great, I could play again right now," he said. "That was the kind of game that can energize you instead of taking energy out of you. I'll be proud of this one for a long time."

The MVP of the tournament so far? Flip between Collison, Arizona's Luke Walton and Jason Gardner, and Syracuse's Carmelo Anthony. Collison is the rare shining example of why it can be beneficial to stay in college four years. He would have been taken in the first round last year, but now he'll be a lottery pick. He'd look good with the Bulls, joining Tyson Chandler and Eddy Curry on an impressive front line. "I always knew I'd be here my senior year," Collison said. "I'm having so much fun, and I wasn't ready to give that up. I'm confident I'm a better player one year later, and I'll be in a better position in the draft."

By staying, Collison was able to practice with the NBA-dominated U.S. team last August. With more hearts like his, perhaps Team USA wouldn't have embarrassed itself in the World Championships. "I think he should have had a spot on the team, if for no other reason than it would have been important to him," said Oklahoma coach and U.S. assistant Kelvin Sampson, oozing of sarcasm. "At first, the NBA players called him 'kid.' But Nick's a quiet warrior, and I think because of his attitude, his work ethic, and how he banged, he earned their respect. After two or three days, they were calling him Nick. Usually, a post player has some kind of hole in his game, but not Collison. There isn't anything you want a big man to do that he isn't good at."

Williams loves telling anecdotes about Collison's attitude. On the offhand occasions he makes a major mistake, this is how their conversation goes:

"What happened there, Nick?"

"I screwed up."

"What were you thinking?"

"I wasn't."

Reflected Williams, smiling: "It's refreshing. It's just Nick being Nick. He always takes responsibility and moves on."

It should surprise no one that Collison's father is a coach. In fact, he and Hinrich played for their fathers on small-town teams that won

Iowa state titles. When Nick was five, he already was taking mental notes as a water boy. "One of the best things I learned from my dad was how not to be," Collison said. "I'd hear him complaining at home about kids who were selfish, who didn't play hard, or who never played much defense. So I was like, man, I'm never going to be like that when I play."

If Tim Floyd had stayed at Iowa State instead of plunging into the Bulls' big sham, Collison might have signed to play in Ames with Hinrich, who had orally committed there. And despite the protests of Krzyzewski, there's clearly a sour taste about who rejected whom four years ago. Did Collison dis Coach K, or vice versa?

"Actually, when I called to tell [Krzyzewski] I was going to Kansas, he said, 'Okay, we got a commitment from Casey Sanders anyway,'" Collison said. "I didn't know if I still had an offer or not."

K's loss is Roy's gain. America is conditioned to believe Kansas is just teasing every March, with Williams's quest for a national title bordering on boring after 15 years. "My goal and my dream at Kansas is every year we have a chance," he said. "I'd like to be that last guy standing." But he was in a chipper mood Friday, locked in Collison's comfort zone.

"I told him, 'Man, did you play your buns off,'" Williams said of the Thursday gem. "He's had some big-time games for us, but never one as important. If you'd told me before the game that Kirk was going to go one-of-nine, I'd think we would have a bad night. But Nick wouldn't let us lose."

He might not have those powers against an Arizona team peaking accordingly. In January, the Wildcats strolled into Allen Fieldhouse and won 91–74. "They beat our tails the last time, so I'm going to be fired up," Williams said. "Fortunately for Kansas, I won't play."

No, as he has every game for four seasons, he'll dispatch Collison to the scene. This time, a special inspiration is driving the horse. When his grandfather died, Nick pulled out a paper he'd written about Arden and read it at the funeral. Then there's the shoe initials, which might have a deeper meaning.

AC. Isn't that short for A Championship?

Jason King, *The Kansas City Star*

WAYNE'S WHIRL

The 2004–05 season for the Jayhawks is remembered by many away from the state of Kansas as the year that Bucknell shocked KU in the first round of the NCAA Tournament. For Jayhawks fans, though, the season will be marked by a talented group of seniors—led by Wayne Simien from nearby Leavenworth, along with Aaron Miles, Keith Langford, and Michael Lee. Simien, the Jayhawks' 11ᵗʰ first-team All-American basketball player, knew that there was more to life than hoops, as The Kansas City Star*'s KU beat writer, Jason King, showed readers in this feature article that ran the day of the Bucknell game.*

The lights from the squad car flickered in the rearview mirror as Wayne Simien veered his 1978 Toyota Corolla coupe onto the shoulder of Leavenworth Road.

Simien, then a high school senior, hadn't been speeding, his tags weren't expired, and everyone knew he didn't drink. So why, Simien thought to himself, was this police officer pulling him over as he headed home from a night of movie-watching in his friend's living room?

"Wayne," chuckles his mother, Margaret, "was out about 10 minutes past his curfew that night, and the guy just wanted to make sure he was on his way back to the house. Everyone in Leavenworth knew what time Wayne was supposed to be home."

She pauses.

"It's been that way his whole life. People around here have always looked out for Wayne."

Four years later, Simien will begin the final phase of his Kansas basketball career when the Jayhawks open NCAA Tournament play against Bucknell tonight in Oklahoma City.

Exhilarating as the next few weeks could be for KU fans, there are sure to be some sentimental moments, too.

Sure, the Jayhawks are losing their all-time assists leader in Aaron Miles and a top scorer in Keith Langford. With Simien, though, it's as if the entire state is parting ways with a favorite son.

"Wayne has become a real influence in Kansas and across the whole Midwest," said Lafayette Norwood, Simien's AAU coach. "In some ways everyone can relate to him because of where he's from. He's our own homegrown star."

Indeed, from Kansas City to Lawrence to Wichita to Topeka, we've all watched Simien grow up.

Could be that you live on Fourth Avenue in Leavenworth, where neighbors used to look out their window and see Simien riding his bicycle up and down the block until sunset. Maybe you gloat to your friends about the time you played against Simien in high school and somehow beat him for a rebound.

Or perhaps you were walking across KU's campus that day nearly two years ago when Simien climbed atop a flight of steps and announced to nearly 700 onlookers that he'd become a born-again Christian.

Everyone, it seems, has a story to tell about the 6'9" forward who's enjoying the best college career of any homegrown player in the state's history.

Whether his time as a Jayhawk ends tonight or in the national title game on April 4, Simien said it always will be rewarding to know that he helped bring recognition to the state where he's lived his whole life.

"I'm lucky that I got to stay so close to home," Simien said. "I love it here. Everything is so convenient and comfortable. I'll always be proud to say that I'm from Kansas."

For Wayne Simien, infatuation with Kansas basketball began on a summer afternoon back in 1996, when former Jayhawks coach Roy Williams pulled his Cadillac into the parking lot of a Lawrence junior high school.

Then a seventh-grader, Simien was inside the gymnasium shooting hoops with the other kids at Williams's basketball camp. But that didn't stop Williams from approaching Simien's parents, who were waiting in a van outside.

"We were starstruck," Simien's father, Wayne Sr., said.

Margaret Simien: "He just stuck his hand through the window and introduced himself. We talked a while, and he told us he was going to be following our son. If you'd have asked us, it was pretty much a done deal right then and there."

The whole episode came as a surprise to Simien, who used to sit at Kansas games and lament his chances of ever playing for the Jayhawks. Simien said he would buy game programs and look at the hometowns of the players on the roster.

"Barely any of them were from Kansas," Simien said. "And the ones that were never really got to play that much. I kept thinking, 'Man, I'll never be able to get out there on that court.'"

Things began to change, though, shortly after Simien joined Norwood's AAU team, the 76ers, as a sixth-grader. A former KU assistant,

Norwood was nothing short of a legend in summer basketball circles, having coached players such as Antoine Carr, Derek Hood, and JaRon and Kareem Rush.

Norwood said Simien was an average player during his first few years with the team. But even then, he could see the intangibles that would one day make Simien great.

"He wasn't the most agile youngster, but he was a nice kid that came from some very concerned and interested parents," Norwood said. "Wayne had the maturity about him. He knew it wasn't just about dunking. He saw the overall game. He knew he had to develop the all-round skills that were necessary to go on to that next level."

Eventually Simien became the focal point of a squad that included future college players such as Jamar Howard (Wichita State), Jeff Hawkins (Kansas), and Nick Sanders (Furman). The 76ers won the AAU national title after Simien's sophomore year.

"After that," Simien said, "the inferiority complex everyone had about being from Kansas took a backseat."

As a junior he led Leavenworth High School to the Kansas 6A state title. Simien committed to Kansas before his senior season began. Once rated the 78th-best player in his senior class, Simien catapulted to number 20 after excelling at the prestigious Nike Camp against Tyson Chandler and Eddy Curry, two players who went straight from high school to the NBA.

"Wayne knew that he was as good as those guys," said Simien's father. "They just had not discovered him yet. It was hard for him to get noticed being from the Midwest."

Even with time missed for various injuries, Simien's KU career will be remembered as one of the most successful in recent memory.

This season's Big 12 Player of the Year, Simien probably will become only the second consensus All-American from the Kansas City area in the program's storied history. Charlie Black, who played at Southwest High School, accomplished the feat in 1943.

Although names such as Antoine Carr (Wichita), Lucius Allen (Kansas City), and Darnell Valentine (Wichita) come up in discussions, KU coach Bill Self said no player from the Sunflower State has excelled quite like Simien.

"Wayne Simien is the best college player ever from this state, at least from my memory," Self said. "This isn't exactly a hotbed for players. Look at where we've had to go to get kids: Alaska, New York, Florida, Chicago, Seattle. It's always nice when there's one right there in your backyard."

Walk into Simien's off-campus apartment, and you're sure to find some of his most prized possessions: a cowboy hat, cowboy boots, and a fishing pole. Rather than a sleek sports car or an SUV, Simien drives a red GMC pickup truck.

"Yeah," Simien said, "I guess I'm a country bumpkin."

Simien always has taken a laid-back approach to life—which is why he so relishes the peaceful, sheltered towns in which he lives.

Margaret and Wayne Sr. said they can count on one hand the times they had to discipline their son during his early years. Heck, he never had time to get into much trouble. If he wasn't meeting his Leavenworth High School buddies at Applebee's or watching movies at a friend's house, Simien was either on the baseball field or the basketball court.

"He'd get in the van after a game and change uniforms as we drove to the next one," Margaret said. "Once Wayne chose to stick with basketball, we made a commitment to do everything we could to give him a chance to get to that next level. All of a sudden we were traveling all around the country. There hasn't been a time Wayne stepped on a basketball court when we weren't there to support him."

Still, Simien's most enjoyable moments have always involved the Leavenworth and Kansas City area. His apartment walls are covered with Chiefs and Royals paraphernalia. Some of his favorite moments in the summer are spent at Kauffman Stadium.

"Once I leave here, I don't watch basketball," Simien said. "I don't go home and watch four college games a night or the NBA. I like to go home and check out NFL and major league baseball. I just like having the chance to be a fan. I appreciate that now more than ever."

Simien said he now calls baseball stars such as Mike Sweeney, George Brett, and Joe Randa his close friends.

"I see George Brett all the time at the games," Simien said. "It's funny. I'm starstruck when I see him, and his sons act kind of starstruck when they see me. It's a weird feeling."

That's the thing about Simien: the bigger his name gets on a national stage, the more humble and appreciative of his roots he seems to become.

These days more than ever, Simien cherishes his visits back to Leavenworth. Simien attended the Pioneers' playoff game against Lawrence Free State a few weeks ago, and he always makes a point to see George Furch, his longtime barber, at Professional Hair Care.

It's a given, too, that Simien will stop by the Hallmark Cards plant, where his father is a manager. Machine operators, forklift drivers, janitors—all of them stop what they're doing to reminisce with "Little Wayne," the kid they've watched grow up.

"He's always been very low-key," said Wayne Sr., who played college ball at Avila. "Wayne doesn't like a lot of attention, but if it comes his way, he handles it the right way. There's no arrogance about him at all."

Self said Simien has exuded joy ever since he enhanced his relationship with God two summers ago.

"He's a very mature guy who almost seems too good to be true," Self said. "He doesn't feel he has to impress anybody. He is totally at peace with himself.

"My wife says, 'Gosh almighty, does he ever have a bad day? Is he ever not polite? Does he ever not open the door for somebody? Has he ever not said thank you? Ever been late? Ever miss a class?'"

Self stops and begins to laugh.

"The answer, of course, is yes. But we don't know about it."

Every now and then, a throng of reporters stands in the main tunnel leading toward the Allen Fieldhouse court, waiting to interview Simien.

Five minutes pass, then 10 and 15. Practice begins, and Simien is nowhere to be seen—until he sneaks through an entrance on the other side of the gym, joining his teammates without facing the media.

"I guess it just makes me a little uncomfortable sometimes, you know, being singled out like that," Simien said. "All that talk about the accolades and awards...I just want to play ball."

Modest as his intentions may be, Simien knows the demand for interviews and photo shoots are only going to increase. His scoring average has jumped nearly three points in the last six weeks. Simien will enter tonight's 8:50 PM game against Bucknell averaging 20.2 points and 11.1 rebounds, making him the only Big 12 player to average a double-double.

"He's getting more rebounds per minute, and he's becoming a better offensive rebounder," Self said. "He's becoming a better passer, and he's scoring away from the basket more and more. That turn-around jump shot he has from the baseline...it's a hard shot for even a tall guy to contest, because he jumps away from contact."

Simien said his spiritual walk has helped improve his play on the court.

"I'm just playing with so much more peace out there," Simien said. "My success isn't being defined by circumstances on the court: points, rebounds, wins, losses. The game has been a lot more fun since my transition.

"I'm not playing for myself. I'm not playing for the roar of the crowd. I'm playing for the glory of God. The great thing about that is that He's going to be pleased with you no matter what you do. As long as you go out and play as hard as you can, every game is a great game."

Professional scouts and analysts say Simien is a sure bet to be a first-round pick in this summer's NBA draft, and he may even go in the lottery. In the meantime, though, he said his thoughts are hardly on where he may be picked or how much money he could end up making.

Too much still lies ahead at Kansas.

Because second-leading scorer Keith Langford has been battling the stomach flu, Simien knows he'll be counted on more than ever to help the Jayhawks advance in the tournament.

"It could all be over with right now, and it would definitely be a success," Simien said. "It's been great, but if I didn't have any accolades or team accomplishments, the experience has still been awesome.

"Luckily, though, it's not over with. I don't plan on settling on what we've accomplished as a team or the things I've accomplished as an individual. I'm not going to stop here."

On May 23, the day after he's handed his college diploma, Simien will join his father on a fishing trip to southern Alberta.

"No cell phones, no interviews or schedules to worry about," Simien said. "Just straight-up outdoors."

More than anything, Simien's biggest vice is fishing. For years Wayne Sr. took his son along when he entered professional tournaments. Since he arrived at KU, Simien has been fishing more and more, thanks to numerous fans who have invited him to their private property.

"It will be good for him to get away from basketball and all the stress and pressures that go along with it," Wayne Sr. said. "He doesn't care for a lot of attention. When he can just get out there and relax, out in nature, he'll be able to release everything that's built up."

Eventually, though, Simien realizes he'll have to ponder his long-term future. Soon he'll be living in a new city—a big city—with traffic and noise and hustle and bustle. He'll have millions of dollars and people pulling at him from every direction.

"Wayne has always been here in the Midwest," Wayne Sr. said. "We've always been able to get our hands on him really quick. For him to be headed to some big city...it's scary. He's ready to take that next step. He's ready to be an adult on his own without Mom and Dad being right there."

Those close to Simien say the spiritual changes he has undergone will help him with the transition.

"Two years ago that's something I would've really worried about with Wayne," said Nick Sanders, Simien's close friend and former Leavenworth teammate. "But now the turn that's occurred in his life and with his faith, I know he'll surround himself with quality people."

Indeed, Simien said Morningstar Church, where he goes for fellowship and worship, has branches all over the United States. He even wants to help start another branch at the Country Club Plaza someday.

Just as Simien has support groups here, he's confident he'll find the same thing wherever he ends up. Not that he won't miss Leavenworth and Lawrence and Kansas City and everything else about the Sunflower State.

Simien picks up a plate of cookies given to him by the wife of KU assistant Joe Dooley. It's his 22nd birthday, probably the last he'll spend in these parts for a while.

"I've been here for 22 years now," Simien said. "I know this area like the back of my hand, whether I'm coming down I-70 and seeing The Hill as you come into Lawrence or driving into Kansas City and seeing downtown and Kemper Arena. It's going to be tough leaving here. I love it here.

"It's all I've ever known."

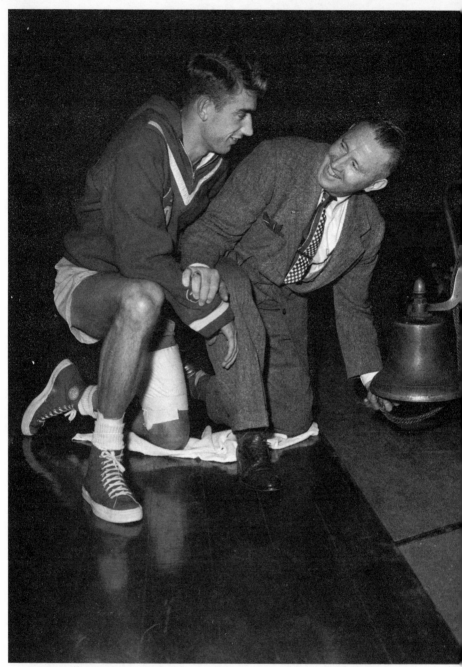

Legendary coach Phog Allen rings a fog bell with his team captain Jerry Waugh as the Jayhawks arrived in New York for a contest with St. John's on December 11, 1950. Photo courtesy of Bettmann/CORBIS.

Section III
THE COACHES

Bob Broeg, *The Saturday Evening Post*

THE BASKETBALL MAN

The stories about James Naismith's thoughts on basketball as a sport are legendary. He saw basketball as more of a physical activity than as a game that is coached. That might partially explain why he's the only losing coach in the program's history. Bob Broeg, who was the former sports editor of the St. Louis Post-Dispatch, *offers this wonderful look at when he met Naismith in 1937.*

A short, stocky old man with a bristling mustache and a thick, powerful neck that belied his age wandered into a gymnasium some years ago. He was asked by one young chap to referee an impromptu basketball game.

Another youth interrupted and said in a semi-whisper, "Oh, you're wasting your breath. That old guy can't know anything about basketball."

James Naismith, the man who invented the game, told me that one about himself. When I repeat it, people think I'm so old I must have been the official scorer when Naismith came up with the greatest invention since indoor plumbing.

Truth is, though basketball now ranks internationally behind only soccer as a team sport, the great American game—invented by a Canadian with a Scottish accent—really isn't *that* old, but neither was Doc Naismith when he devised it; nor was I when he talked to me about it two years before he died.

As a sophomore at the University of Missouri, I visited the University of Kansas at Lawrence on Thanksgiving 1937 for the annual football game between the oldest rivals west of the Mississippi. At my social fraternity's KU chapter house, I met with delight the professor emeritus. A widower, Dr. James Naismith was wooing the chapter housemother, who would become his wife a few months before his death two years later at 78.

With a twinkle in blue eyes framed by severe gold-rimmed glasses, Naismith told me about meeting the kid who hadn't thought "that old guy" knew enough about basketball to referee a game. Naismith told me he'd been the featured speaker that night on the young man's campus. The "old guy" noticed the younger man in the audience and gave the red-faced kid a good-natured ribbing.

I found the inventor grumpy about the only two changes made in the 13 rules he had set down for the game in 1891. Five years earlier, in 1932, the rules committee had instituted the rule giving the defensive team 10 seconds to move the ball beyond midcourt. Now, in 1937, they were eliminating the center jump after each score.

"They've spoiled it," Naismith said, a bit peevishly, yet with a pretty sound argument. Naismith recognized that the 1932 10-second rule had been installed primarily to keep a team from playing patty-cake with a ball in its half of the court. But elimination of the center jump, he felt, created a disadvantage to the team that had scored.

But, Doc, weren't they trying to speed up the game, increase the scoring, and make basketball more interesting?

"But have they?" Naismith asked rhetorically. "They've cut the court in half, requiring 10 men to play in it, but they still haven't eliminated the stall, which they tried to do. A player scored against now has five seconds to throw the ball in and 10 seconds more to take it over the center line. With the center jump after each basket, it took only an average of four seconds to take the ball to midcourt and toss it up.

"Spectators don't like the stall, I don't, and I believe most coaches don't. I saw one game where one side passed the ball 343 times, and a great referee, Ernie Quigley, stood there 12 minutes watching them. I still say that eliminating the center jump penalizes the team that has scored."

Naismith talked about time, i.e., the modern shot clock, and about bonus points for outside shooting, both of which came long after he was gone. "Scoring is important," he said, "but not all-consuming. I think speed is. Speed, passing, and the unexpected. To curb the stall, I'd put in a time limit on the team with the ball. To make the defense come out, I'd penalize the defense after, say, 30 seconds, or to draw the defense to the ball, I'd give the scoring team four points rather than two for a basket scored from 30 feet out."

Naismith's suggestion became pro basketball's 24-second clock nearly a quarter-century later, and more recently the 45-second shot requirement in college ball. Even more prescient was his proposal to double the point value for a shot from nearly 10 feet farther out than the current distance for three-point shots.

Born in Almonte, Ontario, in 1861, James Naismith was a son of Scottish immigrants. Orphaned at age nine, he was reared by an uncle and an older sister. Rugged both physically and in spirit, James was interested in hunting and the outdoors. He was a high school dropout. To envision his becoming an honorary doctor of divinity, a medical doctor, and an honorary master of physical education would have been difficult—as difficult as suggesting that a person who reveled in rugby, soccer, lacrosse, and wrestling would devise the scientific poetry of motion that is basketball.

The young Jim Naismith suddenly saw the spiritual light. He went back to school and graduated in theology from McGill University at age 26 in 1887. He didn't smoke or drink, and he rarely swore. In fact, he had a purity of heart that made him the counterpart of college football's Amos Alonzo Stagg.

The divinity graduate with muscles turned his interest to youth, recalled his daughter Mrs. Hellen Dodd when visiting her own family 20 years ago in St. Louis. (Mrs. Dodd, one of Doc's five children, was named Hellen "with two *l*'s," she quipped, so her father could say, "'Hellen blazes,' his only curse word.")

Naismith began teaching at the YMCA's training school in Springfield, Massachusetts. The head of the physical-training department, Dr. Luther H. Gulick, told Naismith he wanted a winter activity that would keep budding young physical culturists in shape for spring. Something that could be played on the gym floor, Jim.

Naismith studied and borrowed from various games. "Duck on a rock" suggested the use of a ball tossed in an arc rather than hurled. Lacrosse contributed the arrangement of players. Rugby furnished a hint of putting the ball in play, and soccer—well, association football, as they called soccer then, offered a ready-made ball.

A goal on the floor, as in hockey, wouldn't do because it would be too easy to defend, especially if Naismith were trying to accommodate Dr. Gulick's 18 students. So Jim got himself a peach basket and a ladder. He installed the peach basket at a height the Y's gymnasium floor would permit—nine feet from the floor. He began the game with nine players on a side.

The players wore woolen sweaters and turnverein trousers. A referee tossed up the ball, and—as prescribed by Naismith to keep the game from becoming indoor football—a player was required to dribble the ball and to take only a stride before passing the ball to a teammate.

Because the court was only 35 feet by 45 feet, Naismith reduced the number of players from nine to seven, and then to the current five. Where permitted, he elevated the basket to 10 feet, still the current height (even though Naismith's prized product at Kansas, the coaching legend Forrest C. "Phog" Allen, later urged an increase that today would negate dunking—12 feet!). I wish I'd asked Doc Naismith about that one in our meeting 51 years ago.

Even though rugby still bore the name of where the sport began at a British school [Rugby School] in 1823—a guy named Ellis picked up a soccer ball in frustration and ran with it—Naismith declined to have his new game named for him. So, heck, since they were using peach baskets, why not call it "basket" ball?

Peach baskets weren't always easy to find, and after a score, using a rod to poke the ball out—or, even worse, a stepladder—was troublesome too. So a carpenter's aid made the game more sophisticated and, at least temporarily, seemed to make rule number eight laughable. In part, the rule stated: if the ball rests on the edge of the basket and an opponent moves the basket, it shall count as a goal.

Even in our own era of height matched only by agility, or vice versa, it's still a two-point no-no to goaltend against a ball in downward flight in the basket's perimeter and, just as Doc wrote it in 1891, two points if a defensive hand disturbs the basket.

By 1893, at which time Yale had already become one of the first colleges to adopt the game, a carpenter devised a wire cylinder to replace the original peach basket. At first, chicken-wire netting under the cylinder kept the ball from swishing through the nets as it does now.

By '94, also, the first basketball had replaced the soccer ball's size and weight; a 30-inch circumference limited the size of the ball to 20 to 22 ounces. Over the years, smart alecks like me have called the game "round-ball" because in the early days of rubberized inflation the ball often became a tad lopsided. Yet it wasn't until 1938, the year after I met Naismith and shortly before his death, that the rules were amended to state that a spherical basketball could not vary more than a quarter of an inch in diameter.

To Oklahoma State's "Iron Duke," Henry Iba, like Phog Allen an early-day legend, "true bounce" has always been the gentle synonym for the game he loves dearly (in effect, if you will, a dig at what Iba calls "bad bounce," i.e., the crazy caprice of a football).

Over the years, added safeguards made Naismith's game as good as Doc wanted. To keep spectators in shoebox gyms from deflecting shots, backboards were devised—wood at first, then glass. Ultimately, played on stage auditorium floors, basketball required a net to keep the ball from bouncing away—which generated the term still seen in an occasional newspaper headline: "cagers."

Jim Naismith next left for the foothills of the Rockies. There, at the present-day University of Colorado, he studied to become an M.D. because, as his daughter Hellen Dodd explained, he felt he could better direct young men's physical activities if he knew as much about the body as...well, yes, a physician.

Over the years, as an intellectual roughneck, an academician with muscles, Naismith lived with a head-in-the-sky attitude toward such mundane things as money. For instance, he twice lost houses to a foreclosure gavel. Even though he might have earned much from the game he invented, the royalties he received belatedly from a basketball named for him didn't cover what he had spent.

Naismith was interested in body and soul; ergo, what better job than to serve as the director of chapel and physical education?

Naismith moved to the University of Kansas in 1898. He was 36 then, already burning the candle at both ends, in the nicest sense, Hellen recalled. Not only was he supporting a family, but he was studying and teaching as well as working.

One night he didn't come home. The family was alarmed, as were the faculty and the university kids. An alarm was sounded. Finally, searchers found him, asleep on a park bench. "Like Rip Van Winkle, utterly exhausted, he'd sat down and fallen fast asleep," his daughter remembered fondly.

Kind, soft-hearted, and considerate—that's the way they remembered him at Kansas, where he lived out his last 41 years. Loosely coaching KU's first eight basketball teams through 1908, he was barely a break-even coach, yet he helped establish a tradition. The defending NCAA champion Jayhawks have more basketball victories than all universities except Kentucky, North Carolina, and St. John's. KU became NCAA champions in the tournament's 50th year, 1988. Kentucky's longtime coach, Adolph Rupp, was a Kansas man, and North Carolina's famed current coach, Dean Smith, also played under Phog Allen.

Allen, an osteopath who played under Naismith, coached Kansas for 38 years, through 1956, and achieved a .729 record (590–219). The university's field house is named for him, but it also contains a handsome painted portrait of that stocky, thick-necked little man who began it all, James Naismith.

Allen maintained constant affection for Naismith. When basketball first became an Olympic sport in 1936—imagine how far, fast, and strongly it has come in the quadrennial games since then—Phog Allen practically horsewhipped the NCAA to send Naismith to Berlin for the ceremonies.

Doc came back as exhilarated as when he had been stationed on the Mexican border with the U.S. Army in 1916 or served as a [chaplain and YMCA representative] in Europe in World War I, as happy as when he worked on a road gang with one of his sons "just for the fun of it."

He'd seen basketball go from narrow, low-ceilinged gyms and parish basements to dance halls and haylofts, then ultimately to giant field houses and arenas. The year he died, 1939, the NCAA began its annual postseason tournament that now, through its Final Four, rivals the Super Bowl and the World Series.

Naismith said on his return from Berlin that basketball had "grown tremendously [overseas], and I think it will continue to grow, perhaps not in this country, but in foreign countries."

Jim Naismith was both right and wrong. The round ball, not the snowball, is the symbol of winter now, and really, winter hasn't been the same since 1891. But then, the master of the game always thought there was too much ado about his sport. Like the time early in the century when Baker University near Lawrence wrote him to inquire about hiring a young KU athlete as part-time basketball coach. Naismith called in young Phog Allen to announce the news.

"I've got a joke on you, you bloody beggar," Doc Naismith said with a laugh. "They want you to coach basketball down at Baker."

Phog bristled. "What's so funny about that?"

"Why, Forrest," explained the man who invented the game to one of the greatest who would ever coach it, "you don't 'coach' basketball. You just play it!"

Howard W. Turtle, *The Saturday Evening Post*

GIVE THE BALL TO JUNIOR!

Talk about being way ahead of one's time. Even though he was mocked for wanting to coach basketball—by James Naismith, no less—Dr. Forrest C. "Phog" Allen became the most successful coach in basketball and is still known as the father of basketball coaching. He was in the news often, trying to implement rule changes or speaking out against the NCAA. He also had the distinction of coaching his two sons at Kansas. This piece by Howard Turtle appeared in The Saturday Evening Post *on December 28, 1940, the season after the Jayhawks lost in the national championship game to Indiana.*

Southern California was ahead, 40–38. Two minutes were left to play in the semifinals of the national collegiate basketball tournament last spring, and a Kansas City crowd of 10,000 was yelling like mad. A midget University of Kansas basketball team was up against a California squad of sun-bronzed giants rated the greatest in the nation. The Jayhawkers looked puny in comparison. They were guarding furiously to keep California from running up a bigger lead, when out of the big blue bowl of the Municipal Auditorium came the derisive yell: "Give the ball to Junior!"

Everyone knew what it meant. "Junior" was Bobby Allen, center on the Kansas team and son of the Kansas coach, Dr. Forrest C. "Phog" Allen. Bobby, who is not "Junior" at all, was having a bad night hitting the basket. The long ones he tossed from out on the court would roll around the rim, then drop out. He was guarding for dear life, and the yell came again: "Give the ball to Junior!"

Before anyone could see very well what was happening, Junior had the ball. He was dribbling forward. A Trojan guard leaped at him. Bobby gave the ball a flip and it settled prettily through the hoop. The crowd screamed and howled. The score: Kansas 40, Southern California 40. Allen was to have a free throw. Just as he had shot, the guard had fouled him.

Bobby stepped to the line, a pale, almost frail figure against the giant opposition. There was no hoot now from the balcony. The ball rose toward the basket, and a yell went up that almost shook the building. The throw was good. All the Middle West rejoiced. Families sitting in their living rooms across Missouri, Oklahoma, Nebraska, and Kansas had forgotten their bridge games and were listening on their radios. The score was 41–40—50 seconds to play.

Southern Cal took the ball. Kansas set its defense. The bronze giants went sweeping down the floor, and zowie! They had a basket. Jane Allen, Phog's handsome daughter, fainted. The crowd crumpled. The game was virtually over, and Southern California led, 42–41.

Then Phog Allen, squirming and thrashing on the Kansas bench, experienced a brain wave. He receives them every once in a while, usually when he is asleep or when tremendously excited. They come without reason, without logic, but they come, and he follows them without cavil. This time the message was: "Engleman can score!"

"Engleman!" Phog yelled to a blond boy warming the Kansas bench. "Report!"

A Brain Wave's Aftermath

Howard Engleman, student president of the university school of business, ran out on the floor. Southern Cal was stalling again. Engleman streaked forward. [Jack] Lippert, of Southern Cal, a sure and steady player, pivoted easily out of his way. But Bobby Allen, playing a hunch of his own, was running out of position, too. As Lippert pivoted, Allen drove in from behind and stole the ball. The timer's finger was twitching on the trigger. Bobby was dribbling for his own basket. Lippert rushed him.

Engleman ran down the sideline. Bobby feinted as if to shoot, Lippert jumped, and Bobby push-passed to Engleman. Far to the side of the basket, Engleman blazed away. A high arching shot looped toward the ceiling. Sam Barry, Southern California coach, hid his face in his hands. The ball floated gently downward.

Swish!

Engleman had scored. The timer's gun went off before anything else could happen. Kansas had won by one point, 43 to 42. Phog's hunch had worked. Jane Allen revived, too late to see her dad's team win.

It was another miracle in Kansas basketball. Kansas fans should be getting used to them by this time. For 21 years, Phog Allen has been producing miracle teams at KU. Last year was just about the same as usual. At midseason, the Jayhawkers looked mediocre. At the end of the season they had tied for the Big 6 conference championship and held second place in the national standings. Defeat came in the finals of the national tournament, when a red-hot band of Indiana Hoosiers sped with twinkling feet into the basket and blazed from all angles to hit a phenomenal 36 percent of all their shots.

In the 21 years Phog Allen has coached at Kansas, his teams have won or tied for 16 championships. Of the lads who have played three years of varsity basketball for him, all but one own their own gold basketballs signifying a conference title.

Phog has been coaching collegiate basketball longer than any other man alive. Above his office desk hangs a portrait of the late Dr. James Naismith, inscribed in 1936: "With kindest regards to Dr. Forrest C. Allen, the father of basketball coaching, from the father of the game."

Phog has never grown old-fashioned. With each new trend he has changed his tactics, and in many instances has been ahead of the field. Today he is one of the cagiest of the world's coaches in the hell-for-leather scramble of the modern game.

This year Phog figures to have his troubles. Two of his crack juniors did not come back for their senior year. But Phog is bringing along his other veterans, including "Junior," confidently. The legions of the faithful expect to see him up there again before the season's over. He says his team is going to be quicker than ever on the break, risking a tight defense now and again to make that quick-passing, coordinated dash for the basket.

It is the trend in basketball—this pell-mell sprint for the goal, Phog says. When his team gets the ball, it will cut lickety-split for the basket. The idea is to make the scoring thrust before the opposition defense can form.

Phog will combine the fast break with his set scoring plays. A championship team, he says, must use both. When his own team outnumbers the opposition in the area of the basket, he will use the fast break. When the opposition is stronger in that region, his boys will attempt to lure them out of position by the set scoring play.

Phog is 55 years old now, and looks more like 40. Six feet tall, trim at the waist, he still can play about 10 minutes of the fastest basketball. He wears loud clothes. A gray or brown imported tweed is his chief joy. The bigger the spots in it, the better. He'll wear a canary-yellow tie without a qualm. His varsity basketball players, tricked out in the latest collegiate regalia, look drab beside him. He has lots of brown hair, close-clipped at the temples; a pink face; tiny lines at the eyes; and overall a look of awareness.

When visitors are in his office, he talks a blue streak, all the time voraciously engulfing horehound candy. He buys 60 pounds at a time. He presses it on visitors, piece after piece, explaining it is good for the larynx. Phog needs it because in practice he talks and yells himself hoarse.

He is known as "Phog" by thousands who never heard his real name. Many years ago, as a baseball umpire, he called out the strikes and balls in such a loud, sustained yell that the fans began calling him

"Foghorn Allen." A sportswriter shortened the nickname, and inexplicably spelled it "Phog." The name has stuck for all except Phog's four grandchildren. They call him "Phoggy."

Unlike many other coaches, Phog has no fears of black cats or the number 13, but he plays his hunches for all they're worth. The brain wave that told him Engleman could score against Southern Cal was an example. Also he follows with implicit faith the things he dreams at night. He admits he dreams most of his tricks between two and five o'clock in the morning. When the heaven-sent strategy has been revealed, Phog will spring out of bed, pad in pajamas across a cold floor to his dresser, and jot down on paper the fiendish plot by which his team will bedevil the daylights out of the opposition.

In 1920 he had his most outlandish dream. He was temporary coach of football at Kansas and had the lightest team in the school's history, 162 pounds. It was the night before the Iowa State game. Iowa State that year was solid brawn. Phog was sleeping at home, and an airplane went soaring across his mind. It was loaded with Kansas football players, but only six of them were regulars—the others were substitutes. The airplane sailed off to the left, turned east, and flew past a giant set of goal posts. Phog woke up and made his jottings.

Next day in the dressing room he told his squad of the dream. He called out the names of his starting lineup—the six regulars and five substitutes he had seen in the airplane. Then he gave his final instructions to his quarterback, Arthur (Dutch) Lonborg, now basketball coach at Northwestern University. If Dutch won the toss, Phog told him he was to receive the kickoff. On the first formation he was to call number 46—the signal for Harley Little, right half, to take the ball around left end. Phog said Little would carry the ball in the airplane route over the east goal line on the first play.

Dutch won the toss. Kenny Welch, 133-pound Kansas fullback, received the kickoff on the Kansas goal line and ran it back 15 yards. Lonborg called out Harley Little's signal. The ball was snapped. Little started around the end. Down went the Iowa State huskies in front of the bowling Kansas substitutes. Little streaked toward the sideline, cut back, and started toward the goal, 85 yards away. Ahead were two big Iowa State defensive backs. Sweeping down to attack came a couple of the Kansas substitutes. Down fell the Iowa State tacklers. Harley Little breezed across the goal line standing up. When the final gun went off, the only score of the game was the "dream" touchdown, and Kansas won 7–0.

The victory helped work up the enthusiasm by which Phog received the first contributions for a $660,000 stadium at KU. It is a horseshoe seating 38,000 persons, and it never has been filled. Some Kansans point with pride to the great gray structure, and others speak of it as "Phog's Folly."

The heart and soul of Phog Allen, however, is not in football; his life is basketball.

When he was growing up, he played with his five brothers in a livery barn in Independence, Missouri. They called themselves the Allen Brothers Basketball Team. They played all comers. Basketball was only 10 years old, and the rules provided that one member of the team should toss all the free throws. Phog performed that duty for the Allen boys, and was good at it. In coaching his champions of today, Phog requires every boy to throw 100 free throws at every practice.

"You win or lose games on your free-throw record," Phog says.

In 1905, when he was 19, Phog left the Allen team temporarily to join the Kansas City Athletic Club Blue Diamonds. He became star forward, free thrower, and manager. The Blue Diamonds won the world championship by beating the Buffalo, New York, Germans, 41 to 14. In 1907 Phog was captain of the basketball team at the University of Kansas, in Lawrence. In 1908 he became a collegiate coach, traveling daily from Lawrence, where he was a student in the law school, to Baldwin, Kansas, to coach the Baker University basketball team. When he told Doctor Naismith, then director of physical education at KU, that he intended to coach at Baker, the inventor of the game snorted, "Why, basketball can't be coached; you just play it."

Phog's team at Baker beat all opposition that year. The other teams didn't have coaches. Scheduling a game for Baker with the Allen Brothers, Phog played for the Allens and was beaten by his Baker boys by one point.

After being graduated from KU, Phog went to Warrensburg, Missouri, in 1912, as coach of the state teachers' team there. In seven years his team won seven championships. For three years he studied osteopathy and gained the skill by which he is now famous in the treatment of athletic injuries. He is licensed to practice in both Missouri and Kansas.

Phog has watched basketball come through all its changes. Finally, after years of dreams, hunches, experience, and plain horse sense, he came up with a system of his own. It is the present super-colossal, invincible "Stratified Transitional Man-for-Man Defense with the Zone Principle."

"It's impenetrable," Phog modestly admits. "The only time the other team can score is when your own team makes a mistake."

A Meaningful System

Every word has a meaning in his "Stratified Transitional Man-for-Man Defense with the Zone Principle." When the opposition starts down the court with the ball, the defense becomes "stratified." Two forwards form the first stratum up toward the center of the court, and the two guards and center stay back near the basket. They guard "man for man" until the opposition begins crisscrossing under the basket and it is impossible to keep up with them. Then the defensive players make a "transitional" swing to the "zone principle," by which they guard given areas of floor space, trading opponents as they run from area to area. Phog says that in big-time modern basketball, neither the straight man-for-man nor the straight zone will work all the time. Consequently, the Stratified Transitional Man-for-Man Defense, and so forth.

Dr. Allen demonstrates every play his team uses. In a gray woolen warm-up suit, he drills two hours every afternoon with his squad. He has an uncanny eye for the basket. At 55 he can flip the ball through the hoop more often than most of his varsity boys. In the heat of scrimmage, when a play isn't working right, Phog will call for the ball and in the next few seconds will give his regulars a large eyeful of the fastest way to smash through a defense and lay in a counter with an overhand hook shot.

Phog insists on rigid mastery of fundamentals. That is one reason his teams look ordinary at the first of the season and brilliant at the end. Early in the year he restrains his boys in scrimmage and makes them practice pivoting, dribbling, passing, and guarding. It takes some time and patience, but in the end, his lads are smoother, more deceptive ball handlers than the opposition. They have mastered their set team plays, and they know the way to win in close, man-for-man fighting for possession of the ball.

A boy has to train to be on Phog's team. A few athletes have been dropped for violations. Phog never drinks or smokes. "I've always been tempted by a cigar after dinner, and I don't think it would hurt me much," he says, "but I ask the boys not to, so…"

Until a few years ago he would invite an athlete suspected of breaking training rules to the gymnasium and beat him soundly in handball. Defeat from a grandfather was usually lesson enough for a prodigal youngster, without a word said. Several years ago, however, when his All-American forward, Ted O'Leary, got the invitation to the handball court, Ted trounced Phog soundly. Players have noticed a marked decrease in the frequency of handball invitations.

Phog believes he wins most of his basketball games because of rigid attention to detail on the day of battle. His boys get up at the usual time, eat the usual hearty breakfast, go to classes in the morning, and eat their regular luncheon. After that their time belongs to Phog. At 3:20 PM they report to a designated rooming house, where Phog puts them all to bed. Undressed and in between clean sheets, Phog says, the boys always sleep. The purpose of the rest, Phog says, is to relax the big, fundamental muscles in the legs. Usually Phog gets in bed and sleeps too. After an hour and a half, they all get up, dress quickly, and walk a mile. When they return, the grogginess from sleep has disappeared, and they sit down to eat.

It is now 5:30 PM, some two hours before the game. Their meal is rather skimpy; Phog wants no heavy stomachs. He tells his ravenous charges they are not going to play on what they eat at that meal. It is the type of food they have eaten a couple of weeks or a month before that is important. It is the glycogen, or muscle sugar, in their liver, Phog says, that is going to give them the old spizzerinetum in the last minutes of the game. So their menu is half a grapefruit, a small cup of honey, two pieces of whole-wheat toast, half an order of celery, and a cup of hot chocolate.

After dinner, for about 15 minutes, the boys sit in front of a fireplace with their feet close up toward the coals. Phog says the feet of every basketball player get cold before a game. The cause is nervousness. "Get their feet warm," Phog says, "and the kids will calm down."

An hour and a half before game time Phog hustles his players into heated taxicabs. He sees to it that no one gets chilly. They go in cabs to the dressing room. Thirty minutes before the game they take the floor in red woolen warm-up suits for 25 minutes of practice. Phog has his boys shoot only short shots, no long ones. He says he's afraid that if they sink quite a few long ones in practice, they might get the idea they can hit all the time and try too many in the game. Besides, in the heat of battle, players hit a much higher percentage of long shots than in practice, he insists.

The Dressing-Room Thespian

After the warm-up period, Phog calls the boys back into the dressing room. He calls the names of the lads who are to start the game. They take their places, side by side, seated on the training table. Then Phog usually pulls something unexpected. He knows good theater in the dressing room. Sometimes he switches out all the lights. In the darkness he quietly tells them they're up against a tough team, but he has a hunch they can go out there and beat 'em. He never lets his boys believe the other team is any better. Once when his players seemed sluggish, he feigned anger, swung a chair over his head, and yelled, "Get out of here, all of you!" Kansas won the game.

Under different circumstances he may simply say, "Boys, I haven't a thing to tell you. The old rule applies tonight—run their hearts out, then whip them. That's all."

Phog goes with his squad out onto the floor. One minute before game time the first team makes a quick flash on the court, passing the ball fast and running like the wind. A few seconds before the referee's whistle, they form the familiar "pod," circled around Phog crouching on the floor. Their hands are piled together in the center. A bottle of smelling salts is passed, for the opening of nasal passages. Phog says to his team, "All right, boys. You can do it. Go get 'em!"

In the fury of the game Phog consumes water like a steam engine. He keeps the players' water bottles at his feet. Every few seconds he reaches down and takes a swig. He says a moist pharynx keeps down nervousness, and if that is true, he needs plenty of moistening. He bleeds when his team is out there playing.

While he is squirming, 10 Kansas students in the balcony are keeping his special records in a system Phog invented. The students work in pairs, each pair assigned to an individual player. When the player commits an error, such as letting the man he is supposed to be guarding sink a basket, it is a demerit. When he captures a rebound off the basket, it is a credit. At the end of the game Phog has a record on every one of his men.

By the time the final gun goes off, Phog has consumed about six quarts of water. If he has won, it is a pleasure to watch the way he steps out on the floor and benignly receives the congratulations of fans swarming out to shake his hand. If his team has been beaten, Phog gets up at the sound of the gun, pushes past those who speak to him, and goes straight to the position of the rival team. Not until he has congratulated the other coach does he have time for anything else.

After the game, Phog's players begin satisfying their appetites by eating as many grapefruits as they want. Then they may have ham and eggs, or all the cereal with cream they can hold. No steaks, Phog says, because they're too heavy to go to bed on. Ice cream? "By all means. Order a double dip," Phog advises, "and then order up some more."

Basketball rules get a lot of attention from Phog. He is chairman of the research subcommittee of the National Basketball Rules Committee. Today he advocates one main change. It is in the interest of the fellow of ordinary size who would like to play basketball. For his sake, Phog believes the baskets should be raised to 12 feet. They are now 10 feet high, and a tall man can virtually reach up and "dunk" the ball through. Phog says the only reason for the 10-foot baskets is that when Dr. Naismith rigged up his first indoor court, in Springfield, Massachusetts, he nailed the hoops to the gymnasium balcony, and the balcony just happened to be 10 feet high.

"If we raised the goals," Phog says, "these mezzanine-popping goons wouldn't be able to score like little children pushing pennies into gum machines. They would have to throw the ball like anyone else. They would have to make the team on real skill, not merely on height."

Phog also believes it would be good basketball to bring the center jump back. He thinks the rule change has put a little too much emphasis on the fast break for the good of the game. Even if the center jump were not returned, Phog would like to see a 10-second respite before play is resumed after baskets, out of deference to the players' hearts and kidneys.

But Phog says he'll play under any rules, because the fundamentals stay the same. The only time he ever got really good and mad over a rule change was when the dribble was abolished 10 years ago. At that time he quickly called a meeting of coaches in Des Moines, Iowa, after the Drake Relays. He worked up so much dissension that the dribble was returned. Out of the protest meeting the National Association of Basketball Coaches was formed, and Phog was elected its first president.

Phog's two sons, Milton and Robert, have both played on his basketball teams. Milton, now a law student at KU, won letters in 1934, '35, and '36. Bobby is expected to star this year, and the fans will hear "Give the ball to Junior!" loud and often.

The boys had a couple of goals out in their backyard for practice when they were kids, but after they got to college Phog enforced a strict rule that playing or talking basketball at home was taboo. They were going to have to make the Kansas team just like anyone else. And they did. In his book *Better Basketball,* published in 1937 by Whittlesey House, Phog says: "It is always difficult, if not unwise, for a father to attempt to coach his own son. A relative will sometimes unwittingly presume upon such a relationship."

The most obvious father-and-son strain came when Milton—called "Mit" by his pals—was on Phog's "Ever-Victorious Team" of 1935–36. He was playing center, or "quarterback," and started all offensive plays.

It was the day before the final game that would decide the conference championship. The opponent was Nebraska, at Lincoln. Phog was drilling the boys on a slightly different style of attack. The new plays weren't working right, and Phog's boy, Mit, made some suggestions. Phog called a halt. He gave the reminder that he was running the team. He told the players that the trouble was in their timing—a pass too forcefully thrown, or thrown at the wrong time, was upsetting the smoothness of the combination. Play started again. Still the freshmen, using the Nebraska defense, smeared everything. Phog set himself. His boy Mit passed carelessly and the play went haywire. Phog's reprimand was sure and quick, and Mit's reply was curt. Phog dismissed Mit from the floor.

The newspapers made much of the incident. It was said Phog was not going to let Mit play in the championship game.

The next night 9,000 spectators jammed the Nebraska coliseum, dead set that Nebraska should win its first Big 6 basketball championship. Mit sat beside his dad on the bench at the start of the game. Roy Holliday, substitute quarterback, played well, but the old spark wasn't there. Nebraska was threatening strongly. Phog turned to Mit and said, "Report."

The boy ran out on the floor, and there were hoots from the gallery: "Naughty boy, sonny. Do what papa tells you, sonny boy."

Mit paid no attention. He engineered a few successful scoring plays, and Kansas got in stride—and won.

The team didn't lose a game all season, either in the conference or outside. Phog had the satisfaction of knowing that his own son was a potent factor in every victory.

His other boy, Bobby, now has the center, or quarterback, position for Kansas. He has had to overcome the disadvantage of being small. It is phenomenal the way he can stand under the basket and steal the rebound from a fellow with a 12-inch reach advantage.

Bobby says the main thing is to know when to jump. He always gets behind the big fellow he's guarding. About the time the ball is ready to strike the backboard, Bobby has a way of slipping his knee between his opponent's knees and his thigh close under the other's hips. That way he can gently and painlessly prevent the other fellow from crouching for a spring. Then, just at the strategic instant, Bobby leaps to one side and upward. He usually comes down with the ball.

Like Mit, he is cool in the heat of combat. In the Southern Cal game, Bobby played his best when they were yelling, "Give the ball to Junior!" The next week he was knocked unconscious at the opening of the championship Indiana game. They carried him, limp, to the sideline. Indiana quickly found the basket a couple of times. On the sideline Phog was working with his boy.

Two minutes later, Bobby was wobbling out on the floor again. Many of the spectators thought he should have been kept on the bench. But Phog knew the courage of his son. By the time the game was over, Bobby had scored more points than any other player on either side. The fans forgot to yell, "Give the ball to Junior!"—awed by his exhibition.

While Bobby was going to the national peak in basketball, he also was making A grades in school. As a premed student, he had no snap courses, and in basketball season he was known to stay up all night studying. He is now a candidate for Phi Beta Kappa.

In picking his teams, Phog gives the preference to good students. He says boys with brains are the most likely to outfox the opposition. He makes a big point of his belief that the boys are in school first to study, then to play basketball. He is disappointed when his stars accept positions as professional basketball players after graduation. He reminds his athletes a thousand times, "When you train your muscles, you have four to nine years; when you train your mind, you have 50."

Ian Thomsen, *Boston Globe*

THE WIZARD OF KANSAS

When Larry Brown took over the coaching reins of the Kansas basketball program before the 1983–84 season, no one really knew what to expect. Oh, sure, they knew he could win some games, likely eclipsing the 13–16 record of 1982–83. But with his winning tradition came baggage that never really seemed to get unpacked anywhere. However, Brown led the Jayhawks to the NCAA Tournament during each of his five seasons in Lawrence. Along the way, he instilled a new confidence in his players, as Ian Thomsen pointed out in this March 28, 1986, article.

Looks like Coach Brown's going to stay in Kansas for a while. The Jayhawks want to wear his red shoes. Tap them three times and say, "There's no place like Dallas." As the sign said at Kemper Arena last weekend, "Larry Brown is the Wizard of Oz."

His team has brains, heart, courage, and Danny Manning, to go with the best record (35–3) in school history and the Big 8's first trip to the NCAA Final Four since Kansas qualified in 1974. Yes, Brown does believe in spooks. He does he does he does he does he does. But he believes in good spooks—the spirits of James Naismith, who taught basketball at Kansas seven years after he invented it (and is the only losing coach in KU history). Phog Allen was winning his 590 games at KU before anyone ever heard of Adolph Rupp, and Brown figured Lawrence, Kansas, was good enough for him. Enough of this Lou Saban stuff.

So he quit the NBA one more time (understandable, since he was coaching in New Jersey) and hired an assistant named Ed Manning and put him in charge of recruiting the nation's number one high school star—Ed's 6'11" son, Danny. Ed Manning probably does a good job at practices, but during games his main responsibility seems to be wiping clean Coach Brown's clipboard, along with watching Danny lead the team in scoring (17.1 points per game), steals, minutes, and blocked shots. Ed Manning might be the most important assistant coach in the country.

He works for maybe the best head coach anywhere. Brown's 14 professional and collegiate teams have won 571 games (65 percent). The Kansas group he inherited had won only 13 in 1982–83; Brown's introductory crack at the job produced 24 victories and the first of three consecutive NCAA Tournament bids. This was not a casual matter of pouring a water bucket onto Margaret Hamilton. Several Jayhawks fought Brown's system, and Calvin Thompson—a senior guard currently shooting a remarkable 57 percent—almost quit the team.

How times have changed. "I've learned that Coach Brown is never wrong," senior center Greg Dreiling said while sitting next to Coach Brown. "All the time I've been here, if we do exactly as he says, we win. If we've lost, I've looked back at it and seen that it was because we didn't follow his instincts."

One wonders whether KU's instincts are exclusively Brown's. His players—all of them—seem to constantly seek his advice, whether or not the ball is in play. Yet Brown insisted Manning and Dreiling decided whom each would guard against North Carolina State in the Midwest Regional final Sunday, and that the Jayhawks chose among themselves to go to Manning when he was scoring 12 straight to control the second half.

Brown seems to be a good coach for Manning, who as yet has not been pressured into Larry Bird/Indiana State duty. "Danny was in a slump early this year," said KU assistant Mark Freidinger. "For the Kentucky game, Coach [Brown] put in two new plays for him, one out of bounds and one in the offense. It turned out to be a good move. When the kid was down in a slump, Coach was saying, 'Hey, we're still going to you, big fella.'"

Manning could have the basics to dominate college basketball next year as no one has this season. As a freshman, he led KU in rebounding and steals and was second in scoring and assists. This season he was Big 8 Player of the Year while shooting an amazing 61 percent off moves borrowed from the 6'7"s of the world. "At the beginning of the year, his freshman year, we wanted Danny to want the ball a little bit more and he did become more assertive," Brown said. "The *Sports Illustrated* story you saw about him not being assertive enough was written in January, early in the year. Every time he's played against great players, he's played great.

"I'm not surprised by anything he does. He is the best player in the country. He plays the whole court. At times he is a complementary player, but when he finds himself open, he takes over. What he does I haven't seen anybody else do."

He provides that greatness required by other good players. The 7'1", 250-pound Dreiling (11.7 points, 6.7 rebounds) is allowed to be slow when Manning is roaming the baseline behind him. Dreiling broke out of a late-season slump Sunday with a nifty sidestep/dunk around and behind Chris Washburn and with a teammate's advice during a timeout late in the game. "You don't want the ball," senior forward Ron Kellogg told Dreiling.

"I thought about punching him," said Dreiling, who almost did...then smacked Kellogg with a towel. "It was almost a fight. The other guys on the bench shook their heads. No one likes to see that. But Ronnie is an intense guy and knows how to get me going." Dreiling followed Manning's spurt with nine straight points to finish off NC State.

The 6'5" Kellogg (55 percent shooting, 15.7 points), Thompson (13.4), and 6'6" junior Archie Marshall (51 percent, 6.8) are outstanding perimeter shooters, and Manning's chest-heave jumpers also tend to splash in twine. Of course, the Jayhawks' 56 percent shooting this season can be credited to junior munchkin Cedric Hunter (7.2 assists), whose defense last Friday against Michigan State's Scott Skiles (20 points) is the reason Kansas is still playing.

"When you're at Kansas, everybody complains that we've never had a point guard since Darnell Valentine. That's because when you compare them to Darnell, they fall short," Brown said. "I've always felt you don't win 20 games a year without good point-guard play. Considering the personnel we have, we put a lot of pressure on the position and Cedric."

Considering the personnel Duke has, this Blue Devils–Jayhawks semifinal might turn out to decide the national championship. "I told the kids we didn't want them to think it was any small accomplishment getting to the Final Four," said the man who has returned Phog Allen's traditional red shoes and uniforms to KU. "But now that we're there, we might as well try to win it."

Looks like they just might.

Thomas Boswell, *Washington Post*

FOLLOW YOUR HEART— AND HISTORY

Despite his about-face three years later, Roy Williams shocked the world from Lawrence to Chapel Hill with his famous "I'm stayin'" speech in 2000. Thomas Boswell shines some light on why Williams stayed.

Everybody claims to be shocked that Roy Williams didn't accept the job as basketball coach at North Carolina this week. Soon, maybe, you'll understand why he stayed at Kansas. Why, in a sense, he had no choice if he was to remain true to himself. Williams has a unique and powerful history. So does Kansas basketball. They were mated, fated it seems, to be one of the few true sports marriages.

Williams was raised in North Carolina, dirt-poor. As a boy, his dream was to have 10 cents so that, after playing basketball with the other boys, he could buy a Coca-Cola at the gas station vending machine. But 10 cents was what his mother charged to iron a shirt. Some days she'd leave a dime on the kitchen table. Sometimes not. A few years ago, Williams showed his old high school coach a big refrigerator in his garage. Inside, shelf upon shelf, were Coca-Colas.

At North Carolina, Williams made the freshman team, but never the varsity. But he took notes at Dean Smith's practices, kept statistics, did anything to be near the program. After five years as a high school coach, he came back to Carolina to serve 10 years as an assistant to Smith—the first five seasons at $2,700 a year.

Then in 1988, after leading Kansas to the national championship, Larry Brown—just the sixth coach in the program's history—resigned.

That's where Williams's history and Kansas basketball history merge. To many who haven't lived near Kansas, it's hard to understand the depth of passion for KU basketball. Maybe this will give a hint of the 102-year-old love affair in Lawrence.

James Naismith, who invented basketball, brought the game to Kansas and was the school's first coach. One of Naismith's players, Phog Allen, became the first great basketball coach, leading the

Jayhawks from 1907 to '09 and again from 1919 to 1956. One of Allen's players was Adolph Rupp, who won more college games than anybody in history until—yes, you guessed it—Dean Smith broke the record. Smith was born and raised in Kansas and played for Allen, too, on Kansas's 1952 national championship team.

Nobody, it was thought, could be more steeped in KU hoop tradition—the lore of Naismith, Allen, Wilt Chamberlain, Clyde Lovellette, and all the rest—than Smith. So, when the Jayhawks job was open—first in '83, then again in '88—it was natural for KU to telephone the great Deano.

In '83, Smith recommended Larry Brown for the job. At Kansas, being recommended by Dean, who learned from Phog, who learned from Doc Naismith, who got the whole idea direct from God, is akin to being anointed. To complete the symmetry, Smith's choice—Brown— won that national title in just five years.

When KU called Smith again in '88, he said, "Roy Williams." Roy Williams? Perhaps no one so utterly unknown and untested—he wasn't even Smith's top assistant—had been pushed forward for such a hallowed job.

In the horrified words of the wife of the KU athletics director, "You're not going to hire that no-name assistant from Carolina, are you?"

But Williams was hired. Now, he, too, is a Kansas legend. He never curses, seldom screams. Yet he may run the toughest practices in the sport. Somehow, he manages to combine a choirboy look and an aw-shucks modesty. After 12 years, he has the highest winning percentage of any active coach. He has been to two Final Fours.

When Williams flew into Lawrence to accept the KU job, it was night. He awoke with a new life in a new town—and he'd never even seen the place in daylight. What a shock! The campus is lush, wooded, and so hilly that many students wish it were flatter. Allen Fieldhouse is a purist's shrine. "Pay Heed, All Who Enter—Beware of the Phog," one permanent sign says.

Williams was home. Little had he understood the irony in Smith's parting words, "You'll be perfect for Kansas." Smith is corny on the surface but with some Kierkegaard underneath. Williams is all Norman Rockwell, all the time—and proud of it. "I loved being a high school player and I loved being a high school coach," he said. "And Allen Fieldhouse is just an old high school gym, the way I look at it."

Kansas basketball either rolls off your sophisticated back or it sinks into you deeply. It's hard to figure out who it'll hook. For decades, Chamberlain would not return to campus, even to have his jersey retired. The most prevalent theory was that incidents of discrimination in the '50s had soured him on Lawrence. Then, two years ago, the world-hopping Chamberlain came back as part of the program's 100th anniversary celebration. Crying, he told a packed Allen Fieldhouse that he'd never come back because he was ashamed his '57 team had lost the national title by one point in triple overtime. To—who else?—Carolina.

"I thought I let Kansas down and my teammates down," the late Chamberlain told the crowd. "When I came back here today and realized not the simple loss of a game, but how many people have shown such appreciation and warmth, I'm humbled and deeply honored. I'm a Jayhawk, and I know now why there is so much tradition here and why so many wonderful things have come from here."

Then, Chamberlain screamed the KU fight chant, "Rock chalk, Jayhawk." And everybody in the joint, including Williams, had a good reconciliatory blubber.

This week, a national consensus was quickly reached: Williams would return to Carolina. More prestige. More fame. Maybe more money. Add in his profound debt to Smith. Williams's wife and son are Carolina graduates, and his daughter attends Chapel Hill. Williams doesn't just have Carolina roots; you practically have to exhume him.

However, in Lawrence, everybody wasn't so sure. In Kansas, Williams's return—at Dean's behest—has come to be seen as the perfect closing of a very long circle. Naismith begat Phog. Phog begat Dean. Dean begat Roy. Even Bill Guthridge, who replaced Smith as Carolina coach for three years, is from Kansas.

This week, Williams and his wife, Wanda, were spotted walking past the Chi Omega Fountain on campus. Williams put his bare feet in the water as he pondered. Oh, that was a good sign. Maybe he'd even take one more run in Lawrence Park and Oak Hill cemeteries where, so many times before big games, Williams had interrupted his jog to touch the monuments of Doc Naismith and Phog Allen.

All over the map, old KU grads hoped against hope that everything embedded for a century in corny Jayhawks basketball—loyalty, decency, unselfishness, perhaps just comfortable old stolid rootedness—would come to their aid.

On Thursday, they won. Williams called a news conference and said: "I'm staying. ... People can say a lot of things about me, but nobody can ever accuse me of being a phony." In the end, Williams was true to everything that has meant the most to him, from the dimes his mother left on the kitchen table to those old verities—Kansas values—that Dean Smith taught him.

All over America, people are scratching their heads. Why didn't Roy Williams make the smart play, the glamour move, and take the last step to the top?

An enlightened minority, however, gets it. One of my *Post* editors once was the Kansas mascot. Before Roy Williams ever got to Lawrence, she was the Jayhawk.

"I have two cats, Doc Naismith and Phog Allen," she said, summing up the pure Kansas view of the matter. "I've told them that one of them may have to become Roy."

Dennis Dodd, CBSSportsline.com

KANSAS COACH FREE TO BE HIM-SELF

When the rumors started that Roy Williams was leaving Kansas after the 2003 season, Bill Self's name immediately started popping up. Within a week, he was KU's new coach. The following March 2005 column by Dennis Dodd is a testament to Self and the personality that his Jayhawks have taken.

Bill Self has become more comfortable at Kansas in two years than Roy Williams ever was in 15.

Williams used to worry about petty stuff like perception and image. His infamous "wine-and-cheese crowd" crack about Kansas's fans still sticks in their minds like gum to a shoe. They'll never forget because Roy eventually forgot who he was—the humble assistant selling calendars door-to-door at Carolina.

At some point Ol' Roy became more millionaire than man of the people.

At this point, Bill Self still can be a million laughs.

That's the basic difference in this remake of the Kansas program. Williams's cornpone "suckers" and "friggins" have been replaced by Self's actual sincere humanity.

Peek behind the curtain for a second: the coach of basketball royalty bounds into the coaches' dressing room at Allen Fieldhouse with juicy info. He blurts out breathlessly that San Antonio Spurs guard Tony Parker is now dating Eva Longoria, the naughtiest of the Desperate Housewives.

That Parker's dating habits seem to fascinate only Self is kind of the point. Take it or leave it, boys. Just trying to lighten your day a little bit.

"I wouldn't say he's a bullshitter," says close friend R. C. Buford, the San Antonio Spurs general manager and likely source of the Parker dish. "A bullshitter implies lack of sincerity. He can maneuver in many systems and many scenes. Sarcastic people would say that's bullshit. This person is too sincere."

"He makes everything fun," said Texas A&M's Billy Gillispie, who used to be in the frat, er, on the staff with Self at Illinois. "It's not a job. You're awfully lucky if you can be in that type of environment."

March Madness bearing down? Bring it on. This is the time of year Self's teams peak. Williams recruited the core Jayhawks who will play Bucknell in a first-round NCAA Tournament game on Friday. The real turnover won't come until next season.

Maybe that's why his team has embraced a possible regional final against Williams and the Heels.

"It put a little smile on my face," said senior Michael Lee after seeing the bracket. "I would love to get a chance to play against my former coach."

"North Carolina is not on my brain at all," Self said.

Maybe not but the possibility of crossing paths has crossed his mind. A North Carolina, Kansas, Illinois, and Oklahoma State Final Four is now impossible. The schools share so many bloodlines that Dick Vitale would have spontaneously combusted trying to describe them all.

Still, Self might have to go through the Tar Heels in the Syracuse regional and beat either Illinois (his former team) or Oklahoma State (his former boss, Eddie Sutton) in the national championship game.

"If you made it to the Final Four, you would think that would be something a coach would enjoy," Self said earlier in the season, "but that wouldn't be any fun."

This is how you climb the ladder: from Oral Roberts to Tulsa to Illinois to Kansas. The last three programs he took to the Elite Eight. With the latest, he has the rest of his life to chase The Next Level.

Right or wrong, there is still that feeling here that Williams "jilted" the school after giving heart and soul for 15 years. Self is younger, more personable, and has a blueprint—along with about 20 years to share it with you.

"He got the best players in America," Self said after being reminded how Williams complained about being able to recruit players to little ol' Lawrence. "If you've got a product, you can sell it."

And as product lines go, Kansas is one of a handful of Lexuses on the lot. The others belong to Kentucky, North Carolina, and Duke. That's it for this exclusive club that doesn't readily admit new members.

He's already pretty much overcome the biggest obstacle he'll ever face at Kansas: convincing Jayhawks everywhere that he's not just the next one, he's the one.

The one to lead Kansas to its first national championship since 1988. Because no matter how much Jayhawkers blather on about tradition and rock chalks and Phogs, they want that next title. A Final Four, at least.

"I think we build our basketball program for longevity," said Kansas chancellor Robert Hemenway, who took seven days to hire Self two years ago without a full-time athletics director in place. "You don't see coaches here four or five years and moving on.

"There was a general consensus that, frankly, Bill Self was the best basketball coach in the country."

So on the eighth day Hemenway rested. He hired the school's eighth coach at a place that traces its roots back to the guy who invented the game. Confident that Self basically has a lifetime to contribute his own championship flag—or two—to the Allen Fieldhouse rafters.

This love of everything KU for Self started more than two decades ago. He met his wife during a road trip to Kansas while he was playing for, and she was cheerleading for, Oklahoma State. As Self progressed up the ladder, it was assumed he would one day succeed Eddie Sutton at Stillwater.

Then the planets aligned that April day in 2003 when Williams left and it took Kansas only a week to find his replacement.

"I thought all along I wanted to be the coach at Oklahoma State, my alma mater," Self said. "I told people at Illinois I was here for the long haul, which I thought I would be. [But] I felt like five years from now I would think back and say, 'God, I could have been the coach at Kansas.'"

None of it would be possible without the cachet of winning, of course. It brought him to Kansas. It has endeared him to the legions of crimson and bluebloods.

"He's such a chameleon type of personality because he fits in with almost any crowd," said Illinois sports information director Kent Brown, who became close to Self in his three years there.

Webster's defines *chameleon* as "a changeable or fickle person." Changeable? Yes. Fickle. No. People like Self are measured like carbon dioxide, in parts per million. They don't come along very often.

Coaches like Self are so rare they exist on the subatomic level. Successful *and* personable. Not in an are-the-TV-cameras-on-yet? way, either. Self is to interpersonal relationships what Jack Webb was to interrogation. Which is to say, intense.

Press, point guard, president, and publicist all say the same thing.

"He has a rare sense of charisma. I don't think there's very many people in the world that have that type of charisma," Kent Brown said. "He's kind of like a guy who is going through life and enjoying life. Bill is one of those guys [who] if I had to spend an evening sitting around drinking a couple of beers watching sports, he's the guy."

That Brown is among many that have done exactly that makes Self somewhat of a legend at age 42. How many major college coaches sit with the unwashed—also known as the media—at lunch? Self does, exchanging gossip knowing none of it will show up in print because, you know, it's just us guys. Sorry, can't picture Coach K or Tubby or Ol' Roy bringing any more than paranoia to the table this time of year.

Gillispie recalls idle moments on long bus rides at Illinois. He and Self would break into one of their impromptu trivia challenges.

Don't argue about this one true fact. Self's favorite player: Barry Bonds, warts and all. End of story. Turn-ons: defensive rebounding. Turn-offs: oh, maybe Illinois coach Bruce Weber, who continues to shoot barbs at Self from Champaign two years after replacing him.

"Bruce has said several things since he's become head coach that, if I was thin-skinned, I could take personally," Self said, "but I don't take that personally at all."

A noble statement from a coach who was declared "dead" by Weber last season as a way to emphasize to Illini players that their old coach was gone. Weber wore black to a game one night to drive home the point.

Self has had a heck of a honeymoon at Kansas. In his first season, the Jayhawks won 24 games and came within an overtime loss to Georgia Tech of advancing to the Final Four for the third consecutive year. This year they head into the dance as Big 12 co-champs, but having lost five of their last eight.

That represents a net gain, considering the turmoil involved in convincing Roy's red-carpet stars to have blind trust in Bill.

"When he came in, I think he thought we were a lot more spoiled than we needed to be," guard Michael Lee said. "He had to convince us his system works."

Sophomore J. R. Giddens had to be re-recruited after committing to Williams.

"My question for Coach Self was: if you inherit a pair of shoes, they're comfortable and they fit. But do you really want those shoes? I wasn't thinking about leaving but then I was like, hey, I don't know."

One pundit put it this way: under Williams, Kansas players were made to feel like gods. Self had to make them feel like soldiers. If a sometimes-rocky transition almost turned into a Final Four berth, the position truly looks like what Self wants it to be—a retirement job.

"It's almost not real-world," he said. "These guys are treated, in a lot of respects, like rock stars. It's our responsibility each and every day [to remind them] they're no different than anybody else."

Self's biting sarcasm is his defense mechanism in practice. He'll pick a straggler from the herd in practice and send him to the sideline for perceived lack of effort.

"When Coach Self gets on you, he stays on you," Lee said. "He knows how to get under your skin. He tries to make you feel as uncomfortable as possible because he knows there are times in the game when you're not going to be comfortable."

"It's something no player wants to go through because we all feel he's picking on us more than he's picking on the next person sometimes."

"I know my sarcasm can go overboard," Self admitted. "I'm too sarcastic too often."

But there is a fine line between practice tactics and abuse.

"I understand what he's trying to do," Lee said. "When he first got here, I didn't. I can honestly admit I struggled with it at first. He just wants you to perform at your best."

There were casualties. Omar Wilkes and David Padgett left after Self's first season. In a private moment, Self says the inconsistency of his freshmen—Alex Galindo, Sasha Kaun, Russell Robinson, Darnell Jackson, and C. J. Giles—is maddening at times.

It takes a master manipulator, though, to smooth over every crisis. Here's the difference: in his later years, Williams needed constant stroking. Self just needs an outlet for his personality.

"Love" for Kansas is not too strong a word for a kid who grew up in Edmond, Oklahoma, and played at Oklahoma State. Buford, then a Kansas assistant, got Self on to work at a Larry Brown summer camp.

During a pickup game with KU players, Self sprained a knee. He limped around with just a touch of self-pity. Brown felt so bad, he uttered one of those if-there's-anything-I-can-do-for-you lines.

"Well, there is one thing..." Self said.

He played the pity card enough to be hired as a graduate assistant. It was enough to light the fuse on Self's career. The Jayhawks went to the Final Four in Self's one-and-only season in 1985–86. Self then went back to Oklahoma State for the next eight years, learning under Leonard Hamilton and Sutton.

It's hard to imagine Self has been a head coach only 11 years. You don't talk about your desire to someday, maybe, coach at KU when you're 6–21 in your first year at Oral Roberts. In fact, the frat boy/good guy basically lucked into his first point guard at the school after bumping into him at a Subway restaurant.

"Coach Self, sir, I'd really like to come out for the team, sir," Earl McClellan said. "If you let me come out, I promise I won't embarrass you."

McClellan walked on and ended up starting four years because, Self says, he was "the only guy who called me 'sir' five times in a sentence."

Fast forward. The seat Self occupies is hot. Games at Kansas tend to be events, picked apart like a turkey on Thanksgiving. Lose before the Final Four and the seat is going to get hotter.

At least he's comfortable—which is more than can be said for the guy who occupied the seat for 15 years.

The Kansas-Missouri rivalry is one of the fiercest in all of sports—so fierce, in fact, that there was talk of ending the heated border war back in the 1950s and 1960s.
Photo courtesy of AP/Wide World Photos.

Section IV
THE MYSTIQUE

David Halberstam, *The Kansas Century*

THE PASSION, THE INTENSITY, THE HISTORY

Without question, David Halberstam is one of the premier writers of his generation. It's fitting, then, that Halberstam wrote this essay on one of the nation's premier college basketball programs for the book The Kansas Century.

A week before big games, hundreds of students, even though they already have general admission tickets, start lining up to get even better seats in Allen Fieldhouse. Roy Williams, the team's head coach, not unaware of the acoustical benefits that derive from this kind of passion, arrives at his office early in the morning and often hands out dozens of doughnuts to those in line. In the evening before he goes home he often stops by with slices of pizza.

Passion, bordering on madness, is very much encouraged. The ticket itself is very simply the dearest in the state of Kansas and among the dearest in the Midwest. On occasion season tickets are passed on to the next generation in people's wills. When a local couple gets a divorce sometimes there is a bitter dispute over who gets custody of the tickets. Not surprisingly, the passion and the noise generated in Lawrence are almost without parallel, even in college basketball.

Winter, after all, in Kansas can be long and bleak, and, therefore, the light and energy and excitement found inside at a Jayhawks basketball game are singular. On those special nights when the team is at home, this arena becomes a universe all its own, a community within a community; a citadel of both adventure and pleasure, however momentary, in a region that does not offer many alternatives for several cold, hard months.

Rival coaches consider a visit to Allen Fieldhouse not unlike a visit to the hangman and with good reason: in the last 13 years the Jayhawks' home record is 178–14. And Kansas will open this forthcoming season with a run of 44 straight home victories. Inside the arena hangs a banner: "Pay Heed, All Who Enter—Beware of the Phog," a reference to Phog Allen, the formidable coach who essentially created basketball's preeminence here, and for whom the field house is named. Legend has it that in close games, the spirit of Phog Allen will enter the arena and cause a crucial turnover, or at the least slip inside the soul of a referee and help pressure him into a call against the visitors.

What we have here is not just sports, of course. What we have is theater disguised as basketball, where some 15 times a year, good takes on evil and almost always triumphs. Good, of course, is KU; Evil is Kansas State and Missouri and all the other unfortunate visitors whose somber, melancholy duty it is to play the role of the villain. Lawrence is a perfect venue for that: Allen Fieldhouse is both big-time and yet old-fashioned. It was one of the first of the modern basketball arenas, erected in 1956, but it was built to Allen's shrewd specifications, with the impact of the crowd very much in the mind of the by-then venerable coach. It is not like some of the more modern but rather genteel arenas, places where the best seats are somewhat removed from the action. Instead the fans are right down there in front, as close to the action as possible; indeed, in any real sense they are a part of the action. In addition, unlike a lot of the newer basketball emporiums, the best seats do not go to the wealthiest (but occasionally slightly subdued) alumni, but to the students themselves. Phog wanted it that way and for a good reason: it may well be worth two or three home wins a year. No wonder then that Roy Williams, his lineal descendant, becomes for a few minutes a day a doughnut and pizza deliveryman.

This is a basketball school. Almost from the start, probably because of the force of Allen's personality and his systematic success against historic rivals, Kansas became one of the rare big-time state universities in America where basketball was more important than football. Allen Fieldhouse was one of the first of the super arenas. If, in its sense of luxury and skyboxes, it is a bit behind the contemporary curve, it was well ahead of that curve in the mid-1950s when it was completed. In that first year a season ticket for every home game cost all of $16, with free parking thrown in. A year later a freshman named Wilt Chamberlain arrived in Lawrence, and the athletics department, sensing that a big-time program was about to become even bigger, jacked the season ticket price up $4, an unheard-of increase of 25 percent. There was a good deal of grumbling, but few people turned in their tickets, which was a good thing: Chamberlain played two full varsity seasons for Kansas. As a freshman he was not eligible for varsity play in that era, but in his first game at KU, his freshman team beat the Kansas varsity, and in his first varsity game he scored 52 points.

Over the years the cost of the season ticket has gone up until today it costs $289—with no parking thrown in. But given the madness it produces, it still remains something of a bargain. Contemporary Kansas basketball fever, of course, is nothing less than the proper legacy of an unusually rich history. For if the game as we know it was born in Springfield, Massachusetts, then in any real sense the college game began here, and local aficionados take justifiable pride in thinking that this is the cradle of a sport that has now transfixed not just the nation but the rest of the world. It is not by chance that Dr. James Naismith, who invented the sport, was Kansas's first coach and that he is buried here; and that his successor and protégé was the fabled Phog Allen. Allen was not only the reigning coach of the early era, but he was the father of modern basketball coaching. It may be that Kansas basketball, located far from the dual media centers of America (New York and Los Angeles), does not quite get the national notoriety it deserves, but any visiting coach who has come here knows that Jayhawks teams are consistently among the best and toughest-minded in the country.

It is a long way from the time a century ago when its coach made about $2,000 a year and had several other major responsibilities to the sport—which, because of the speed of its action, shares center stage with football in America today and whose professional players earn salaries in the tens of millions of dollars a year.

Technically Naismith invented the game at a Springfield YMCA, using two peach baskets and hanging them at a height of 10 feet because that was the height of the available balcony he was using. Six years later, Naismith, more a man of God than of sport, was asked to come to the University of Kansas to teach and coach. His arrival was hardly an auspicious start for the birth of a big-time sport. The chancellor of the university, Francis Snow, had wanted a religious man more than a physical education man; among other things, Snow wanted someone to lead all his students in prayer at the daily mandatory chapel sessions.

Naismith did not seem particularly passionate about the basketball job or the game that he had invented, least of all about winning with any regularity. He seemed to like the idea of hearty, youthful physical exertion as an end in itself. On occasion he would pull a player from a game and check his heartbeat, worried the player might be overexerting himself—not something that one expects to see Pat Riley or Phil Jackson doing these days. Naismith believed in a strong body and a clean life. He was a seriously religious man who turned down an endorsement from a cigarette company because he did not believe in tobacco. He drank, as far as his friends could tell, on only one occasion, when he wanted to check out alcohol's effect on athletic performance. He took drink after drink to measure what quickly became an obvious decline in his skills as a fencer.

Naismith handled the team's schedule, but he did not necessarily travel with his players. If he did travel, it was often to referee the game—things were, it seems, quite different then. Competition as the driving purpose in collegiate sport seems not to have interested him at all. No wonder then that he remains not merely the father of basketball, but the only one of Kansas's coaches with a losing record. Later, after retiring as coach (as Blair Kerkhoff points out in his book on Phog Allen), Naismith would continue to attend KU games, where he would always sit in the same seat in the second row, ever impassive, showing neither pleasure nor passion, and never, apparently, cheering.

The real era of modern basketball began not with Naismith but his protégé, Phog Allen. From the start Allen wanted more than to upgrade the physical condition of his young players—he wanted to win. He began coaching at Kansas in 1907 at the grand age of 22 years and five months old, which, as fans here point out, means that he still remains the youngest head coach in NCAA Division I history. Though he briefly left Kansas to coach elsewhere, he returned, and in the end he recorded 590 wins and 219 defeats. Over the years Allen became recognized as the game's foremost coach, and in time his progeny took his gospel and spread it throughout the country. Slowly and steadily under his tutelage a formidable basketball tradition was created here; other young men who believed they wanted to play—or to play and perhaps one day coach—began to arrive. In the days before big-time recruiting, Allen on his own had helped create a dynamic that drew young men to Lawrence. He became in time the progenitor of a long line of other prominent coaches, including Adolph Rupp of Kentucky, Dean Smith of North Carolina, and Ralph Miller of Oregon State. That means that among his contemporary lineal descendants in the family tree of coaching are Pat Riley, who played at Kentucky, and the current Kansas coach, Roy Williams, who played for a season for Smith at Chapel Hill and then coached alongside Smith for 10 years.

Over the years Kansas has produced a prototype kind of team: tough, smart, disciplined. Tradition has turned into trademark. Not surprisingly, the 1996–97 team was one of the school's best, and two of its players, Scot Pollard and Jacque Vaughn, became first-round choices in the NBA draft. If the world of sport has changed dramatically from that time a century ago when a handful of white players gathered around Naismith to experiment with this new and largely unheralded sport, then there is nonetheless a powerful connection to the past that one senses here. College basketball in recent years has gone from something of an athletic afterthought, a wintertime filler between football and baseball seasons, to the nation's new high-profile sport, one which is being embraced at an astonishing rate by the rest of the world. The reason for that growing success is obvious: in an era where the velocity of daily life is ever faster, and where spectators demand more and more action per viewer minute, basketball showcases the fastest, most powerful, and most versatile athletes in the world, and it reflects the changes in our society far more accurately than, say, baseball.

It is a long way from the simple beginning when Naismith was a young man and Allen was still a boy to today's game with its amazing athletes, its big-time professional salaries, its high-powered college recruiting, its media hype—but it is nice to remember that it all began here. And lest people doubt the influence of Kansas and Allen on the game, they should only remember that it was Phog Allen who probably saved the game for today's stunningly quick and brilliant athletes by preserving its tempo. When other NCAA officials wanted to limit the sport to one dribble per player per possession, something that would have killed the game's speed, it was Allen who mustered the opposition and held the line, opening up the way to the future by that one decision.

Lawrence Daily Journal-World staff

HIGHEST TRIBUTE TO BEFALL PHOG AT FÊTE TONIGHT

On March 2, 1955, Phog Allen received the highest compliment possible during the dedication of Kansas's newest venue, Allen Fieldhouse. This article, which was written by a member of the Lawrence Daily Journal-World*'s staff, ran the day of the dedication game between KU and Kansas State. Incidentally, the Jayhawks won that first game, 77–67.*

Kansas's newest and biggest state-owned building—Allen Fieldhouse—will be dedicated tonight in honor of the famed Kansas University basketball coach, Dr. F. C. "Phog" Allen.

The two-and-a-half-million-dollar athletic plant, with a capacity of 17,000, will get the "Allen" tag officially between halves of the 129th cage meeting between KU and bitter rival Kansas State College of Manhattan, Kansas. The contest starts at 7:35 PM.

The game itself means little in the Big 7 conference standings since both teams were knocked out of the running some time ago. Colorado clinched the title by beating Missouri 66–57 at Columbia Monday night.

But there is tremendous feeling in any KU–K-State game, and this is no exception. KU ruined the dedication of State's Ahearn Fieldhouse with a 78–68 upset win on February 12. Now the Wildcats would love to repay that questionable "favor."

Allen's record as a coach surpasses even the vastness of the new field house, which is second only to Minnesota University's 18,250-capacity arena among the nation's on-campus physical plants.

Allen Record Is 755–223

Beginning with his first season as a coach, Allen-coached teams have won 755 times against only 223 defeats. His teams have 20 collegiate championships and have shared the bunting nine times since 1908. In 1952 Kansas won the national collegiate championship.

Allen will be presented a new car at the dedication. The car, obtained through contributions, drew criticism from a university economics professor. In a letter to the student newspaper, Charles E. Staley suggested it would be better to give the money to something like cancer or heart research or an academic scholarship.

The 69-year-old coach, in reply, pointed out that a $1,000 Phog Allen scholarship had already been established. He said the suggestion was a good one but since his old car had been traded in on the new one, he would be converted to "a limping pedestrian instead of an aloof and cold-blooded representative of the upper crust."

Other Uses for Structure

Allen Fieldhouse also will be used for such things as indoor baseball and football drills. A balcony, which will seat about 65 percent of the capacity crowd, surrounds the arena. The running track has six lanes of 220 yards.

Phog gets the full treatment in his third move into a new playing area at Kansas. He had champions in the first two—Robinson Gymnasium and Hoch Auditorium, which had been his home battleground since 1929. Hoch had a seating capacity of no more than 4,000.

Among the speakers at the dedication ceremonies will be Governor Fred Hall of Kansas, members of the Board of Regents, and administrative officials and coaches of the rival schools.

Pageant, March Slated

Included in the halftime ceremony will be a pageant tracing the history of basketball and the vast role Allen has played in its development. Over 100 KU lettermen will take part.

Another feature will be the playing of a special march, "Mr. Basketball," dedicated to Dr. Allen. The march was written by Professor Russell L. Wiley, director of the KU band that will play it, and will be presented to the public for the first time tonight.

Doors of the field house are to be opened at 6:00 this evening to allow visitors to inspect the arena fully. Parking will be at a premium and KU officials are asking that as many persons as possible take public transportation or walk. The recent damp weather is likely to make the parking situation even more critical, and it was never ideal to begin with.

Gary Bedore, *Lawrence Journal-World*

FANS PART OF FIELDHOUSE'S MYSTIQUE

In March 2005, Allen Fieldhouse celebrated its 50th anniversary. The following is Gary Bedore's look at the basketball venue that many consider to be the best in the nation, college basketball's equivalent to Chicago's Wrigley Field.

Lew Perkins, who played college basketball at the University of Iowa and worked as athletics director at Connecticut, Maryland, and Wichita State, has attended games in some fabulous, historic hoops venues.

"You name it, I have been there. I have seen them all—Madison Square Garden, Rupp Arena, Cameron, the Palestra," said Perkins, KU's second-year AD. "There is none better than Allen Fieldhouse. None."

Perkins, who is committed to improving the building by sandblasting the outside and by adding a new floor, windows, seating, lights, and sound system, said it was more than the structure itself that made the 50-year-old building so spectacular.

"The first time I walked in this building, I looked around and felt the history and tradition," he said of the field house, which at 8:00 tonight officially celebrates its 50th birthday when KU takes on Kansas State.

"Seeing it full with our great fans, you realize it is a building, but it's the people, the fans that truly make it the best."

People who have rocked the field house for 50 years indeed have had a love affair with the players and coaches. This love affair might have best been described by Jo Jo White in his acceptance speech during his jersey retirement ceremony.

"Every time I stepped on that court I gave you everything I had, everything," White said, "and you gave me everything you had. It made for a great relationship. Yes, a relationship is what it was."

Much has been said about the field house and great games in the tradition-rich structure in the months leading up to today's 50th-anniversary game.

Not much has been said of the folks who have cheered the players and coaches for so many seasons.

"I get goose bumps every time I walk through the tunnel onto the court," KU coach Bill Self said, echoing a statement repeated by almost all KU players interviewed since the inception of the building. "I get goose bumps every day before practice when I walk past the students camping out for the games."

Dozens of fans line up outside the KU locker room all the way to the court, waiting patiently for the Jayhawks to appear, then applauding them wildly before, during, and after games.

"I love that. It's one of the things that makes this place special, how much they care and how much they want to show us they support us," senior Aaron Miles said.

The Jayhawks try to pay back their fans by remaining long after the games to sign autographs for those who line up five deep outside the locker room.

There's an obvious affection between the Jayhawks and the fans, especially the young children who seek autographs and pictures.

"I've never seen a place where so many people stick around to get autographs," Self said. "Different players, like Wayne [Simien], if he wanted he could sign for two and a half hours after every game. I don't think they can sign every one. They've got to go do their deal from time to time. I do think our players have a good relationship with the kids."

Self said the fans who have attended games in the field house for many years don't seem to mind any of the inconveniences—such as how cramped the seats are.

"I would say how the people view Allen Fieldhouse, and what a historic place it is, is even greater than what I thought it would be," Self said. "There are so many things about it that are old and need to be modernized. I don't think you ever want to change the feel in any way, shape, or form, because if we did, I think it would really disappoint a lot of people.

"You could say, 'Don't you guys want a few more inches per seat to spread out just a little bit?' I think the consensus would be, 'No, we like it just the way it is.' I think it is what makes it classic."

Self is thankful that those who built the building 50 years ago did it right.

"First of all, they had the foresight to build it big enough," Self said. "I'm sure back then it was one of the largest in the country. I'm sure we look at [how] the outside needs to be cleaned, windows replaced. At its foundation, they did such a good job taking care of it. I love the windows. I love the building."

So did his predecessor, Roy Williams, who paid the ultimate compliment.

"What is that old saying that imitation is the sincerest form of flattery? I'm trying to make our people understand here that I want the Smith Center to be the Allen Fieldhouse of the East. And that's the biggest compliment I can give," said Williams, now coach at North Carolina.

"Walking through that tunnel every night for 15 years, I always got goose bumps. And every night it was a thrill. I've seen other big-time places, like Duke University and Indiana and Pauley Pavilion. There's no place like Allen Fieldhouse."

Malcolm Moran, *The New York Times*

A TRIUMPHANT HERITAGE REBOUNDS WITH JAYHAWKS

Despite the detractors who thought he wouldn't stay very long, coach Larry Brown led the Jayhawks to the Final Four at the end of his third season, 1985–86. Since the Jayhawks had struggled for a few seasons, publications were readdressing KU's remarkable past. One such was this article by Malcolm Moran for The New York Times.

Mark Turgeon was nearly born too little and too late. Even now, in his junior year at Kansas, he is generously listed as 5'10" and 150 pounds. In his freshman year, he wore braces on his teeth.

Which is fine, except that when Turgeon was growing up in Topeka, he hardly looked the part of someone who could help Kansas relive its days of basketball greatness. Just like all those dreamers who twisted radio dials to listen to the Jayhawks decades ago, Turgeon wanted, more than anything else, to play basketball for KU. "When I was little," he said, "I just wanted to be on the team. Even if I could be that guy on the end of the bench. I just wanted to be him."

Turgeon has become a backup guard and a co-captain of the team that has reminded Kansans of their basketball heritage. He represents a time when schoolboys dreamed that Dr. Forrest Clare Allen, the coach for 39 seasons spread between 1907 and 1956—Phog to the fans and Doc to his friends—would choose them for his team.

Gone are the days when Dr. Allen chose players rather than recruited them, or even when the huge field house named for him was the second-largest campus arena in the nation. Kansas is just one school that refers to itself as Big Blue. The other schools to reach the Final Four have their own memories, traditions, and phobias—Duke has its cynical wits in the stands, Louisiana State has Mike the Tiger, and Louisville has Kentucky.

But only three Division I schools—Kentucky, North Carolina, and St. John's—have won more basketball games, and two of those schools have been coached by former Jayhawks. There can be no other people on earth that can possibly find inspiration from these words:

Rock chalk, Jayhawk, KU
Rock chalk, Jayhawk, KU
RockchalkJayhawkKU
RockchalkJayhawkKU
RockchalkJayhawkKU

The explanation is that the rhyme refers to the limestone formation that appears on Mount Oread, a bump in the Plains where a campus now jumps in anticipation of this weekend. The significance is that the words have been screamed since 1898, when Kansas teams played their games and when Kansans fought in the Spanish-American War.

It was around that time when Dr. James Naismith, a Presbyterian clergyman who joined the faculty as the director of chapel and a professor of physical education, coached the school's first basketball game. Seven years earlier, he had invented the sport in Springfield, Massachusetts. Dr. Naismith viewed his invention as exercise more than as fierce competition.

The first time the Jayhawks took the floor, against the Kansas City YMCA, Dr. Naismith acted as both the coach and referee. Kansas still lost, 16–5, playing under rules that awarded one point per basket. Dr. Naismith's career record was 55–60, a percentage of .478, the only losing record among the eight Kansas coaches. When Allen decided to go into coaching, Dr. Naismith is said to have told his protégé: "Forrest, basketball is just a game to play. You don't coach it."

After Rupp and Smith

His descendants have had another view. Turgeon was right about the importance of being even the least important member of the team; just a seat on the Kansas bench has proven valuable. Look in the upper left corner of the picture of the 1923 Helms Foundation national champions. That serious-looking one, who did not play much, is Adolph Rupp. Look at the first row of the 1952 team, the one that defeated St. John's for the only NCAA Tournament championship in Kansas history. The third one from the right, the substitute with the ball in his lap and the half-smile on his face, is Dean Smith.

Rupp moved on to Kentucky, and Smith to North Carolina. Each has had a gigantic arena named for him, and each coach has been enshrined in the sport's hall of fame, the Naismith Memorial Basketball Hall of Fame.

Surely, tradition does not guarantee championships. "Tradition now means who has been to the Final Four the last three years," said

Larry Brown, the Jayhawks coach who played for Smith, worked on his staff at North Carolina, and who has educated these Jayhawks on the subject of those who came before them. "Tradition is now whoever ESPN puts on."

His players are proving that is not entirely so. With their 35 victories this season—including two emotional, come-from-behind efforts to win the Midwest Regional and advance to the national semifinal against Duke, the Jayhawks are reminding their followers of a time when they all believed that wearing the word *Kansas* on one's chest provided an important advantage.

Ted O'Leary, a star from the 1930s, once said of Allen: "Somehow he convinced you that when you played for Kansas you were supposed to win. If you didn't it was a fluke."

Just this week, Greg Dreiling, the 7'1" senior from Wichita, said, "I didn't know who Phog Allen was, to tell you the truth. But with Naismith bringing the game here and things like that, it gets into your subconscious. You feel like you've got the breeding or something."

Evolution to Modern Era

The tradition has been preserved with adjustments to the times. Dick Harp, who succeeded Allen in 1956, recalled when his old boss came to the realization that more active recruiting was a necessity. Kansas State was offering a serious challenge. Allen had always looked ahead; he advocated that the basket be raised to a height of 12 feet, he predicted that a national college tournament would be a financial success in the days when it was in the red, and he foresaw the fix scandals of the early 1950s. In 1948, 40 years after his first season as coach, the Jayhawks were 9–15 and Allen decided something had to be done.

So he sent a message to the recruits. Harp remembered: "He told me to tell each of them that not only are we going to win the national championship in their senior year, but we're going to win the Olympics in their senior year. That was his challenge to himself to get back on top."

Allen suggested that Clyde Lovellette, the 6'9" center recruited from Terre Haute, Indiana, was better off at Kansas because the height of Mount Oread was good for his asthma. The fact is that Mount Oread is not high enough to stop a speck of Salinas dust from settling beneath a Kansas City eyelid. But Lovellette came, Kansas won the 1952 tournament, and seven Jayhawks played for the United States team that won the gold medal at the Helsinki Olympics.

And the demands increased. The Fieldhouse was completed. Allen reluctantly retired at the age of 70, just before Wilt Chamberlain's first varsity season. "With Wilt and four cheerleaders, you could win the national championship," Allen was quoted as saying, but the Jayhawks never did.

Togetherness for Brown

Chamberlain said last October that Kansas boosters paid him about $3,800, an amount that "would make it look like I was not worth very much" by current standards. Harp denied knowledge of the payments. The Jayhawks lost to North Carolina in triple overtime in the 1957 championship.

After Kansas lost to UCLA in the 1971 national semifinal, Coach Ted Owens received a telegram that read, "You couldn't coach a girls volleyball team."

Brown, who was hired away from the Nets in 1983, released Jo Jo White, twice an All-American and an assistant coach who some thought should have become head coach. Brown changed the housing policy that once called for players to live together. "I didn't like our guys being separated from the student body," Brown said. "I wanted them to be independent, to pick and choose their own friends rather than have me picking for them."

"I think it helped," said Danny Manning, the 6'11" sophomore, Big 8 conference player of the year who was named the outstanding player of the Midwest Regional. "We played together. We practiced together. We showered together. We ate together. That gets old. It gets like a brother and sister. You get into little fights."

"This year we split up," Turgeon said, "and we're just a lot closer team."

The 35 victories seem to have made everyone happy. The Waving of the Wheat—the arm-swaying ritual that must wait until victory is assured—has taken place with a giddy regularity. Twice this season the Jayhawks wore red uniforms instead of the usual blue. The reason: the 1952 champions wore red. Kurt Unruh, the head manager, said the red uniforms were packed for yesterday's departure for Dallas, but no decision has been made.

And Turgeon, among other Jayhawks, has shaved his hair into a flattop to complete a vow made long ago. They would do it if they reached the Final Four.

They may never pass this way again. "It's really weird," Turgeon said. "I never really considered myself good enough to play at KU. Now that I'm on the team, and I'm part of one of the best teams ever at KU, that makes it all the more special. When things are going bad sometimes I think about how lucky I am."

Joe Posnanski, *The Kansas City Star*

KU RETIRES CHAMBERLAIN'S JERSEY

Although he'd stepped foot in Allen Fieldhouse in the 1960s and '70s (including playing in an NBA exhibition game there) since playing for the Jayhawks, Wilt Chamberlain had not returned for any of the reunions or other celebrations. But on January 17, 1998, more than 40 years since he last donned a Kansas uniform, Wilt Chamberlain returned to Allen Fieldhouse. Award-winning writer Joe Posnanski explains why Chamberlain stayed away so long and what brought him back.

Wilt Chamberlain did not know how much they loved him.

See, he left Kansas a long, long time ago, in a different world, a different time, when the floor at Allen Fieldhouse was dirt, when black children and white attended different schools, before shot clocks, when Elvis had just begun rocking.

Chamberlain lost the most famous game in school history, triple overtime to North Carolina in 1957, and then he left, blazing. He would play for the Globetrotters, and he would score 100 points in an NBA game, and he would score 50 points a game for a season, and he would tell himself to slow down because it was too easy, and he would meet most of those 20,000 women, and he would become one of the most famous men on earth. He did not think of Kansas much. Who has the time?

"I've been away a long time," he told those Kansas players Friday when they gathered around him. "That's my fault. I just never got back." He did not know how much they wanted him back. He did not know how desperately they wanted to claim him as family, bring him in, hug him. No. They asked him to come back, sure. They asked him and asked him, and he never said no, but he never said yes, either. Who has the time? There was talk of bitterness, and maybe some of that bubbled inside Chamberlain. Maybe not. He never came back. He was busy being Wilt Chamberlain.

Funny thing, though, Saturday he did come back. He wore his old Kansas letter jacket. He sat with the students. He listened and nodded as radio voice Max Falkenstien told the crowd of Chamberlain's accomplishments, the 56 NBA records, all the points, all the rebounds, how nobody has ever dominated the game like Big Wilt, and the retired jersey unfurled, and the crowd stood, and the fans cheered, all of them, and Allen Fieldhouse shook, and Chamberlain clapped 19 times, then he tried to speak, but his voice was drowned by the sound. And he looked and saw children, and he saw college kids, and he saw people his own age, all of them, pounding the stands, clapping, shrieking.

And that's when it hit him.

And he began to cry.

"Rock chalk, Jayhawk," he said softly.

He did not speak long. There is not much a man can say after 40 years of being away. Especially when you think about how much life Wilt Chamberlain has lived. He left a skinny kid, barely more than 200 pounds, angry, frightened, disappointed, alone. He returned Wilt Chamberlain, dominant player, trailblazer, ladies' man, social critic, and, some would say, the best to ever play sports in America.

He did not speak long.

"Forty years ago, I lost a heartbreaking battle, toughest loss of my life, losing to North Carolina by one point in triple overtime," he said. "It was devastating because I felt like I let KU down." The fans screamed no. He raised his hand to silence them.

"But to come here today and feel the appreciation, the love and warmth." He stopped to catch his breath. The cheers lingered for a minute.

He raised his hands again. The noise slowly faded.

"I've learned in life that you have to take the bitter with the sweet. And how sweet it is." And they cheered him again. He raised his hands, but this time the noise would not fade. The building shook. Wilt Chamberlain was a Jayhawk again.

Here's what the folks at Kansas say about Wilt Chamberlain.

"He's got those python arms, man," Lester Earl says. "The only arms I've seen like that is Hulk Hogan."

"He's huge," Billy Thomas says.

"Huge," T. J. Pugh says.

"He's huge, but he's got small feet," Ryan Robertson says.

"Size 14 feet, man," Earl says.

"It's weird, those small feet," Robertson says. "That's what sticks with me."

"He's like a legend," Paul Pierce says. "I'll be able to tell my kids I saw him."

"I'll tell my kids I met him," Robertson says.

"Little tiny feet, man," Earl says.

"That's a big man," coach Roy Williams says.

"Looks like he can still play," Thomas says.

"I don't know that he's ready to come out and play with us," Pierce says. "I wouldn't go that far."

"They changed the game for him," Earl says. "He had to be the best."

"Big man," Robertson says. "Fills up a room."

Wilt Chamberlain signed autographs for more than two hours Saturday after Kansas beat Kansas State 69–62. Nobody expected it.

Nobody planned it. Chamberlain, overwhelmed by the moment, enjoying the cheers, happy to be home, turned to KU athletics director Bob Frederick and said, "I'll sign autographs." They set up a table at the free throw line, and the line went out the tunnel, halfway around the track, and Chamberlain sat in a chair too small for him and signed autographs for kids and parents and grandparents. He signed tickets and posters and hats and shirts and his autobiography and Kansas coffee-table books and popcorn boxes and dresses and basketballs and teddy bears and signs and Jerod Haase's book, *Floor Burns.*

He laughed for every little boy, every little girl, firmly shook hands with the big fellas, smiled for cameras, nodded whenever someone asked whether Wilt remembered the old days. "Time moves fast, my friend," he told one man from those days, and their eyes clicked.

"Good to have you home," the man said.

And Chamberlain kept staying, he kept signing, on and on, an endless line, and people kept wandering up to ask whether he had enough. Security guards asked whether they should shoo people away.

Old friends asked whether he needed any help. Chamberlain kept signing.

Roy Williams came out to shake his hand. "You've got a great team, Coach," Chamberlain said. "Really. They play hard." Cameras swirled around him. "In a day for old legends," one broadcaster said as the camera pointed at him (foreground) and Chamberlain (background), "Kansas needed some young stars." And Chamberlain kept signing, until the last person, shy as all of them, walked up, and Wilt Chamberlain carefully scripted his name by a picture of a younger man. "I looked good, didn't I?" he asked, and he got up, stretched his giant legs, flexed his python arms, and limped slowly out of Allen Fieldhouse, his number retired, his place in Kansas history back where it belonged.

"Thank you for coming back, Mr. Chamberlain," a woman said.

"Thank you," Wilt Chamberlain replied, "for letting me come home."

Dick Jerardi, *Philadelphia Daily News*

WHERE PHOG NEVER LIFTS

The 1996–97 season ended as one of the more disappointing in the decade. Along the way, though, the team linked itself with other great teams and fantastic seasons, as Dick Jerardi found out when he traveled to Lawrence for the KU–George Washington game in December.

Head out a mile or so east of Massachusetts Street, the main road through downtown Lawrence, where the parking is slanted to the meters that give you 90 minutes for a quarter and where the Granada Movie Theater shows Kansas basketball games live, and you come upon Lawrence Memorial Park Cemetery.

Just inside the gate is a huge monument to Dr. James Naismith, the inventor of basketball, the first basketball coach at the University of Kansas and its only coach with a losing record.

Inscribed in marble in front of the monument are the names of Kansas's coaches, a legacy that stretches from Naismith to today.

Naismith coached the Jayhawks from 1898 to 1907. One of his players was Dr. Forrest C. "Phog" Allen, a Lawrence native. The story about Allen goes like this: he told Naismith that he wanted to be a coach, and Naismith replied: "You don't coach basketball. You play it." Allen proved his mentor wrong, coaching it for 39 years at Kansas, winning 590 games there and 746 overall.

Allen retired in 1956 as the all-time winningest college basketball coach, until one of his players, Adolph Rupp of Halstead, Kansas, eclipsed him by winning 876 games as coach at Kentucky. Another of Allen's players, Dean Smith of Emporia, Kansas, who has won 858 games as coach at North Carolina, is likely to break Rupp's record late this season or early next season.

Ralph Miller, of Chanute, Kansas, played for Allen. He won 674 games at Wichita State, Iowa, and Oregon State. John McLendon, of Hiawatha, Kansas, who in 1936 was the first black man to graduate from Kansas with a degree in physical education, won 523 games as a coach at North Carolina College, Hampton Institute, and Tennessee

A&I, three of the south's traditionally black colleges. Each man is enshrined in the Naismith Memorial Basketball Hall of Fame in Springfield, Massachusetts.

Naismith is buried in the southern end of [Lawrence Memorial Park] Cemetery. Allen is buried across the street in Oak Hill Cemetery. The man entrusted with all this tradition, Kansas coach Roy Williams, finds that when he goes jogging, especially when a big game is scheduled that night, he often ends up at the cemeteries. He pats the grave markers.

The game might have been invented 105 years ago in Massachusetts, but, for 99 years, they haven't coached it or played it anywhere else quite like they do at Kansas.

Stroll down Naismith Drive, smack in the middle of campus, and there, with three stories that spread over what seems like several football fields and windows that make it appear like some mammoth classroom, sits Allen Fieldhouse. A week ago Wednesday, the relic was crammed to its 16,300-person capacity for a game between number one Kansas and George Washington.

In an era of arenas, centers, forums, and pavilions, Allen is something different: a true field house. It smells of popcorn even when there is no game. Its seats are a bit dirty, the paint is chipped in spots. In some spots, upper-level rows run smack into girders, leaving no place for a fan's head. Allen is scarred, lived-in, and absolutely wonderful, as good a college basketball atmosphere as there is anywhere. And it has been since its opening on March 1, 1955.

"I think it's the best place there is to play college basketball," Williams said. "Everybody says, 'Well, you should say that, you're the coach.' You can't picture it. You can't understand it unless you've been there."

Wilt Chamberlain played there, as did Clyde Lovellette, Danny Manning, and Jo Jo White. Kansas is 446–94 there, 109–11 under Williams. The Jayhawks have won their last 32 at Allen, 23 shy of the school record. A permanent banner high in the stands reads: "Pay Heed, All Who Enter—Beware of the Phog."

"It's in the rafters," said Jerod Haase, the starting shooting guard. "Looking at the banners and the people that have played here. One of my favorite quotes is [teammate] Scot Pollard saying, 'It's original air.' It's the air that Wilt breathed and the same air that all these great players breathed."

Kansas (9–0) recently earned its 1,600[th] victory. Only North Carolina and Kentucky have won more. But they needed Kansas guys to get there.

These Jayhawks are large, quick, experienced, and absolutely fearless.

If a ball is on the floor, the only danger is that they will hurt each other. They all dive. And their best player, point guard Jacque Vaughn, is still several weeks away from being ready. He suffered ligament damage to his right wrist in a pickup game at Allen on September 10 and underwent surgery. He was cleared to return to practice Tuesday.

No matter. Kansas wins. The Jayhawks always win.

Williams, 46, is in his ninth season. And in a twist in this tale, he is a North Carolina graduate who coached under Smith for 10 years.

No matter. He is 222–56 at KU. His team has won at least 25 games in each of the last seven seasons. The Jayhawks have won five of the last six Big 8 regular-season titles. The legendary Everett Case, of North Carolina State, and Williams are the only two coaches to win 200 games in their first eight NCAA Division I seasons. Only John Wooden, Rupp, Clair Bee, and Jerry Tarkanian have better career winning percentages than Williams.

Naismith. Allen. Rupp. Smith. Williams.

A native of Asheville, North Carolina, Williams wasn't born to basketball. It was an acquired taste.

"Baseball was my real love," Williams said. "I signed up [for basketball] in my eighth-grade year. First game, I remember it like it was yesterday. I passed it and the guy shot it and missed. The next time, I brought it down, the guy shot and missed. The third time, I brought it down again, passed it, and the guy shot and missed. So I said, 'Well, the heck with this.' The fourth time, I shot it and it went in. So, that was it. After that, a lot of them went in and I just fell in love with it."

Williams could have taken an engineering scholarship to Georgia Tech or accepted one of seven basketball scholarship offers from smaller schools. But he had decided he wanted to coach after ninth grade. His high school coach, Buddy Baldwin, suggested he go to North Carolina and learn from the best. He did.

And when Williams was ready, after playing on the freshman basketball team, umpiring softball games to help pay for college, and learning basketball as a student and an assistant, Smith suggested that his alma mater hire him. They did.

Williams knew little of the Kansas tradition before he took the job on July 8, 1988, just three months after Larry Brown and Manning gave KU its most recent NCAA championship. Now a history student himself who had been told of the tradition by Smith and Dick Harp—Wilt's coach at Kansas and an administrative assistant at North Carolina when Williams was there—Williams finds himself caught up in it.

"I'd never been on this campus until the night they offered me the job," Williams said. "I got here at dark, took the job, and thought, 'I haven't even seen what the place looks like.' So, the next morning my eyes were wide open."

In a time of coach as savior, coach as showman, coach as ugly American, Roy Williams is none of these. He's just one wonderful basketball coach—in both a strategy and people sense.

"He has a passion for the game of basketball," Vaughn said. "And he tries to give that passion to us every day. It's hard to imagine somebody having the uniqueness that he has as far as caring for an individual, not just on the basketball court. When he says his door is open, he really means it."

Nobody has ever questioned Williams's basketball IQ. Nor should they.

He has to be near the top of any list of college basketball minds. And nobody has questioned his life skills, either.

"I've watched a lot of coaching techniques," said Ron LaFrentz, a player at Northern Iowa, a coach, and the father of Kansas power forward Raef LaFrentz. "There is no vulgarity in his vocabulary. He's a class guy and he's very tough. I told Roy when Raef decided he was going to Kansas that I think, and I don't want to flatter myself or my wife, that we're sending you a good boy and I want you to make a man out of him.

"There's a certain amount of competitiveness that is there, he never got where he is right now by being docile. I have great respect for him. ... We were flattered to think that Roy Williams recruited our son as hard as he did to play for the University of Kansas."

Twenty minutes before the GW game, Williams strolled onto the floor with the sounds of "Roy, Roy" in his ears. Unlike many of his peers, he does not wait until the last minute to make a grand entrance. He just relaxes in his chair, arms over the backs of the chairs next to him.

"He's very genuine," said Pollard, he of the muttonchops and bizarre sense of humor. "The guy is almost perfect. He's honest from top to bottom. ... He never berates us and tells us we're idiots or anything.

"He tells us if we do something stupid that that was stupid, but he never says 'You are stupid.'"

Kansas basketball is understated and charming, Williams its perfect spokesman. As he took his team back to the locker room for final instructions, the students, arm in arm, swaying back and forth, began to sing softly, almost eerily. Close your eyes and you could have been in a monastery. The scene was heartfelt, out of another time and not to be missed.

And when they finished by chanting: "Rock chalk, Jayhawk, go K-UUUUUUU," you knew this was a place like no other.

"It's a very unique place," Vaughn said. "If you look from the outside, it doesn't have the fancy banners and surroundings. But there's a certain mystique when you walk in the building. ... There are so many things that were done 30, 40 years ago and you don't see that in too many places. ... It's special. That's the one thing about basketball here. It doesn't matter about your ethnicity or your race or your color or where you come from. The art of basketball brings so many people together."

Kansas blasted the Colonials, 85–56, centered around a 24–2 run that started with a perfectly designed out-of-bounds pass that led to a three-pointer at the halftime buzzer. All great teams win with runs.

Thus far, Kansas has blitzed LSU (18–0, to start the game), California (17–0), Virginia (16–2), Cincinnati (18–2), and UCLA (30–6).

The only thing Kansas has not done under Williams is win the last game.

In 1991, the Jayhawks upset Indiana, Arkansas, and North Carolina to get to the national championship game. But they lost to Duke. In 1993, they lost to North Carolina in the national semifinals. Last season, they couldn't make a shot in the Final Eight and lost to Syracuse.

"It's like Russian roulette," Williams said. "One chamber that's loaded, you're done."

Exactly. And nobody really understands just how hard it is to win those six games.

"Unless you've been on that bench, you have no clue," Williams said. "You can follow basketball as closely as possible."

Williams was an assistant on the 1982 North Carolina team that had Michael Jordan, James Worthy, and Sam Perkins. He knew all season they were going to win.

All of a sudden, with 40 seconds left in the championship game against Georgetown, the Tar Heels were down by one point.

"It was the first time the whole season that I thought we could lose," Williams said. "The enormity of that feeling at that time..."

Jordan made the jump shot, but Williams, up very late, thought how the Tar Heels were one missed jump shot away from not winning it.

When Williams arrived, the Jayhawks really weren't that close. Even though they had just won the national championship, the team was on probation for violations that occurred on Brown's watch. Kansas basketball was no easy sell.

"When we first got here, we couldn't get the top 25 kids in the country to even talk to us," Williams said. "Three years in a row, we picked the top three players in the country, but we couldn't get them to talk to us. Even as late as Chris Webber. He got us into his final 12."

But when he narrowed it to six, Kansas was out. "Now, Kansas is a player. Williams got into California when UCLA was down. The Californians loved Kansas and told their friends." The current 13-player roster has six players—including Vaughn, Pollard, Haase, and Paul Pierce—from California.

"Every other college coach is saying that's flat wheatfields and cornfields," Williams said. "We're saying, give us a chance, come and see. I tell them we're on this little oasis where basketball is the thing."

This Kansas team is good enough. The Jayhawks have a unique blend of players. They have a chance. It clearly is one of maybe 10 teams that can make it to the RCA Dome, in Indianapolis, and win the tournament.

Kansas has been to the Final Four 10 times, with two championships. Twice in the 1920s, the Jayhawks won a mythical national championship under Allen. Rupp played on those teams. In 1952, Allen won his only NCAA championship. Smith was a deep reserve. Brown and Manning won in 1988.

Kansas will win another championship. It might happen in 1997. It will happen under coach Roy Williams. And when it does, the coach can stop by the park and visit the men who were there at the beginning, the coaches who made coaches, the soul of the experience that is Kansas basketball.

Mike DeArmond, *The Kansas City Star*

ROOTS OF A RIVALRY

To call the Kansas-Missouri rivalry just a rivalry would be like calling Elvis Presley just a good singer. It is one of the most bitter rivalries in college athletics. In fact, it was so bad at one point during the late 1950s and early 1960s that there were discussions of ending the games between the two schools. The Star's Missouri beat writer, Mike DeArmond, with the help of Kansas beat writer Jason King, shares some of the history in this January 2002 article.

Where do we begin? Better yet, where did it begin, this Border War between Kansas and Missouri that on Monday night in Lawrence will boil over for the 244th time?

"It's just always been," said Norm Stewart, that storied player and former coach of Mizzou, who even now could make only the briefest of appearances in the stands at Allen Fieldhouse and be told not so kindly to "Sit down, Norm!"

"I loved that chant," Stewart says.

Stewart always looked at this series—which Kansas leads in overwhelming fashion with 153 victories and 90 losses—with an ever-humorous twinkle in his eye. But even he, who played for Missouri before coaching the Tigers for 32 seasons, can't pinpoint the origin.

Some say that, because Kansas won 30 of the first 34 games of a series that began in 1907, Missouri fans learned early to hate the Jayhawks. Of course, Missouri then returned the favor by winning 21 of the next 25.

Max Falkenstien, now in his 56th season as a KU broadcaster, traces the rivalry to the 1951 game when Kansas star Clyde Lovellette stomped his size-14 right shoe into the chest of MU's Win Wilfong.

"Ever since that day," Falkenstien said, "KU and Missouri has always been a tremendous rivalry.

"I don't think the years have changed anything."

Sure enough, the significance of Monday's showdown hasn't been lost on current KU and MU combatants. They understand how important it is, how fans on both sides of the border treat it as far more than just another date on the schedule.

"This is their life," Missouri senior Clarence Gilbert said. "This is what they dream of. This is everything to them, this Kansas and Missouri game.

"You've got to love it."

Stewart, reached by phone this week, first coached against the Jayhawks on December 30, 1967. Kansas beat Stewart's first Tiger team 63–47 in Kansas City. When Stewart finally stepped down, after the 1998–99 season, he was 33–41 in games against Kansas.

Stewart fared much better as a Missouri player against the Jayhawks. From his first year in 1954 through 1955 and 1956, when Stewart captained the MU basketball team, the Tigers won five of six games against KU.

Yet, falling back on one of his favorite stories, Stewart recalls the one game he did lose as a player to Kansas.

It was January 9, 1954. As Missouri arrived at old 2,200-seat Hoch Auditorium—precursor to Allen Fieldhouse—so did a near-blizzard of snow.

At halftime, when MU retired to its dressing room to receive words of wisdom from coach Wilbur "Sparky" Stalcup, the Tigers opened the door on an icebox.

"Somebody had raised the window in our dressing room," Stewart said, "and there was snow all over the floor.

"Spark immediately took the opportunity, for motivation, to tell us that Dr. Allen [Phog, the legendary KU coach] had left the windows up. Spark left the room then. And we had a vote: 'How many think it was Dr. Allen and how many think it was Spark trying to motivate us?'

"It came out a 6–6 tie."

Either way, motivation wasn't what the second half was about. Kansas beat Missouri 86–69.

To generations who trace their interest in MU-KU basketball back no further than the 14 seasons of Roy Williams as the Kansas coach, realize that there was actually a time when the meanest ol' son of a gun in the series might not have been Norm Stewart.

Phog Allen coached 48 seasons at four colleges from 1907 to 1956 and compiled a 590–219 record just in his years at Kansas. Beloved long before his death in 1974, Allen was truly hated by many in his native Missouri, where he was born within blocks of former U.S. president Harry Truman in Independence.

Allen never hid his belief that Columbia, home of the Tigers, was a backwater town compared to Lawrence.

"I noticed that Lawrence had wide, paved streets," Allen once said. "Columbia had muddy streets.

"The storefronts were different. Lawrence had all-glass fronts and the merchants were very progressive in appearance, while Columbia had many of their storefronts boarded up.

"I could see the difference, and I wanted to go to a place that was progressive."

In January of 1947, two days after Allen's Jayhawks lost to Missouri in Lawrence for the first time since 1930, Allen checked into a Kansas City, Kansas, hospital and took the rest of the season off.

Allen went down nearly fighting.

Stalcup had been working the officials during that game. According to accounts of the day, Allen walked over to the MU bench and pushed Stalcup, who was in his first game as an MU coach in Lawrence. Stalcup cocked his arm as if he was about to slug Allen but instead told the Phog to drift back over to his own bench.

Then there was the 1951 game, which Falkenstien alluded to. It was, perhaps, the closest this long and storied series came to blows. It took place in a Big 7 Conference Holiday Tournament game in Kansas City on December 30, 1951.

All heck—to put it mildly—broke loose in Municipal Auditorium when Lovellette stepped on Wilfong. Eventually, Lovellette approached the MU bench to try to help restore order by apologizing to Wilfong. Stalcup stood up, shook Lovellette's hand, then went to the public-address microphone and told the crowd: "The University of Missouri enjoys this rivalry with the University of Kansas."

Players from both teams shook hands. Lovellette and Wilfong hugged. After the game, which Kansas won 75–65, Allen said of Stalcup: "The night will never be too dark or stormy to do him a favor."

The most recent years of MU and KU basketball have been filled with plenty of dark and stormy nights and afternoons.

Just last season, unranked Missouri—behind Kareem Rush's 27 points—upset number three Kansas 75–66 in Columbia. In the return game in Lawrence, number 10 Kansas, with Drew Gooden leading five Jayhawks in double-figure scoring with 19 points, beat MU 75–59.

In each of the last six seasons, the teams have split the regular-season series. KU won a Big 12 Tournament rubber game in 1997. Kansas swept both games in 1995, and Missouri won both games in 1994.

In most of those games—even in 1994—Kansas was favored to beat Missouri. But the Tigers have made a tradition of upsetting the oddsmakers and the Jayhawks, perhaps never in more surprising fashion than when unranked MU topped number three Kansas 77–73 on February 10, 1996, in Columbia.

In Norm Stewart's final visit to KU, on January 24, 1999, Missouri won 71–63. Missouri was not ranked, and KU was number 19. That's the only time Missouri has beaten Kansas in its last seven trips to Lawrence.

But that, as they say, is history.

Another chapter is about to be written, Monday night at 8 PM, when number 18 Missouri takes on number two Kansas in ESPN's Big Monday national telecast.

"I don't know if *hatred* is the right word," said Falkenstien, who then cited a familiar refrain. "KU is a little unique in that it has two primary rivals. Missouri doesn't have that. Their only rival is KU. That's their big game every year."

Let the Border War begin.

William Gildea, *Washington Post*

WHERE BASKETBALL IS HISTORY

The University of Kansas has some of college's best traditions and tales. Shortly before the 1998 NCAA Tournament, William Gildea uncovered several of them for the following article.

Before he hurt his heel last spring, Roy Williams used to jog three miles down the east slope of the University of Kansas's hilltop campus and across the prairie to the Lawrence Memorial Park Cemetery and, directly opposite, to the Oak Hill Cemetery. In one is a monument to the "father of basketball"—Kansas's first coach, James Naismith. In the other is a modest marker to the "father of basketball coaching"—Kansas's second coach, Forrest C. "Phog" Allen. Williams, just the seventh coach in the school's 100 years of basketball and a superstitious sort, would touch each monument before his run back to campus.

Since his foot ailment, Williams doesn't make it quite as far as the cemeteries. No matter, Kansas began a season-long centennial basketball celebration in December by dedicating a memorial that Williams finds convenient to touch as he finishes his five-times-a-week run. That would be a nine-foot statue of Phog Allen on Naismith Drive outside Allen Fieldhouse. The field house, which seats 16,300 primarily on benches, is a limestone structure with a crimson roof like others on campus. But it contains enough steel to make it virtually indestructible, a source of satisfaction to some of its builders in the 1950s, who also considered it a haven from possible attack by foreign countries.

"I have no hesitation in saying that I don't want another place," Williams has said. "As long as I'm the coach I want it just the way it is." And Williams, now in his 10th season, has made it clear he isn't leaving any time soon, to the delight of Jayhawks fans who like stability and the fact that he's won more games than any other college coach this decade. This NCAA Tournament will be the ninth straight for his Kansas teams; they made Final Fours in 1991 and 1993.

A man of medium build and close-cropped gray hair, Williams, 47, affects a laid-back manner (sometimes altered by referees' calls). Sitting behind his office desk before a practice, he elaborated on his affection for his surroundings: "The first night walking in there onto the field house court, walking through the tunnel, I got cold chills. And 10 years later I still get cold chills every night that I walk out there. It's the greatest environment you can possibly have for college basketball. I loved being a high school player and I loved being a high school coach. And what Allen Fieldhouse is is just an old high school gym, the way I look at it."

In this centennial season of Kansas basketball, as the Jayhawks yearn to return to the Final Four after being denied a year ago in the round of 16 by eventual champion Arizona, almost every home game has meant a celebration.

"This has been an incredible year to have been at the University of Kansas," Ryan Robertson, a 6'5" junior guard, said recently. "Wilt Chamberlain came back and we retired his number, and that was huge. I didn't think it could get any bigger than that, but then we had our 100 years' ceremony. I'll never forget seeing all those old players and hearing them talk, and feeling what it's like to be a part of that tradition."

About 300 former Jayhawk basketballers returned for February 7–8, including Dean Smith, whose recommendation of his then-assistant at North Carolina landed Williams the Kansas job in 1988. A capacity crowd filled Allen Fieldhouse simply to see 57 of the 300 take part in the "legends" game; the varsity game against Missouri was played to another full house the next day. Ron Loneski, a teammate of Chamberlain in the '50s, said the weekend had the third-biggest impact on his life, behind his first of three tours of duty in Vietnam and the tragic death of his son.

Being inside Allen Fieldhouse can be affecting. Much is painted crimson or blue, the school colors. Championship banners hang from the ceiling, retired players' jerseys adorn the south-end wall, a banner warns opponents, "Pay Heed, All Who Enter—Beware of the Phog." Allen's ghost is said to help the home team in close games in the building where the Jayhawks have won 60 straight. Rabid students, many wearing "Phog Phanatics" T-shirts, intimidate foes with a game-long din following their pregame mantra known as the "Rock Chalk Chant," "Rock Chalk" being derived from the chalky limestone formations on the school's Mount Oread campus.

The chant goes, "Rock chalk, Jayhawk, KU," repeated three times, although it is virtually indecipherable in its best rendition by bleachers full of students. Teddy Roosevelt said that whatever exactly it was, [it was] the finest chant he'd heard.

Another sellout crowd applauded Kansas players on the afternoon of February 21 as they cut down the nets after a 71–54 victory over Iowa

State to clinch their fourth straight conference title (the last two of the Big 8 and the first two of the Big 12) and seventh in eight years. Each player, starting with 6'11" senior forward Raef LaFrentz, climbed a ladder and cut a piece of the net to keep. The penultimate snip went to a short, white-haired man named Max Falkenstien, who has broadcast Kansas games almost back to the time when Naismith lived. Billy Thomas, senior guard, cut the last strands and draped the remains of the net around his neck as he acknowledged the cheers.

The players then walked to the other end of the court, where a second ladder had been placed under that basket. Williams had wanted the second net taken down for symbolism. The drive for the conference title was signified as completed with the cutting of the first net, but the cutting of the second was a reminder of what they all wanted, to win the NCAA championship March 30 in San Antonio and to cut the nets at the Alamodome. Thomas remarked of Williams: "He said he wanted to signify a new ending to this season as opposed to the last couple seasons."

Two nights later, before and after an 83–70 victory over Oklahoma, Kansas seniors LaFrentz, Thomas, and C. B. McGrath, a reserve guard, were fêted. They'd completed a four-year home record of 58–0. School officials begged students not to throw roses during pregame festivities because they were hard to clean up from the court, but carnations or silk flowers were encouraged. People were urged, for safety, not to throw the flowers from the stands to the court but to give them to the cheerleaders and some others who would do it. So it was they who tossed the flowers gently through the sweetness of the popcorn-scented air.

The Pioneer

Ninety years before Dean Smith recommended Roy Williams, Amos Alonzo Stagg suggested to Kansas officials that they hire one of his former football players at Springfield College in Massachusetts—the good doctor Naismith, who invented basketball there in 1891. Licensed as a minister after studies in his native Canada, Naismith was brought west to join the faculty and head up the physical education department. He also preached in the community. Although it is said that he coached Kansas to victory in its first home game in 1898, he actually refereed it and took time during the contest to explain to an audience of about 50 what was happening. Naismith's seven-season record of 55–60, making him Kansas's only losing basketball coach, is better understood in light of his belief that the game was more a physical activity than a competition requiring a coach.

Phog Allen, one of Naismith's players, respectfully disagreed. When he succeeded Naismith for the 1907–08 season, he took coaching seriously and compiled a 590–219 record in 1907–09 and 1919–56. (In between those stints, he studied osteopathy and coached at

Central Missouri State.) Only a mandatory retirement age of 70 forced him from the bench against his wishes. Allen's players included Adolph Rupp—second only to another of his players, Dean Smith, in all-time coaching victories—and Clyde Lovellette, the hook-shooting Hoosier whom the extremely persuasive Allen talked out of the state of Indiana. Described in his day as a colossus, the 6'9" Lovellette presented Kansas its first NCAA title in 1952. (The Helms Foundation declared Kansas national champion in both 1922 and 1923.) Dean Smith was a reserve on the Lovellette team.

Allen was renowned for his pregame routine:

3:30—He met with his players downtown at the Eldridge Hotel, then had the players take a one-hour nap, "undressed and between clean sheets."

4.30—The team walked one mile.

5:30—The team ate a meal at the Jayhawk Café. The meal consisted of two slices of whole-wheat toast, a portion of honey, half a grapefruit, celery, and hot chocolate. There were no deviations or substitutions.

6:00—The players warmed their bare feet by a fireplace for 15 minutes.

Ninety minutes before game time, they took heated taxicabs to the arena. Thirty minutes before tip-off, they shot around on the court—but Allen allowed them to take only short shots. He feared if they took long shots before the game, they might try too many during the game.

Allen had been a baseball umpire, and to a sportswriter covering his games the arbiter sounded like a foghorn when he called the pitches. The writer thought "Phog" looked fancier in print than "Fog." Allen preferred to be called Doctor, because he was an osteopath; he became one in part because he wanted to treat his injured players himself so they'd get back in action quickly. Players called him "Doc."

As the '52 team was flying toward Seattle and the Final Four, its plane encountered turbulence. Lovellette calmly took some artificial flowers that were aboard and placed them in the coach's hands, saying, "Relax, Doc. If we crash, you've got a good suit on and they can take you right to the funeral home."

The Tuesday night following Kansas's "legends" weekend, Lovellette, back home in Terre Haute, Indiana, phoned Williams, who was on the air doing his radio show, to say that the ceremonies had made for the best time he'd ever had. "Roy is an emotional guy," said Dean Buchan, Kansas's sports publicist. "He had to think about it to keep from crying."

In 1957, the Chamberlain-led Jayhawks played probably the school's most famous game, a 54–53 loss to North Carolina in three overtimes for the NCAA championship. Much of the country listened on radio. It sounded remarkable, and a photographer, for one, who was situated under a table at the edge of the court in Kansas City, Missouri's, Municipal Auditorium vouched that it was. Nevertheless, broadcaster Falkenstien ranks that game somewhat below the mythical status it has attained in some places, most particularly on Tobacco Road. "It was a boring game when you get right down to it," Falkenstien said recently, "because it was so low-scoring."

Chamberlain might have done well to seek solace from Max back then. On his recent return to campus after an absence of 25 years, Chamberlain, wearing his old KU letter jacket, told a field house throng: "Forty years ago I lost a heartbreaking battle, toughest loss of my life, losing to North Carolina by one point in triple overtime. It was devastating because I felt like I let Kansas University down." The sustained applause told him otherwise. Wilt, the "Big Dipper" and self-proclaimed macho man, wept.

The nomadic Larry Brown, Kansas's sixth coach, stayed only five years, a blink in Kansas annals. But it was long enough for Falkenstien to write in his book *Max and the Jayhawks* that because of Brown's success, fans almost were ready to change the town name from Lawrence to Larry. Every morning Brown bought six glazed doughnuts for his office workers at the Carol Lee Doughnut Shop. He also hired one of his former players, Ed Manning, as an assistant coach, leading to the enrollment of Manning's son, the coveted and future All-American Danny. With the 6'11" Manning, Kansas won its second NCAA title, in 1988.

A photograph of that celebration shows Brown's dark-rimmed glasses at risk as his smiling face is scrunched into some taller person's shoulder—it is a happier-looking Larry Brown than the richer one seen these days on the Philadelphia 76ers' bench. Shortly after winning the NCAA Tournament, Brown called a news conference in the field house and declared he was, to the surprise of most, staying at Kansas. A month later the predictable happened after all. Brown left to become coach of the San Antonio Spurs.

The "No-Name"

Most Kansans believed another well-known coach would succeed him, but Dean Smith let his opinion be known by phoning KU athletics director Bob Frederick and recommending the Tar Heel Williams, born in Asheville, North Carolina, and educated at Chapel Hill. Besides having won 879 games at North Carolina, Smith came from Emporia, Kansas, and attended Topeka High before gravitating to "Phog" Allen. Smith's imprimatur counted. "Let's be honest," Williams said, "there's no way I would have gotten the job if it hadn't been for the respect that people around here have for him. I wasn't a household name. I was a no-name. I was barely a name in my own house."

Williams believed that last season might bring the Jayhawks another national championship. But when Arizona eliminated them from the tournament, he felt as distraught as Chamberlain once did. "It was probably the most painful feeling I've ever had relating to basketball," Williams said. "Not because of my own personal feelings. It was that I had six seniors—four of them were recruits, two of them were walk-ons—and, in my opinion, it was the perfect group of kids who were very talented. All six of them got their degrees in May, nobody had to go to summer school, and I'm very naïve—I thought it was just right for them to get to go to the Final Four.

"And when we lost to Arizona my whole thought process was, 'What can I say to these kids to relieve some of that pain because they're never going to go to the Final Four?' I hope Roy Williams"—he often speaks of himself in the third person—"will have more opportunities. But those seniors would not. And it was the...I don't know if I'm over it yet. You know, those kids meant so much to me. ... The relationships that I had with those kids and the feelings we had for each other almost made me feel like I was cheating every time I got a paycheck."

Williams was praised recently when he delivered a comeuppance to a Kansas City, Missouri, high school blue-chip prospect named JaRon Rush, who said that he might not attend Kansas after saying he would because "Roy substitutes too much." Williams announced he no longer was recruiting Rush.

"I've always said I want to recruit and coach the kind of kids I want to be around every single day," Williams said. "And last year's kids were the epitome of college coaching as far as I was concerned. A couple of weeks ago was just a very small blip. I have very definite feelings about how recruiting has soured over the last couple of years, with the involvement of outside people in the recruiting process, maybe much more than ever before. [But] I think the negative feelings that I had for that recruiting situation were a little ant compared to the biggest, biggest dinosaur in the world—that feeling of goodness that I had for last year's group."

This year's group includes a 6'8" sophomore named Lester Earl, a valuable substitute. He became eligible December 20 following his transfer from Louisiana State, where he remains the focus of an NCAA investigation because he reportedly received improper payments there. It is beyond the imagination of anyone who knows Williams to think that he's opened the Allen Fieldhouse doors to trouble, and he emphatically stated in his January 22 weekly news conference that Kansas did nothing improper while recruiting Earl when he was a high school senior and when he left LSU after one semester and transferred to KU. "Since the day we walked on this campus until the day we walk off, we'll never fail to do it the right way," Williams declared.

Unlike Kansas's powerful team of a year ago, this one, according to Williams, is still "developing," although its record is 33–3 and it is ranked third in the nation. But clearly, the coach and his players hope to win the NCAA Tournament. "We're one of those 12 to 14 teams that has a chance," Williams said.

LaFrentz agreed. "That's definitely something we're going to be pushing for," he said. "That's something this team can achieve."

Jim Caple, ESPN.com

JOURNEY TO THE HEART OF HOOP

In the days leading up to the 2003 Final Four, ESPN.com senior writer Jim Caple traveled to the four campuses to experience each one. Even though he wasn't in Allen Fieldhouse for a game, he found all that Lawrence has to offer. This is what he discovered.

As a young man, Bob Dole was a good enough basketball player that he set his sights on earning a scholarship to play basketball at Kansas. He never did, though. While serving in World War II, Dole suffered such horrible wounds that he returned from Europe paralyzed and in a full-body cast. He spent three years in and out of the hospital. He nearly died twice. He lost more than 70 pounds. And though he eventually recovered the use of his legs and left arm, his right arm remained so shattered that he couldn't lift it above shoulder height.

Yet Dole still so desperately wanted to play for Kansas that, as Richard Ben Cramer describes in his masterful book *What It Takes*, he would strap that useless right arm to a beam in the family garage and hang there, hoping to straighten it out so he could play basketball again. One day, he dangled from the beam so long that his family found him there unconscious.

Kansas basketball has that sort of power over people.

Is there a school with a longer, prouder basketball heritage than Kansas? Sure, there are a handful that have as rich a tradition as Kansas, but richer?

Kentucky? No. Remember, Adolph Rupp learned his game here at Kansas as a player and, when [Rupp] still was years away from allowing blacks on the Kentucky roster, Wilt Chamberlain was leading Kansas to the Final Four. Indiana? Maybe, but the man who invented the game didn't coach there (Bobby Knight just acted liked he did). Duke? Please. No amount of those "clever" Dukie chants can begin to touch the haunting "Rock chalk, Jayhawk" chant. North Carolina? Perhaps, but then again, Dean Smith played here, too.

How good a basketball school is Kansas? Look at it this way: the only coach with a losing record at Kansas was the man who nailed up the first peach basket, James Naismith.

"Answer this: How many basketball arenas are named after Jayhawks?" Rob Farha asked. "Rupp Arena. The Dean Smith Dome. Allen Fieldhouse. What does that tell you about Kansas basketball?"

Farha is the owner of the Wheel, a KU drinking institution since Chamberlain was a student here. (Larry Brown ate here several days a week and Roy Williams eats here Friday afternoon.) He bought it from John Wooden.

Okay, sure, he wasn't *that* John Wooden, but after experiencing Kansas as the third campus on my Final Four tour, I wouldn't have been *that* surprised if he was.

How big is Kansas basketball? When the Jayhawks returned from winning the West Regional late last Saturday night, thousands of fans showed up at Allen Fieldhouse at three in the morning to welcome them. "Of course," one student said when I visited the Pi Kappa Phi fraternity Wednesday, "half of them don't remember being there."

But it wasn't just drunk college students. Parents woke up their children, got them out of bed, and brought them to the gym to pay their proper respects.

This stuff is barely even worth mentioning at KU, where the morning after a game, students head to Allen Fieldhouse to go through a lottery that establishes their spot in the waiting line for the *next* game. But there's a catch. Someone from every student group with a number must be present inside the field house from six in the morning until 10 at night *every day* until the game. Roll is called regularly, and if you aren't there, you've lost your space.

"It's surprisingly civil, too," senior Kevin Seaman says. "It's not sanctioned by the university, or at least not as far as I know, but everybody just goes along with it. They don't need any police to keep us in line.

"Roy Williams is always at the field house, and he always takes time and always treats us with such respect. One time, he came out and showed a group of us the locker room. He brings us pizza. He brings us donuts."

If all this sounds insane, consider that in the old days there wasn't the 10:00 PM to 6:00 AM grace period. Students had to be at the field house 24 hours a day, morning, noon, and night. And no matter the weather, they weren't allowed inside, either.

How big is Kansas basketball? At the Hawk, the eight-decade-old bar down the block from the Wheel, the jukebox plays the Rock chalk, Jayhawk chant.

Rock chalk, Jayhawk, K-U...

The Jayhawk—so revered that Kansas basketball players aren't allowed to step on its image in the center of their locker room—is everywhere at KU. There's the main drag, Jayhawk Boulevard (which runs parallel to the old Oregon Trail). And there is the Jayhawk statue in front of Strong Hall. And there are the Jayhawk logos on the walls and floors throughout the Union. And there are all the Jayhawks on the caps and shirts of thousands of students.

And then, of course, there is the Jayhawk mascot itself, the big goofy bird that looks like Woody Woodpecker on steroids.

The current Jayhawk is in his second year, and he would like to continue but isn't sure how many years of eligibility he has remaining. "I think I could keep going if I went to grad school," the Jayhawk says, "but it's a little fuzzy whether I'm considered a student-athlete or just another employee of the university."

Even if he has eligibility, he must survive the intense audition that takes three days and includes one afternoon in the costume spent learning cheers and moves. "They'll yell, 'Your tail is on fire!' and you have to show how you would react to that."

The Jayhawk is so popular that KU fans occasionally request its presence at their weddings. "We usually come in during the reception, and then play the fight song and meet and greet people," the Jayhawk says. "I don't kiss the bride, they mostly kiss us on the beak.

"I've heard we've gone to funerals, too, but that was before my time. I think *that's* a little frightening."

It isn't easy being red and blue, though. The temperature can get as high as 120 degrees inside the Jayhawk suit, so you need to stay in shape. You certainly don't want a weak mascot in the Big Dance. Look what happened to the Oregon Duck, who had his headpiece torn off by the Utah State mascot in the tournament's first round.

The Jayhawk swears it won't happen to him. "I could take the Duck."

Maybe, but what about the Stanford Tree?

"Last year during the second round of the tournament when we played Stanford, I put a couple KU stickers on the tree and he didn't even know about it. He never noticed until someone told him about it at the end of the game, and then he was pretty mad. So, yeah, I could take him."

How about Pete Purdue, the Boilermaker?

"Pete's a pretty big guy. I'd like to see that fight. It would be tough, and it would take a couple rounds, but I could take him."

Rock chalk, Jayhawk, K-U...

Maybe it's the Final Four. Maybe it's the 85-degree weather. Maybe it's the trees blooming across the gorgeous campus. But whatever the reason, these Jayhawks are the friendliest people on earth. One student chased me down on Jayhawk Boulevard to invite me to his fraternity. A minute later, Molly Kocour invited me to the Kappa Alpha Theta house.

I swear, this never happened to me when I was in college.

The favorite woman I met Wednesday, though, was Claudine (Scottie) Lingelbach, who was among the fans who cheered on the team as it left for New Orleans. Lingelbach has been a Jayhawks fan since 1940, when she was an unmarried freshman named Claudine Scott and a member of KU's Jay-Janes cheer squad.

Following her freshman year at KU, she volunteered for the WAVES (Women Accepted for Voluntary Emergency Service) and was assigned as a staff assistant to the Joint Chiefs of Staff. Her job was delivering top-secret documents between the war department and the White House and, as such, she was one of the few people privy to the most important secrets of the war, including the date of the D-Day invasion of Normandy.

"The night before, I knew it was going to take place so I asked them to give me a call as soon as it started," she said. "I received the call and I immediately phoned my parents. I said, 'Turn on your radio. Something big is happening.'"

When the war ended, she married her University of Kansas boyfriend, Dale Lingelbach, who had been so severely injured fighting in the liberation of France that his recovery took two years. "So I don't have much patience with the French right now," she says.

At least Dale Lingelbach came back alive. The interior of the campanile that rises off Memorial Drive is lined with the names of the KU students who died in World War II. The union building and the football stadium are dedicated to the students who died in World War I. Just down the road from all three is a Vietnam memorial.

"I've always found it so sad that you can stand in one spot, right by where you parked, and you can almost see all the war memorials from there," Lingelbach says, as her voice cracks and she fights to hold back tears. "I had hoped we wouldn't have had to build any more war memorials."

Meanwhile, in front of Strong Hall are new bright yellow ribbons that KU Chancellor Robert Hemenway tied around two trees Wednesday afternoon. Hemenway estimated 30 KU students are serving in Iraq, a total that doesn't include assistant basketball coach Joe Holladay's son, Matt, who is there as well.

"We gather together to make visible our feelings of support for all U.S. servicemen and women," Hemenway said. "But we hold especially close to our hearts those students, staff, and alumni who would rather be spending this beautiful spring day on Jayhawk Boulevard, studying for finals or preparing for the Final Four.

"To them we say, 'We treasure you. We value your enormous personal sacrifice, and we look forward to a day when we can welcome you home to Lawrence.'"

Rock chalk, Jayhawk, K-U...

As Williams thanked the fans and boarded the bus Wednesday, the biggest question was whether the man with the highest winning percentage in school history will return to Lawrence. North Carolina needs a coach. Williams went to North Carolina and he doesn't get along with the Kansas athletics director, but would he really leave KU?

Lingelbach dismissed the possibility with a wave of her hand. It can't happen. The rest of the fans around her were just as certain (though the boys on Frat Row weren't so sure). Fiercely proud of their town, their school, and their program, KU fans can't think of a reason why Williams would go elsewhere.

Kansas is the geographic center of the United States and folks here consider Allen Fieldhouse to be the center of the universe.

The gym opened in 1955 and other than a few concessions to the modern age, it still appears as rooted in that era as fins on a Cadillac and *I Love Lucy* reruns. It has survived everything from the widening of the key to nuclear war itself (KU and Lawrence served as the setting for the post-apocalyptic movie *The Day After*).

The limestone exterior is darkened by soot. The paint is cracked and fading on the seats. There aren't any luxury suites. And it's absolutely beautiful. It's like Wrigley Field, only with championship banners. Why, it's so old-school that there's a Longines clock on the wall. You expect to see players in Chuck Taylors and tight satin shorts run from the locker room and start practicing two-handed set shots.

When I walked in Wednesday, the lights were off, the stands and court were deserted, and the Jayhawks won't play here again for seven months, but that was all right. The banners were there. The hardwood was there. The history was there. The spirit of Kansas basketball was there, real enough you could almost hear Phog Allen's whistle blowing during line drills.

How special is Kansas basketball? I'm not saying it's worth hanging from a beam until you pass out, and I'm not saying it's worth wearing a 120-degree bird costume and setting your tail on fire. But had someone started the Rock Chalk chant when I was inside Allen Fieldhouse, I think I would have grabbed a sleeping bag, cleared a spot in the hallway, and camped out in the ticket line for next season.

Joe McGuff, *The Kansas City Star*

SPORTING COMMENT

As a longtime columnist and editor at The Kansas City Star, *Joe McGuff was a fan favorite with his humorous and poignant "Sporting Comment" columns. The one he wrote on September 17, 1974, at the passing of Phog Allen is both a wonderful tribute to Allen and a display of why McGuff was one of the Midwest's most beloved writers. McGuff, who's largely responsible for the Royals being in Kansas City, passed away during the compiling of this book.*

Dr. Forrest C. Allen, who died yesterday at the age of 88, was one of basketball's all-time great coaches. He was also a football coach, an athletics director, an osteopathic physician, a colorful phrase maker, and a man drawn to controversy because of his strong convictions.

His activities were so wide-ranging that his file in the *Star* library fills nine envelopes, the greatest number for any sports figure. The first clipping is dated 1905 and reads, "Forrest Allen of Independence, Missouri, manager of the K.C.A.C. basketball team last year, has enrolled at the law school of the University of Kansas. He does not expect to do much in football this year, but he will be making a good basketball team at KU this winter."

A man as strong-minded and as outspoken as Allen was certain to have enemies. His eastern critics sometimes called him the Big Wind of the West and the Kansas Hayshaker, but in verbal exchanges Doc, as his players called him, gave much more than he got. His flair for phrasemaking made him a favorite with sportswriters.

One time in a Kansas City speech he attacked Colonel Harry Henshel, then chairman of the U.S. Olympic Basketball Committee, saying: "Colonel Harry Henshel—he's probably a colonel in the Brooklyn band."

Henshel was so incensed that he filed a libel suit.

"You have popped off one time too many," he fumed in replying to Allen. "I intend to make you pay dearly for one indiscretion too many." Allen filed a countersuit, but later both suits were dropped.

The AAU [Amateur Athletic Union] was Allen's favorite target. He attacked it, saying, "The AAU is neither amateur, athletic, nor a union. It is an eastern clique." He also said, "The AAU is an archaic, decadent, high-handed, heterogeneous oligarchy." He once sneered, "I like the AAU about the same way that a fellow likes garlic for dessert." He called Olympic officials "quadrennial trans-oceanic hitchhikers."

Before he had big men on his teams, he referred to them as "mezzanine-peeping Toms." Allen campaigned for years to have the baskets raised to 12 feet and once said in frustration, "For some strange reason the height of the basket has become somewhat sanctified, like motherhood."

When one of his centers, B. H. Born, failed to hustle enough to suit him Allen observed, "Born stood around like a Christmas tree, and out of season at that." In a game at Colorado Born fouled out and was hooted as he left the court. Later Allen said, "During those frenzied moments at Boulder my mind kaleidoscopically swept across ages past wherein I could see a captive and tortured prisoner being fiendishly dealt with at the hands of his heathen gloaters."

Allen Berated Eastern Basketball

When a basketball scandal broke out in the East Phog commented, "There are a lot of rotten eggs in eastern basketball, but we only smell them occasionally when one gets broken."

Speaking on the subject of sportsmanship he said, "The father who takes his son to a basketball game and boos the officials is teaching that son the principles of Bolshevism and Communism."

Among Allen's attributes was his sense of humor. When he was asked why Clyde Lovellette, the giant center from Terre Haute, Indiana, had enrolled at Kansas, Allen explained that Lovellette had come to Mount Oread because of his asthma. "The poor boy suffers from asthma simply terrible back there," Phog said. When Wilt Chamberlain announced that he would enroll at Kansas, Phog dryly observed, "I hope he comes out for basketball."

Allen had an inventive mind, and he was willing to take risks and try new things while men with less vision hung back and carped at him. As early as 1924 Allen backed a plan for having two varsity teams in basketball, saying such an approach would provide competition for a greater number of athletes and minimize the overemphasis that was developing in athletics. As collegiate athletics grew bigger and scandals developed, he proposed the establishment of a czar to deal with illegal activities.

Allen was largely responsible for the construction of Memorial Stadium on the KU campus, although when it was built critics called it Phog's Folly, claiming it was too large. When Allen Fieldhouse was being planned, Phog insisted that it have 20,000 seats. A strong movement developed to limit the seating capacity to 12,000, but Phog finally effected a compromise at 17,500. Another of Allen's accomplishments was the establishment of the Kansas Relays.

Many of the rule changes and innovations that Allen campaigned for in basketball have come to pass. His major disappointment was his inability to sell his peers on the merits of the 12-foot basket. But he did succeed in keeping the dribble in basketball at a time when the rules committee had limited movement to a single bounce in an effort to curb roughness.

Allen Showed Great Flexibility

It was said of Allen that while he may not always have been right everyone always knew where he stood. Yet for a man of such strong convictions he showed an amazing flexibility in his personal relationships and his coaching.

For years Allen disliked Sparky Stalcup, the Missouri basketball coach. Their relationship changed completely in the course of one game at the Municipal Auditorium. Lovellette stepped on Missouri's Win Wilfong, and for a few moments a riot seemed to be in the making, but Stalcup personally calmed the crowd, and from that time until Stalcup's death he and Allen were close friends.

In his coaching Allen changed with the times and proved that he could win with all types of personnel. He coached for 39 years at Kansas and won 24 conference championships.

George Mikan of DePaul was the first big man to dominate collegiate basketball, but Allen would have pioneered with the big man except for a freak accident. In the late 1920s he had a center who stood approximately 6'10", but the young man drowned in a freak summer accident without ever playing for KU.

Ted O'Leary, a forward whom Allen ranked as one of his all-time great players, recalls that in the '30s Kansas played a rather informal style of basketball that stressed the skill of the individual.

"We didn't have any plays, except for out-of-bounds plays," O'Leary recalls.

In the '40s the introduction of the block and the pick changed basketball, and Allen changed with the times.

When Mikan and Bob Kurland of Oklahoma State, then Oklahoma A&M, established the era of the big man, Allen recruited Lovellette, who in the early '50s was the most dominant player in the history of collegiate basketball. After Lovellette graduated Allen proved his coaching genius by taking a relatively small team and going to the NCAA finals in 1953, losing the championship game to Indiana by one point. The success of Allen's team was predicated on quickness and the use of the half-court and full-court press, which at the time was a newly emerging technique in college basketball.

When Wilt Chamberlain became the most sought-after player in the country Allen recruited him for KU, but unfortunately Allen was forced to retire before Chamberlain's sophomore year.

While Allen's technical competence was extraordinary, perhaps his greatest asset as a coach was his ability to motivate players and establish a winning attitude. "Somehow he convinced you that when you played for Kansas you were supposed to win," O'Leary says. "If you didn't, it was a fluke. He was a very enthusiastic, positive man, and he made you share his enthusiasm."

And today all who knew him share a great sense of loss.

Jason King, *The Kansas City Star*

JAYHAWK TO THE MAX

In the introduction for this book, longtime broadcaster Max Falkenstien wrote that he's not necessarily a part of the tradition or history of Kansas basketball. Most, if not all, fans would disagree. So, in much the same way that there was no other way to lead off this book than with Dr. James Naismith, there doesn't seem to be any other way to close it than with an article on Falkenstien, who, after 60 seasons behind the microphone, retired at the end of the 2005–06 basketball season. The following article by Jason King on March 1, 2006, the day of Falkenstien's final game at Allen Fieldhouse, helps show why Max was so good for so long.

He's got a hankering for ham and macaroni, but something forces Kansas's most beloved Jayhawk to stop before he ever reaches the grocery store deli.

Max Falkenstien has already had lunch here once this week, but somehow he missed the poster near the Lawrence Hy-Vee salad bar.

"Autograph Signing: Tomorrow 5–7! Come Meet Max!"

Resting nearby is a bundle of white T-shirts bearing Falkenstien's image. Soon, he figures, he'll have signed each one, along with hordes of pictures, pennants, bobbleheads, and basketballs. Falkenstien smiles and points at the poster.

"Can you believe it?" he said. "No one even told me about this. I don't mind doing it, but golly, I just don't understand all this fuss. It really is amazing, isn't it?"

Yes, Max, it really is.

Not the fuss, but the feat.

Kansas's home finale against Colorado tonight will mark the final time Falkenstien, 81, broadcasts a game at Allen Fieldhouse. Falkenstien announced last summer that the 2005–06 season would be his last in a 60-year career that culminated with his induction into the Naismith Basketball Hall of Fame.

Now, with only a handful of games left to call, the man who spent his life describing the achievements of others suddenly finds himself on the receiving end of the praise.

Kansas will honor Falkenstien tonight during a halftime ceremony, when thousands of fans are expected to don the T-shirts that read: "Thanks Max: 60 Years!"

Even at opposing Big 12 arenas, Falkenstien has received standing ovations when recognized by the public address announcer. Every day, it seems as if someone else is marveling at his longevity.

"He may not have been a player, but Max still ranks as one of the greatest people to grace that arena," ESPN commentator Dick Vitale said. "When someone tests time, that's a sign of greatness. Obviously, this is a man who has tested time beyond the norm."

Wilt Chamberlain was only nine years old when Falkenstien called his first game back in 1946. Roy Williams and Bill Self? Heck, they weren't even born.

In all, Falkenstien has broadcast more than 1,750 basketball games. He's been behind the mike for 11 of KU's 12 Final Four appearances and helped make the call for the Jayhawks' national title victories in 1952 and 1988.

Kansas fans say they can't imagine tuning into a game and not hearing good ol' Max—which may be why so many of them are pleading with him to stay.

"People keep begging me to change my mind," said Falkenstien, now enjoying his lunch in a nearby booth. "They keep asking me why I'd want to quit."

He rests his knife and fork on the table and looks away.

"I'm not sure I do want to quit, to tell you the truth," Falkenstien said. "But I don't know. I guess...

"I guess it's just time."

One of the most legendary careers in the history of college sports broadcasting began in a high school biology class.

"Boring as it sounds, one of our teachers took us over to the campus radio station at KU so we could broadcast our biology class on the air," Falkenstien said. "Each of us only had a minimal amount to say.

"After it was over, the lady in charge of the KU station said, 'Have you ever thought about going into radio? You have a really nice voice.'"

Just like that, Falkenstien had discovered his calling.

By the end of his junior year, Falkenstien had been hired as a 17-year-old announcer/disc jockey at WREN in Lawrence, before the station moved to Topeka. He joined the military shortly before the end of his freshman year of college and was later transferred into the Army.

Even during his time in the service, Falkenstien found himself acting as the master of ceremonies when guests and entertainers came through—anything he could do to get behind the microphone.

"I kept thinking, 'If I ever get out of this alive, broadcasting is what I want to do,'" Falkenstien said.

As part of the Signal Corps, Falkenstien's unit was training to sail from Seattle to Japan in the second wave of the invasion of Japan during World War II.

"But then President Truman dropped the atomic bomb, and they canceled our orders," he said. "That may have saved my life."

Falkenstien returned from the war in 1946 intent on continuing his career in the broadcast business. Shortly after resuming his job as an announcer at WREN, his station manager asked him if he'd like to be the commentator for a first-round NCAA Tournament game in Kansas City.

Falkenstien had never called a sporting event before. Still, he didn't hesitate when given the opportunity.

Thus, on March 18, 1946, 21-year-old Max Falkenstien called his first ever Jayhawks game, when Kansas took on eventual national champion Oklahoma A&M.

"Unlike some people who start off doing Great Bend versus Shawnee Heights High, I started off with an NCAA playoff game," said Falkenstien, who had reenrolled at KU.

"I went to class the next week and my math professor said, 'I listened to the game and you made me feel like I was right there.'"

That was all Falkenstien needed to hear.

At 5'8", Falkenstien's hoops career never extended past the playground. But he always had a love for basketball—especially Kansas basketball.

Not that Falkenstien had much of a choice. His father, Earl, was the business manager for KU's athletic department at the same time Falkenstien was entering the radio business.

A close friend of legendary coach Phog Allen, Earl Falkenstien can be seen in a team picture taken of the Jayhawks when they arrived back from Seattle after beating St. John's for the 1952 NCAA title.

Before each and every home game, Earl would stand with young Max as players made "the walk" from Robinson Gymnasium to Hoch Auditorium. Don Ebling, Ralph Miller, Fred Pralle. Falkenstien had his favorites, just like any kid.

"They always had towels around their necks," Falkenstien said. "They seemed so huge and mysterious. The kids all idolized them, just like they do with the players now."

From that point on, Kansas basketball would play a major role in the rest of Falkenstien's life. Instead of looking at the Jayhawks players and coaches as heroes, he began calling them his friends.

Falkenstien golfed with Self, Williams, Larry Brown, and Ted Owens. Dick Harp was one of his closest acquaintances. Former greats such as Clyde Lovellette, Bill Hougland, and Bill Lienhard still keep in touch with Max. So, too, does Al Correll, the first African American team captain in KU history.

"The treasure of my career," Falkenstien said, "is the relationships I formed with these players and coaches."

Falkenstien said his proudest moment was calling KU's national title victory in 1952. That was before the television age, so Falkenstien's voice was the only way people across Kansas could track the game from Seattle.

He also likes to recall Kansas's other national championship, which came in 1988 against Oklahoma at Kansas City's Kemper Arena.

Falkenstien said Danny Manning—the star of that team—is the best player he ever covered. That's a mouthful, considering Falkenstien worked through the Wilt Chamberlain era at KU.

"There was so much going on after that game," Manning said Tuesday. "But I still remember how I kept hearing Max's voice in the hallway. He kept saying, 'We did it! We did it!' We always looked at Max like he was a part of the team."

As many fond memories as Falkenstien has made, there are somber ones, too. He recalls seeing an "ashen-faced" Jerod Haase in the elevator before KU's 1997 loss to Arizona in the second round of the NCAA Tournament.

"You could tell he was in so much pain because of his wrist," Falkenstien said. "That loss was one of the toughest ever to take."

And even tougher was the decision by Williams in 2003 to leave Kansas after 15 years so he could return to North Carolina, his alma mater. Upon hearing the announcement, Falkenstien said he felt "sick."

"I could very well be wrong," Falkenstien said. "But I had the feeling that as soon as Roy made the announcement, he felt like he'd made a terrible mistake. But there was no turning back."

Still, Williams and Falkenstien remain good buddies. The two talked as recently as Monday.

"I know he'll hate this word, but Max is lovable," Williams said. "I always knew he cared about me and about people. When he's asking you about a tough time, he's doing it because he cares about how you feel. He cares about your answer.

"He's really listening to you instead of trying to just pick out one sentence that he might be able to use for a sound bite. That's why everyone loves him so much."

Indeed, Falkenstien has loads of friends—many of whom he's never even met.

Like any avid fan, Kansas guard Stephen Vinson said he grew up watching the games on television. Thing was, he always turned down the volume on the set so he could listen to Max and Bob Davis call the game on the radio.

The practice is one that's become common among KU faithful.

"His voice makes you comfortable," Manning said. "He sounds like he's your neighbor from next door or your grandfather or just your good friend telling you a story."

Former KU assistant Jerry Green said he, too, understands why Falkenstien's vocal cords make him so endearing to people he's never met.

"Max is like Elvis," said Green, who's now on the staff at Oklahoma. "He hasn't lost his voice. It's there and in great shape.

"People have enough problems of their own, so they don't need more by being associated with a negative person. He's always been the crystal-clear image of a person having fun and enjoying life."

Falkenstien has plenty of reasons to have such a cheerful attitude. He's been married to his college sweetheart, Isobel, since 1949. The couple has two children—Jane and Kurt—who were always supportive of their father's career choice.

Even though Falkenstien spent much of his life on the road, he always made sure to make family a priority.

Jane remembers putting a transistor radio under her pillow so she could listen to Dad's broadcasts. Kurt relished the times he got to sit with his father on press row at the Big 8 Tournament in Kansas City. To this day, Isobel still packs Max's travel bag before road trips.

"He treats his regular life just like he does basketball," Isobel said. "He's fair and positive and always optimistic. I think that's refreshing to people. They like that kind of attitude instead of one that's always critical."

So synonymous with KU basketball is Falkenstien that athletic director Lew Perkins is insisting that he continue to contribute to the university in some form or fashion. Maybe he'll do voice-overs for historical videos; perhaps he'll return for special presentations.

Falkenstien says he'll find a way to stay involved. But Bob Davis, his broadcast partner since 1984, knows it will never be the same.

"It's sounds corny, but Max is a pioneer in the radio business," Davis said. "Without even having an idea of what it was about, he just plunged in and started doing it.

"It's going to be tough to lose him. For the last 22 years, I've been to every KU football and basketball game and sat next to the same friend. I know the broadcasts will be different, but I hope they stay fun.

"That's what I hope Max and I have been able to do. I hope we've made the broadcasts fun."

Speaking of fun, we can't end this story without telling you a few Max stories, because there are so many.

"Wherever he goes," Davis said, "humor seems to follow."

Williams remembers a trip to Sea World in Florida where Falkenstien encouraged Williams to feed some of his popcorn to a hungry dolphin.

"I'm sure no one would mind," Falkenstien told the coach.

Moments later, a park employee was screaming at Williams.

"He was yelling, 'Hey, you idiot, what are you doing? Are you trying to kill my dolphins? You can't do that!'

"I turned to the side where my old buddy, Max, had been standing, and he wasn't there anymore. He was retreating so fast, he was about 50 yards away looking over his shoulder."

A few years ago in Oklahoma, Kansas players were forced to evacuate their hotel when someone triggered a fire alarm.

"Max came downstairs and walked outside in this long robe," Self said. "I told him he looked like Hugh Hefner."

Reporters like to joke with Falkenstien about the time he tried to bite into a tamale during a pregame meal in Lubbock, Texas. After watching for several minutes as Falkenstien tugged at the food with his teeth, someone finally informed him that it helps to remove the husk first.

That's right, in 81 years, Falkenstien had apparently never had a tamale.

Back at the grocery store, Falkenstien has finally finished his ham and macaroni lunch. In a few minutes, he'll polish off a doughnut—his reward after a few strenuous games of handball a few hours earlier.

Falkenstien plays three times a week, which is also about how many times he hits the golf course. On days that he doesn't go for a two-mile walk, Falkenstien takes a six-mile round-trip bike ride to Clinton Lake.

He tried drinking just once during his days in the service, but he became queasy and hasn't touched the stuff since. Falkenstien has a soft spot for burgers and barbecue, but his exercise pattern has helped keep him healthy.

"The lifestyle and the traveling...none of it bothers him," Falkenstien's daughter, Jane, said. "He can fall asleep anywhere, and nothing he eats affects him. He's going as strong as ever."

Which makes you stop and think: does Falkenstien really want to retire? He's told people all year that "60 is a nice round number." Other than that, there doesn't seem to be much wearing him down.

"At this point," Falkenstien said, "it's too late to turn back."

Falkenstien gets up and heads toward the front of the store before stopping one last time near the poster and T-shirts. Watch him, listen to him. All these interviews. All this fuss. Used to be that Falkenstien despised this kind of attention, mainly because he never understood it.

But now, after 60 years, you sense he's finally starting to realize just how special he's become.

"I make mistakes," Falkenstien said. "I mess up. I say dumb things sometimes. I've never thought I was great at this. Yet all these people are telling me how it won't be the same around here without me."

Falkenstien smiles gently, gives a mild shrug, and winks.

"Hey, maybe they're right," he says. "Maybe it won't."

NOTES

The publisher has made every effort to determine the copyright holder for each piece in *Echoes of Kansas Basketball.*

"The Passion, the Intensity, the History" *The Kansas Century,* copyright © 1997 by David Halberstam. Reprinted with permission of Andrews McMeel Publishing. All rights reserved.

Reprinted with permission of the *Boston Globe:* "The Wizard of Kansas" by Ian Thomsen, copyright © March 28, 1986; "Kansas Is the Big One" by Jackie MacMullan, copyright © April 5, 1988.

Reprinted courtesy of CBS Sportsline: "Kansas Coach Free to Be Him-Self" by Dennis Dodd, copyright © March 15, 2005. Reprinted with permission.

"Collison a Kansas Classic" As published in the *Chicago Sun-Times.* Author: Jay Mariotti. Copyright © 2003 by Chicago Sun-Times, Inc. Reprinted with permission.

"Kansas Is No Piece of Art; It's Just a Nice Piece of Work" by Skip Myslenski, copyrighted © 2/14/1990, Chicago Tribune Company. All rights reserved. Used with permission.

Reprinted courtesy of ESPN.com: "Journey to the Heart of Hoop" by Jim Caple, copyright © April 3, 2003. Reprinted with permission.

Reprinted with permission of *The Kansas City Star:* "Clyde's Touch with the Ball Makes Him a Great among Giants" by Bob Busby, copyright © March 30, 1952; "Sporting Comment" by Joe McGuff, copyright © September 17, 1974; "KU Was Team Left Standing" by Gib Twyman, copyright © March 31, 1991; "At 21–0, KU Wanted Gold" by Blair Kerkhoff, copyright © February 1, 1997; "KU Retires Chamberlain's Jersey" by Joe Posnanski, copyright © January 18, 1998; "Roots of a Rivalry" by Mike DeArmond, copyright © January 27, 2002; "End Game" by Wright Thompson, copyright © April 7, 2003; "Wayne's